I DRANK FROM THE NILE

AN UNBREAKABLE MEMOIR OF RESILIENCE

KATYA DUNKO

ISBN 979-8-9999484-0-3 (Paperback)

ISBN 979-8-9999484-2-7 (Hardcover)

ISBN 979-8-9999484-3-4 (EPUB)

First Edition – 2025

Published by Katya Dunko

Printed in the United States of America

This is a work of nonfiction based on the author's personal experiences and recollections. While every effort has been made to portray events and people accurately, some names, personal characteristics, locations, and identifying details have been changed, omitted, or combined into composite characters to protect the privacy of individuals. Certain events have been reconstructed from memory, and dialogue has been recreated to reflect the essence of conversations as they occurred. Any resemblance to persons, living or dead, not explicitly acknowledged is purely coincidental.

To my daughter —
may you never run from yourself,
and only feel the power in every struggle.

"The fastest way to change society is to mobilize the women of the world."

— *Charles H. Malik*

BEFORE YOU BEGIN

These pages carry heavy things—addiction, abuse, loss. I share them not to wound, but to show what survival looked like for me. Step gently, and take care of yourself along the way.

PREFACE

Dear Readers,

I'm absolutely terrified to have you holding my memoir. Terrified that you'll see the vulnerable, dirty, gritty, sexy, and painfully human parts of me. But here it is, unpolished and real.

I started writing out of revenge. After taking my daughter from her father and his country, I wanted those who never cared to finally feel my pain. I began with the ending—our escape, the fragile beginnings of freedom. I remember sitting in Becca's kitchen with a bottle of hard cider, her mutant dog at my feet, pouring words into a blank document. It felt like survival.

When I told a literary coach, "I don't want people to like me," she replied, "What do you mean? You're the hero of this story." I couldn't believe her. Writing felt like confession, a way to empty the shame I had carried for years. But slowly, it shifted. This memoir stopped being about revenge and became about learning to love myself when others would not.

It took me seven years to finish. Somewhere along the way, I stopped hiding. I stopped feeling ashamed. I began to see every version of myself—even the broken ones—as worthy of love.

In my culture, you don't speak badly about your parents. But I've learned that while our past shapes us, it doesn't define us. After you read my story, I hope you'll feel braver with your own past, no matter how painful it is. Because it's yours.

The world is full of people saving face, pretending, performing. But the truth always finds its way out.

So here is mine: messy, raw, and real. I hope you see pieces of yourself in it—the hurt, the survival, the triumph, and the beauty of being human.

With love and grit,

Katya

CAIRO AIRPORT
(NOVEMBER 29, 2018)

"Ma'am, excuse me! Ma'am... Wait, please!" yelled a heavily accented Egyptian security gate officer from behind me.

The jetway echoed and vibrated as he took deliberate steps toward us. His concerned tone hit me right between the eyes. Bulls-eye. I clenched my jaw.

I felt weak in the knees, my heart beating ruthlessly in my ears, the color draining from my face. If I hadn't been holding on to the stroller, I would have collapsed.

Damn it. I couldn't recall doing anything suspicious during the boarding process. Maybe it was my face that had betrayed my crime. I'm known to wear my feelings on my face. Walking up the jetway to board that JFK flight out of Cairo, I'd thought I was in the clear. I had been careful to maintain a normal pace and not give away any hint of my victorious escape.

But then again, I will never be in the clear. I have carefully considered all of the consequences for kidnapping my daughter and fleeing to the United States. Until my daughter is eighteen, I will live with the worry that her father will come for her.

This can't be how it ends. Not like this, I thought. *Not after all I've been through.*

Slowly, I turned around to face our fate and stood frozen as the lanky suit-and-tie Arab man approached me.

"Yes?" I replied, clenching the stroller for dear life.

1

CLEAR SKIES, DARK LIES (AUGUST 2012)

You can't run away from yourself: I couldn't get my mother's words out of my head. She'd stated this several times throughout my upbringing.

"Whatever!" I said out loud. For the twenty-three years I'd been on this planet, all my mother had ever done was run away from herself. She used alcohol as her escape from reality and as an excuse to projectile vomit her misery upon us. I despised how she crawled into my head on random mornings. I was already the Wicked Witch of the East at the crack of dawn, and these intrusive thoughts didn't help. Besides, I hadn't spoken to her in almost a year by then, and it wasn't my first instance of no-contact. I shouldn't have been thinking of her.

I finally emerged from our dark beige sheets and planted both feet onto the original 1942 wood floor. It was a picture-perfect Saturday morning in Reno de Janeiro—that was what my boyfriend, Lucas, liked to call Reno. "It gives it more class and culture," he'd say. I couldn't agree more. I could hear the rhythm of his sneakers echoing up and down the concrete steps by the back kitchen door. He was already busy packing the camping gear out of the detached garage for our little getaway to Lake Tahoe, California. We were planning to camp one night at Whale Beach. The locals recognized it as the only undesignated nude beach in Tahoe. We were pros at crafting notable memories.

"Muffy, I hope you're getting ready! I wanna leave in thirty," he yelled toward the open kitchen door.

Lucas embodied the Type-A personality perfectly. I found it an attractive trait in a man. He moved with purpose; each step was deliberate and efficient. I envied him for all his motivation, positivity, and hustle. He was always productive and prepared in any area of life. I could consistently rely on him to be two steps ahead of whatever situation came our way. He was the pinnacle of success in my life up to that point.

"I'll be ready in fifteen, babychka!" I yelled back. Instead of pouring myself a cup of coffee like a normal person, I slithered to my black purse on the linen dresser in our small living room, right by the mustard-yellow-framed French doors leading to an even smaller kitchen. I pulled out my pink, zippered wallet, which my best friend in Ukraine had gifted me, and made a beeline for the bathroom.

Ah, my morning ritual. My prayer at the bathroom counter altar. *Forgive me, Father, Mother, sisters (one, two, three, and four), loving boyfriend, spirit guides, Allah, Buddha, and all those guys up there, for I am a sinner. I'm here to worship my god: codeine.*

Any form my god took on was divine by my standards. I had one rule: I considered a prescribed pharmaceutical drug ending in -one or -ine as the only suitable match. I rationalized that because getting caught in possession of it wasn't illegal, I wasn't a full-blown addict. I steered clear from heroin; it didn't end in -one or -ine. Plus, that shit could kill you. Back then, fentanyl wasn't popular, or perhaps it was, but I wasn't exposed enough to the world of hardcore drug users to keep up with street trends. Prescription pills were easily accessible; one didn't have to turn down dirty streets to find them.

I favored hydrocodone, but I was not monogamous with my opioids. Hydros were a light dose, an instant-release formula, and it was much easier to con a doctor into prescribing them. Occasionally, friends or acquaintances had unused codeine lying around. I told those friends similar tales as the ones I told doctors, claiming, "I take so much ibuprofen. I'm worried I'm damaging my liver, yet I'm still in pain!"

Convincing the doctors was easy for two reasons: first, I didn't look or act like a typical pill addict. Second, I intentionally hadn't replaced a broken crown on a decayed tooth that had no nerves. Physician's assistants were not dentists, and most truly believed I was in pain, judging by the black look of my tooth. As soon as I stepped out of the car in the clinic parking lot, my performance of agony began, just in case they monitored the area with cameras. I found that I had better luck with male doctors because I could bat my lashes at them. If I got a female doc, I'd drop my act immediately and shamefully await my 600mg ibuprofen prescription after the 'I can only recommend seeing a dentist, as I cannot prescribe a controlled substance without concrete evidence you are in pain' spiel.

I lost count of the lies I'd spun for both peers and medical professionals. I still couldn't understand how I managed to get away with years of refills. It was equally baffling that Lucas, my boyfriend of almost two years, never seemed to notice the signs. I couldn't come up with any excuse for why he hadn't caught on; we'd been living together for a year and a half. Surely, he must have noticed the hickeys and strange bruises on my butt cheeks and outer thighs from all the scratching at night—a classic side effect. Not to mention the chronic bowel problems, the erratic mood swings, or the days when I'd be sick and sweating from withdrawal. Maybe he didn't pay attention during the drug and alcohol awareness classes in grade school. Or perhaps I was just that good at hiding it.

But if I could sway a doctor into prescribing medication, then surely I could keep my secret hidden from my significant other—and from everyone else, for that matter. I'd been abusing pills for nine years. I carefully timed my rituals around Lucas being preoccupied with productive tasks, which was most of the time. His constant immersion in his thoughts, plans, and to-do lists kept me in his shadow. I preferred it that way to avoid getting caught while too high. The 'I' I'm referring to here is my alter ego, Katya.

Katya emerged from unfortunate circumstances (no, not in clinical split-personality definition). Neglect shaped her. Traumas, burdens, pills, and the scars of her childhood fed her. She believed she deserved the abuse that happened to her; she carried the weight of everyone's sins and convinced herself she was the problem. She never felt comfortable in her own skin or with the wiring of her brain. She found her own narrative foreign. Deep inside, she knew she was flawed. Codeine offered her a temporary escape from chasing the elusive white rabbit down questionable holes. She lost the true version of herself, Kateryna, in the labyrinth of misfortunes. Katya felt the need to take pills to embody the martyr she perceived herself to be: outwardly strong but inwardly weak.

In addition to being a closet pill addict, I harbored other unresolved issues; the two went hand-in-hand. Lucas confronted me after a drunken outburst one night. I screamed at him, accusing him of being "just like my mother—fucking cold and manipulative!" In response, he locked me outside of the house, and I fought to break down the door. Even in that moment, I loved him deeply, and I vowed to seek help, not only for myself but so he would be happy with me, too.

My therapist, Linda, said I projected those emotional outbursts onto loved ones due to unhealed childhood wounds. She opened up my can of worms and diagnosed me with bipolar depression and generalized anxiety. I agreed with her. My emotions could turn on a dime, and my anxiety didn't like that. My nervous system seemed to go into overdrive in situations that posed no real threat.

Experiencing sudden hostility and feeling my face flush crimson during a simple dinner at our dining table felt incredibly unsettling. I'd resort to coughing to disguise the intense hot flash and my unjustified embarrassment around my own kitchen table. I also experienced an overwhelming urge to urinate and defecate—the result of my adrenaline preparing me for fight or flight—when I first met Lucas's mother in Vermont.

It's hard to admit, but I found myself fighting the urge to smile when I watched Lucas crying at his father's funeral while giving a speech at the altar. That was a very disturbing moment for me, one that only a little sliver of codeine in the church bathroom helped sort out.

My emotional responses seemed beyond my control, and opioids became my desperate attempt at managing them. I struggled to reach for a branch within my childhood memories, seeking stability, self-assurance, and self-esteem—really, anything that resembled a sense of self. But instead of grabbing hold of a core childhood example, I found myself tumbling down from the tree. At times, I felt detached from my humanity.

These inappropriate behaviors and feelings hijacked my brain, leading Linda and me on an endless quest for triggers. "Tell me what thought crosses your mind when you feel like you're losing control?" she would ask. I couldn't tell her! The triggers could be set off by a certain smell, sight, or even a passing conversation from a stranger. I struggled to understand why I felt embarrassed at random times, why laughter replaced tears, and why I felt so uneasy in my own skin.

I also couldn't tell her that I self-medicated with pills. I marked 'no' on the intake form that asked if I had a history of drug abuse. I was afraid of the repercussions if I told the truth. "You didn't cry today. Looks like we're healing those wounds inside. I'm so proud of you," Linda would say.

Poor Linda, she really believed her CBT therapy, double doses of Zoloft, and Wellbutrin XL were making a difference about nine months into our sessions. But in reality, it was only that I had my hands on strong morphine pills. Opioids and antidepressants have a similar effect on behavior—numbness and decreased emotional responsiveness. Linda couldn't tell the difference.

Opioid pills became Katya's best friends. Addiction belonged to her. I wouldn't dare betray their friendship to a therapist. What if Linda sent me to rehab? We would both be lost without each other—the pills and me. I needed them to function in every aspect of life.

Sadly, I was introduced to this addiction by my mother at the ripe age of fifteen. We worked as cleaners and landscapers for a high-ranking government official in Palmer, Alaska, for nine long years, putting in grueling hours after school and on weekends from the time I was twelve years old. Constant work made my body sore; pushing a mower around two acres and tending to trees and bushes weakened my back. One day, when I complained of pain and refused to work, my mother handed me half a Vicodin as we arrived at the gated property and took one herself. Despite the pissing Alaskan rain, I mowed that lawn with a gentle smile on my face. From that moment on, I rummaged through her purse for more pills every chance I got, and she always seemed to have an endless supply. I assumed they came from her daytime job as a phlebotomist at the hospital and her drinking buddies from the pharmacy. I never questioned how she managed to have sandwich baggies filled to the brim with Vicodin in her black purse.

Those magic pills not only alleviated physical pain, but they also numbed the mental anguish of my past. They became my buoy in the sea of instability and neglect I'd been in since my early days.

My father left us when I was around four years old. He made a few brief cameos afterward, taking me to my first day of first grade and the zoo. But that was the extent of his involvement. In general, I felt more drawn to him than my mother; he showed genuine affection toward me. I've missed him every day since he left. I missed his ponytail and stylish leather jacket and the Sandra songs he would play for me at bedtime from his 1970s tape recorder, mostly to mask the sounds of their tumultuous marriage.

I remember witnessing a violent fight between my parents in our apartment in Kyiv, Ukraine. They both threw punches, glass shattered from the kitchen window, and the bloodstain on my mom's white-and-blue-striped robe never faded even years later. The smell of metabolized alcohol filled our room like an air freshener. This smell frightened me, as it was an indicator of the unpredictable behaviors it often accompanied. The three of us squeezed into one small room, a common living arrangement for many Soviet families —multiple generations sardined into a five-hundred-forty-square-foot block apartment. My grandmother told me, years later, that she came home from work once to find me alone in the apartment, in my crib, and eating my own poop. I've tasted neglect in the shittiest of ways.

I don't have any fond early memories of my mother. I can't recall instances of her warmth or affection. And it was true, she never really showed me love. Instead, my grandmother was the one who provided care and food during my early years. My mother left me with memories of her yelling and shaming me for my chronic childhood constipation, her collecting empty booze bottles from the kitchen, and sex sounds: moans, groans, and slaps from random men that came by. She did kill a spider with her bare hands once; I was really proud of her then. I knew what the penis looked like, what sex was, and the color of human flesh from pictures of medical textbooks that were always scattered on the floor. That was educational. I was not afraid of blood or needles. She used to practice blood draws and injections on my small veins for her medical school. I was happy to get that attention.

One incident that Linda dug up was when I fell at a playground at six years old and ran home with a gash on my forehead. My grandma helped to wipe off the blood. Moments later, my drunk mother stumbled in and passed out beside me on the bed. I longed for her comfort or even just for her to notice my injury, but she simply rolled over and vomited undigested mushrooms and vodka all over the bed. Then she screamed at me to clean it up. Did you know you can pour salt on vomit to absorb smells and liquids for a quicker cleanup? I knew things I shouldn't have known at a very young age, and I didn't know things I should have.

Later that year, I tasted vodka from an unfinished shot glass on the messy table I'd been asked to clean. The adults, drunk in their beds, filled me with envy for their carefree joy, and I hated how they confined me to my room until my cleaning shift was done. Curiosity led me to drink the clear liquid. I liked the drowsy warmth I found at the bottom of the shot glass—and that I, too, fell asleep with ease. Before long, I developed a liking for beer, especially when paired with a drag from an almost-smothered cigarette butt in the ashtray.

I believe my parents were simply too young and immature to handle parenthood. My mother was just nineteen, and my father was twenty when I was born. My father's wild oats hadn't been sown, and my mother was too preoccupied with medical school and too beautiful to be tied down by a child. She shamed me for even being born and for being female: "I shouldn't have aborted the boy I was pregnant with before you. Or been with your father! You took my son's place! I wish you were never born. I didn't want you!"

So, it seemed she was prepared to be a mother, just not to me. I felt guilty for being such a burden to her. Seeing how much 'adult stuff' she had to deal with, especially knowing that drowsy liquid was a chore to navigate, I internalized her pain and vowed I would be like the son she desired—strong and helpful. Childhood programming is like drawing a wildcard; the lessons saved on the hard drive can be unpredictable. The innocence of the human condition glitches out while deciphering a hurtful message; my six-year-old mind interpreted this lesson as: "It's not your loving mother's fault; it's your fault for existing."

My father told me he met my mother when she was already pregnant by an older, prestigious doctor. He pleaded with her not to undergo an abortion, but, influenced by my grandfather, she proceeded with it. Since the doctor and she were not married, and premarital sex and abortion were both illegal in the USSR, she had no option but to undergo an abortion at four months gestation. I'm not certain of all the details, but my grandfather had the right connections in the surgery ward. I never dared to ask my mother how she felt; I didn't want her to relive the horror. But it was clear she was not happy with that decision and needed to blame someone. That someone was me, my whole life.

After a few short, lonely childhood years, our destiny took us down a drastically different path. My mother was twenty-seven, I was eight, and my soon-to-be American dad was twelve years her senior. She met him—or, rather, he chose her—through an international dating agency in Kyiv. She went to a casting with her friend as a joke. Dozens of young Slavic brides-to-be recorded their accented intro- ductions. That's right, my mother was a mail-order bride. In the 1990s, before internet dating sites, men would buy VHS tapes adver- tised on late night television through an 800 number.

Six months later, our house phone rang with news that "There's a gentleman from the United States of America that would like to meet you in person." He visited our apartment a couple of times, staying for a total of three months while bringing along his nine- year-old daughter, Fruit Roll-Ups, and Winterfresh gum. She insisted I call him *Dad*, and when I resisted, she replied, "Well, where is your father now? Go to your father then; find him and go!"

They married in Ukraine in late February 1997, and we immi- grated to *Dad's* house in Wasilla, Alaska, in August of that same year. On the morning of our final departure from Kyiv, I knelt beside my mother's hungover body in bed and prayed to God for her happiness. "If she is happy, God, I, too, can be happy."

I wish this had been our fairytale ending, where God, witnessing my innocent tears, granted me my one wish. For years, as I blew out my birthday candles, I made that same wish: "I just want Mom to be happy." However, life fell short of the glamorous American dream, let alone a happy one. Within a year of our arrival, my mother and *Dad* started a pig farm. He had a lot of unused acreage around our home; thus, it seemed logical to put it to good use.

Dad decided that a farm wouldn't be complete without six hundred chickens and two hundred turkeys, as well as some pheasants and rabbits in the mix. He named the farm Triple D Farm and Hatchery (D for daughter, inspired by my new baby sister, Masha). My farm chore list was extensive and included unconventional things, like sifting through wheelbarrows of restaurant crap, picking out toothpicks, creamers, and plastics, then mixing the leftovers with tons of used grains from beer breweries and making gourmet pig food. That was enjoyable compared to the morning routine of walking through the chicken coops collecting dozens of smothered chicken carcasses. Then there was my least favorite chore: shoveling pig pens. The kids on the school bus teased my step-sister and me, calling us the 'chicken sisters.' The whole neighborhood smelled like pig shit, us included.

My mother couldn't play house for too long before she got back into heavy vodka drinking. I'm still not sure if she really pulled a knife on him in a fight, but that was the story *Dad* stuck to, even a decade later. He packed our things and left them on the side of the road in cardboard boxes. I didn't care for them anyways, as they were all hand-me-downs from his daughter, including the underwear. The police arrived with a warrant to make us vacate the property because *Dad* had filed for divorce behind my mom's back.

I was almost twelve when my mom picked me up from a sleepover and told me, "We're never going back to 5840 Hershey Loop." I was actually really happy! No more chickens, smelling like pig shit, and giving *Dad* foot massages. *Dad* graciously allowed us to keep the Chevy van until my mom got her own car. For a few days, home was in that van at a Walmart parking lot until we moved in with my mom's friend, Tina, who was also her drinking buddy and boss. They drank a lot of Crown Royal, and I'm not sure if other substances were involved. I was glad to have the bunk bed in the basement, which I shared with Tina's two chocolate labs.

We struggled to get on our feet. Standing in line at the food bank with my three-year-old sister was too shameful for my mom, so I volunteered to go instead. Mom struggled to accept the divorce, especially the fifty-fifty custody arrangement for Masha. I had to learn to drive a car before I was legally allowed so I could drop Masha off at her dad's place, always making sure *Dad* never saw who was driving, because my mother was often too hungover to wake up. We moved around a lot, living with other families and her drunk friends. She worked cleaning houses with Tina, and I started to help out, too. My mother was never good with money; she needed my help to pay for rent and her two unreasonable car payments.

I think this is a good place to introduce Kateryna, my authentic self. It was during this time that I began to lose touch with her. Kateryna was the voice in my head through these traumas, guiding me to safety like a lighthouse on a distant shore. Kateryna was me, as Mother Nature had intended. She was born with courage, many talents waiting to be discovered, a forgiving heart, and a restless drive for achievement. But no one gave her any attention; no one noticed her. She was wise beyond her years, resilient, proud, nurturing, and motherly, even as a young girl. She even became the strong boy that my mother had aborted just to be acknowledged. When my mother was vomiting and crying in the bathroom, she prayed at the closed door for a different reality—for her mother, not herself.

Eventually, Kateryna began resisting her own reality, constantly asking, *Why me?* The questions kept piling up like a stack of unanswered prison letters and shackled her to the bad memories of childhood. She waited for my mother to acknowledge her, to love her, to build her up, to praise her with even a simple *'Thank you.'* But Kateryna received nothing in return except more grief, negativity, and criticism from her birth mother. Her voice of, *Life is so much more than this, we can turn this around,* faded into a distant whisper. Gradually, I drifted away from her as I stepped into womanhood.

My transition into womanhood was marked by a significant moment: when I received my first paycheck for cleaning houses. This happened before I reached menstruation; I had just turned twelve that spring. Later that same year, my mother beat me black and blue. She did this in front of her boyfriend in his kitchen, kicking me in the stomach, convinced he was hitting on me. She believed that I was instigating his attention since I had become a woman.

The beating continued in the car as she drove on the highway, blackout wasted, and repeatedly elbowed me in the face with full force. I attempted to jump out of the speeding vehicle by opening the passenger door, but she slammed the brakes and pulled me back by my hair. The next day, I applied foundation for the first time to cover my black eye and make it to school. I knew this wasn't right, but I believed that in an alternate universe, things were different—my mother was happy and sober. I believed she could be that person; she had valid excuses for being hurt. I had to accept her ways, continue fulfilling my role in life, and love my mother as nature had intended. I clung to that alternate universe to make it through each day.

At thirteen and fourteen, I was homeschooled, but not by choice. I participated in acting and modeling competitions and won many awards. The idea was both my mother's and mine. Our relationship was sister-like, nothing close to that of a mother and daughter. She saw stardom as a great opportunity to become rich, and I vowed to do it. I was prepared to do anything if it meant her happiness.

So, we took a two-month trip to Los Angeles, where I signed with a talent management company. We lived in our rental car at Santa

Monica beach. I showered in the public outdoor showers, and as I slept in the backseat, my mother would drive all night. I let her sleep during the day, as I kept to the car, watching the homeless people's drama and dynamics. I guess it was kind of cool putting on makeup and heels and going to a few bars with my mother and not getting carded!

I managed to land a few auditions at Fox Studio for a kids' movie and photoshoot for a Sketcher's ad, but that was it. The money my mom spent on me, using funds from the sale of my grandfather's other apartment, weighed heavily on me. The pressure to succeed and repay the investment was too much for a fourteen-year-old to handle. My mother had to return to Alaska so as to maintain the custody order of Masha. I felt bad for my sister, too, only four years old and barely seeing her mom.

She left me in LA and far worse than homeless: in the hands of a wheelchair-bound old Russian man with two lazy eyes. My grandfather had known him back in Ukraine. I was more scared of displeasing my mother than of being left alone in his care. I slept on the couch in his one-bedroom apartment right behind the Chinese theater. He poured shots of vodka for me after our soup dinners and forced me to watch porn in the living room by hiding the remote. He would masturbate loudly in his room a couple times a day so I would hear him. He constantly smelled of piss and vodka. He also insisted on taking me shopping at Victoria's Secret and forced me to model the nightgowns for him.

I attempted suicide after a month of living with him. I stood on top of the roof of the five-story apartment building and almost jumped onto the fence below, hoping to land on the sharp rails. The security guard aimed a gun at me and told me to freeze, thinking I was trespassing. I wished he had pulled that trigger, as it had taken me five weeks to muster up to that suicide attempt. Achieving that level of 'letting go into an alternate universe' had taken a lot of courage, emo-style journaling, and repeating Mandy Moore songs on the edge of a roof. As the guard escorted me back to my floor, I felt defeated; I had to go back to pursuing my dreaded acting career while sleeping on a child molester's couch.

When he drove up in his chair to the edge of the couch in the middle of the night, butt naked, that was the last straw that caused me to finally break my silence to my mother. He pulled off my sheets and threw his paraplegic oily body on top of mine. I threw him off and fell straight for the corded phone. He wrestled with me, managing to unplug it, and I threatened to cut off his dick. He took the phone away completely. Luckily, once a week, a female caretaker came by, bringing his meds and stocking the fridge. But he always kept watch. That week, I passed a note to her with an SOS message, asking her to call my mother and have her take me back to Alaska. My mother came a few weeks later but was angry with me for not sticking to my modeling and acting dream.

"Goddammit, Mom!" I screamed. "I'm done with this modeling shit!" I only wanted friends and to go to school, not because the school system would teach me better ways of adapting to social situations—I'd been educated in that realm beyond my years—but because school gave me one standard of normality in my unconventional teenage life. I felt stuck somewhere between five and fifty-five years old, and I needed a sea of peers to remind me: You are a budding teenager with so much potential.

Then, at fifteen, my mother gave me opioids, and I became Katya. I finally found my alternative universe—and preferred this numbed-out version of myself. As Katya, it was easier to navigate my mother's reality. I would depend on her even more as the shit-storm of my childhood unfolded.

The first memory I have of receiving a hug from my mom was at the age of sixteen. It was after the incident when the DEA and FBI surrounded our house. At the time, we were living in Wasilla, Alaska, cultivating illegal marijuana—another one of my mother's get-rich-quick ideas—and had left the foot-tall female sprouts outside since it was a sunny day. My guess is that our distant neighbor on the unnamed road on the corner of Schrock and Church snitched on us. The agents pulled guns on us as we sat on the front steps, enjoying a sunset cigarette. I ran upstairs and hid all the unboxed grow lamps, bags of dirt, pots, and nutrients under mountains of clothes and bedding. That was the only time I was thankful we didn't have a single piece of furniture, so all our clothes and bedding were already piled on the floor.

They questioned us separately, and we luckily had the same story: "Someone is leaving them here! So glad you're here to help us find whoever is leaving these plants!" I was scared shitless of going to juvenile prison or a foster home, both equally dreadful. I believe the only reason my mother avoided federal prison was because she was wearing medical scrubs and still had on her hospital badge. And she spoke broken English, stood five feet tall, and was stunningly beautiful. She didn't fit the typical profile of a Schedule I drug grower.

Anyway, she rushed over to me and gifted me an extended hug, praising me for being smart enough to hide everything. This is the only letter from Kateryna she ever replied to. Once the adrenaline wore off, she said, "We need to find a better way to hide the plants!" And we did, by digging a hidden cellar under the back patio of our rental house at 3 a.m. My friends and boyfriend helped. She paid us with Vicodin.

Despite all of these downs, and a few ups, I stayed deeply attached to my mother, perhaps to a fault. I stood by her through her self-destructive escapades because I was all she had, and I felt sorry for her. Never did I attempt to run away, and my prayers to God remained unchanged from what they'd been when I was six: "I just want her to be happy."

Looking back, I realize I wasted many prayers on her. Eventually, we abandoned the marijuana project house. Two crazy boyfriends and homes later, we finally went our separate ways. She went to live with her now-husband, Oleg, a pilot. I was not welcome, so I lived with my high-school sweetheart and his family. It was better this way, and it was her only decision that I genuinely supported. I felt liberated not having to clean up her messes anymore. And with my mother, there was always more.

I graduated from an alternative high school for students who were mostly emancipated and expelled (because I couldn't count on my mother to sign school admission papers, and we lacked the same proof of address) with a 4.0 GPA. I was shy about being smart, as that was Kateryna's skill, and Katya was not on speaking terms with her.

My high academics earned me a full scholarship to the University of Alaska, Anchorage, but I never fit the persona of a 'scholarship recipient.' I had a drummer boyfriend, smoked weed and Marlboro Reds, raced motocross and jumped ramps, listened to Metallica in my decal-embellished car that I'd bought with my own money, and paid rent with home-cooked meals for my boyfriend's family of seven. I was a fully grown adult by sixteen, equipped with a closet substance abuse disorder and a nineteen-dollar-an-hour cleaning job. Badass.

With my dynamic rough start, you can see why I still guarded my pill habit. The only person who might have suspected I was an addict would have been my mother, but she never checked in even after she noticed her stash disappearing quicker than usual. The codeine high provided an escape from the dark world that was my mother and our past. It numbed me to the wounds of my upbringing and made the colors of the long Alaskan winters more vivid. Since I wasn't ready to confront the past, I attributed them to Katya, along with the pill habit.

Opiates finally smothered the nature-intended Kateryna, and I locked her up in prison for good. Poor girl, she was desperately fighting the seventeen-year current of instability, neglect, and abuse. She still wore her big white bow and thick red Soviet tights on the night of her imprisonment when my mother officially left me alone in the United States. On that night, I begged my high school sweetheart boyfriend to "lock this fucking door behind me or I will kill someone" as I raged in a hall closet, flying high on morphine, about my mother's final decision to abandon me. She ran back to Ukraine and took my eight-year-old sister with her. They had been my only family here; now, they were gone.

Fast forward to 2012, I was now twenty-three, chopping a morphine line in Lucas's bathroom. Katya had done a great job making it this far, thanks to codeine. With my past silenced and locked up somewhere in Wasilla, I pushed forward, chasing my daily bliss. I did all the necessary things to seem normal: I ate healthy, practiced yoga, showed up to therapy, and had close friendships. I put myself through college and pursued my entrepreneurial goals. I kept Kateryna quiet and numb with a little dose of opioids through the food hatch. "Sit! Stay! Leave it!" the pills commanded her, and she obeyed.

I didn't choose this life of hardships; this life chose me.

That morning, I only had a quarter of the 15mg blue morphine pill left. Doctors prescribe these for severe pain and an inexperienced user would be glued to the couch if they snorted the compound. Narcotics release endorphins in the brain, and that gave me a rush of energy and willpower—not drowsiness and relaxation. All I had to do was hide my glazed-over eyes and control the grin on my face for the first thirty minutes after ingestion—and remain unnoticed.

Dammit! This won't last me until next week when I meet with Gary, I thought to myself. *Maybe I'll just take the rest on Wednesday.* By skipping days, I could taper off my doses and avoid withdrawal symptoms like the shakes and sweats. Besides, I never had large quantities of the drug in my system at once. I took just enough to keep the major withdrawal symptoms manageable.

Yes, that would be fine, Katya replied.

I began my ritual by carefully chipping a piece off the pill with a razor onto the granite stone vanity—careful not to let it go flying across the room. Using my plastic rewards card from a local store, I crushed the small amount into a pea-sized pile. I always kept a rolled-up dollar bill in my wallet, one end designated for my nostril.

Three, two, one...inhale.

I licked the card and the vanity stone clean then checked to make sure nothing was stuck in the bill. That was it. Just the tiniest amount of opioid. Nature produces this stuff from poppies, and we simply mass-produce it in a lab. NO BIG DEAL, folks. Nothing to see here.

"Katya, are you packing? Let's go!" Lucas broke the vibe of my sacred ritual.

"Yes, I'm coming!" I yelled back.

Looking in the gold-framed oval mirror, I thought, *Any second now, it will hit me.* I liked watching my pupils shrink as the drug kicked in. As my pupils constricted, so did the pain behind them, sealing tight for no one to notice.

BAM! There it was. I put a little water on my fingertip and snorted that, too. It helped to wash it all down. The butterflies came, and I felt energized, as though I had just done twelve sun salutations. I instantly felt productive and excited, ready to take on the day. I felt loved and full of joy. Not too much joy, just enough to keep out random intrusive thoughts like the one from this morning. I felt as normal as a normal person who wasn't carrying my baggage. "Put down the rocks," Linda would say. I had done just that with that pea-sized amount of a blue pill.

I glanced at the plastic card I had just used to organize my drugs before putting away all my paraphernalia. 'JUNKEE,' it read. It was a thrift store in Midtown, Reno, known for its outrageous Burning Man attire and random trinkets. The irony was just too much. I had been using this card for months now, but that morning, I made the connection.

"When will you stop?" I asked the mirror while brushing my teeth.

The pain will soon be gone. What's a couple more pills? the addiction answered.

"Sure, I've heard that before," I talked back to it. These inner thoughts really did get in the way.

I found that the pros of taking my pills outweighed the cons. Katya did a great job of damming up despair. She functioned enough to be loved by her boyfriend, and belonging felt wonderful. The cons would be to face Kateryna and to hear her longing to rebuild a foundation on solid ground instead of sand. I didn't want to dive deep and fix my broken pieces; the anxiety and depression Linda and I were working on gave me plenty to deal with. I was not brave enough for the two girls to meet. Not yet.

I said my daily prayers, and with twelve minutes to spare, I dressed in hiking clothes. I couldn't wait for another beautiful day with my twin flame, Lucas. Our story was one of serendipity, transformative in ways I only now fully understand. Meeting Lucas changed me forever.

We met in October 2009 on campus at the University of Reno, Nevada. I was exiting the Nazir Ansari Business Building amidst the sea of students flooding in and out of the heavy double doors. I usually looked down and kept a death stare through this transition, but for a moment, I lifted my gaze and met a pair of hazel eyes under a Gatsby hat; he was holding the door open for me. I smiled, and fate sealed the deal. Certain he would come and talk to me, I sat on the bench and pretended to read. It felt as though we were acting out a scripted scene. I caught sight of him approaching me in my peripheral vision. My heart raced, and I could feel the invisible quantum particles bridging us closer together.

"Devushka, mozhno (Young lady, may I)?" he asked.

I sprung up, not believing my ears. "Da, mozhno (Yes, you may)," I replied.

He sat down next to me.

"You speak Russian?" I asked.

"I traveled to Russia and studied it for a while, but it's a hard language to navigate."

"How did you know I speak Russian?"

"You look Slav," he replied.

I laughed back. "Ukrainian, yes! I look pissed, I know."

"What do you think—brown belt with black shoes doesn't look good?" He changed the subject abruptly and stood up.

I quickly processed the question and pondered a couple of reasons why he would ask a beautiful stranger this. Was it to show his openness with insecurities? Was it to provoke me to check out his body? Or was he fishing for a compliment?

"I don't think it matters. It looks good. No one is noticing," I said, struggling not to blush as I scanned his athletic body, muscular legs, and the bulge in his groin. "What is your name?" I asked.

"I'm Lucas," he replied.

"Katya, or Kateryna," I said.

"Oh, Katyousha! The Russian missile!" He impressed me more. "Well, I am late for class, do you want to meet up for coffee sometime this week?"

"I have a boyfriend, but...yes, sure, let's meet up," I replied.

We exchanged numbers and a few more stories of the Slavic world, and he told me of his experience of teaching English in Cambodia. He left on his blue road bike, switching the flat Gatsby-style hat backwards and mounting his shoulder bag high up on his back. I admired him as though I'd just seen a unicorn in real life.

When he was gone, I sat there in complete shock. It had taken only seven minutes for me to stumble, trip, and fall deeply in love. Seven minutes of subconscious processes, pheromones, and hormones, for me to realize that I had manifested him into existence. He was everything I wanted in a man: confident, charming, athletic, cultured, a man that was aware and made the first move. I was ready to jeopardize everything just to meet Lucas with the flat Gatsby hat for a coffee. I knew with every cell of my being sitting on that bench that we would be together. That night, I laid in bed so high on those hazel eyes that I felt I was going to explode. I was desperately in lust for the first time.

Later that week, we met for lunch. He ordered a stromboli from a pizza place and effortlessly charmed the Greek guys, leaving me in awe. I felt proud and honored standing next to him as I admired his confidence. He radiated energy, filling the food court with inspiration and intrigue, as though he was an undiscovered celebrity.

As I watched him meander through the busy lunch crowd, I longed to be his equal: chatty, cultured, and charismatic. But I was quiet, rigid, and repelling—at least, on the surface. Deep down, I believed he'd be the one to discover a part of me that was just like him. A year before, I had envisioned traveling the world, and Lucas's stories of his adventures in fifty countries assured me that I would be sharing my dreams with him.

"Where is our coffee?" I asked during lunch, though my feelings for him made me too nauseous to eat.

"I don't drink coffee. Hate that stuff. I love tea," he said.

"So, you invite me for coffee, don't even drink coffee, and have lunch instead?" I flirted. I admired his assertiveness, something I wasn't accustomed to from men.

"Would you like some? I have to go now to drop off some paperwork for my business. Um, you can ride with me, and we can have coffee at my house or a coffee shop if you like," he said.

I was in.

He took us to his house and showed me the objects on his walls —knives, art, carpets. He made tea, not coffee, as I sat at his table in the fading auburn light. I admired his René Magritte painting, *The False Mirror*. He said that the eyes were the mirror to the soul. *Then in yours I see mine*, I thought to myself. We fell silent after the first couple sips of tea.

"Do you have sugar?" I asked nervously, swallowing hard.

He brought sugar in a plastic hand grenade dispenser, and I poured too much. When he sat back down, he placed his hand on my knee. My face flushed as I watched his hand—strong, veined, twelve years older than mine. His hands looked capable of both creation and destruction, and I hoped for creation. He pulled me into his kiss.

I had never felt so weak and wanted in a man's arms as I did then. Time warped, and we traveled beyond this galaxy. How could anyone ever again compare to the energy of my muse? We were so consumed by the divine power of reproduction. I was so doomed.

Getting dressed, I didn't feel shameful for what I had done. I felt alive but so confused about what would come next.

"What does this mean?" I asked him, pointing to the massive Chinese character on the wall.

"It means 'soul.' I just love how it looks." He smiled.

Of course, I thought, *you are so passionate, deep, and complex. Not to mention cultured, an entrepreneur, a writer, a competitive runner, a professional air drummer, and at times a Puritan fresh off the* Mayflower. *All wrapped up in one hazel-eyed, half-Greek package.*

He dropped me off on campus, and I broke down. I could still smell him on me. Would he write again? Did he do this with other girls? Did he feel what I felt? The gods had thrown their dice, but I didn't see where they landed. Lucky number seven? Please. I had never felt such a sudden shift, something I called love, after only hours of knowing someone. It wasn't like me to trust so quickly, but this force was beyond my control.

In the weeks that followed, I spent nights in the bathtub, drinking wine from the spout and listening to *Protection* by Massive Attack on repeat. I let the water go cold, my hands pruned, lying there knowing I had to have him with every cell. I wanted him inside my pituitary gland, releasing all my oxytocin.

Another week went by, and I blatantly announced to my Alaskan high school sweetheart that we were over. I felt disgusted doing so because he was my best friend. I had lived with him and his family when my mom left me; we were inseparable, moved to Reno together, shared a dog and a car. I was close with his parents and loved his siblings. I was an idiot to let him go, but Lucas had a hold on me I couldn't explain.

Shocked, my boyfriend kept asking why, and I kept crying, telling him I had fallen out of love. I couldn't admit I'd cheated; our relationship was steady, but my broken twenty-year-old self knew he was too sweet to bear my darkness. It wasn't fair to him to be with an addict. As hard as it was seeing him cry, Lucas's maturity told me: *This is a real man who will have your back, no matter what.*

I chased Lucas for forty-eight weeks. Over three hundred thirty-six days of nonstop Lucas propaganda played in my head. Despite my efforts not to, I wrote to him on topics like travel and politics. I lingered around campus until 10 p.m., hoping to catch a glimpse of him on his road bike. I wandered the campus grounds, pretending I was the main character in a serendipitous love story with a whole camera crew hidden within the student body.

I was completely consumed by this unreciprocated love, which bordered on obsession, but I maintained a calm exterior around him so as not to frighten him off. I'd never seen my mother love like this or suffer from love like this, and the novelty of profound emotions within myself reaffirmed my belief that I was capable of genuine love, regardless of the lack of her example.

Lucas and I would meet on campus for sushi once a month. I learned how to use chopsticks at home just for these sushi dates. He had a girlfriend his own age then, a beautiful, tall, blonde Eastern European athlete, but I knew I still had a chance with him.

During those forty-eight weeks, I changed so much. I grew from my secret and physically distant love for him. I approached strangers and made friends with them, just like I had Lucas; I loved life and did everything with passion, just like Lucas did. He had already transformed my life in profound ways. We had a soul contract, and he was my teacher without even knowing it.

My mother would tell me as a little girl that, "If you want something, anything, you just have to want it bad enough, and you will get it." I spent that summer with my family in Ukraine at the Black Sea. As I lay on the water, I bargained with the universe: "If I let him go and he comes back to me, I will cherish and protect him at all costs." I had to let him go for my sanity. That last week of August, before the start of the next semester, I did just that; I let him go.

We met at a college gathering, Pub n' Sub, on a hot Tuesday night in August. We sat outside, sipping on Sierra Nevada Pale Ale, his go-to brew on tap. I gifted him chocolate from Ukraine. He was particularly happy that night, but I was so drained. I gave him the last of me in those sunset moments.

"Lucas...I need to tell you something. I'm sure you can see that I really, really like you. I mean, Lucas, I love you. I do, and it fucking hurts. I can't be friends anymore, as it's hard for me to sit here without you wanting me back. I wish you all the best. You deserve it all and more. We can't see each other, though." I said it all in one breath.

He stared blankly into my right eye, gently nodded his head, but said nothing.

"Thank you for the beer. Hope you like the chocolate. Good luck this semester," I added, grabbing my purse off the table and leaving the bar patio from the side gate.

"Katyusha! Wait!" he shouted.

I froze in my tracks.

"I want to be with you, too," he said breathlessly, jogging up to me.

Tears rolled down my face, and he pulled me into his chest.

"I have to first end things on a good note with my girlfriend, but soon, after my work event. I just can't handle all of this right now. Please don't leave," he pleaded. His eyes were full of sincerity and vulnerability.

Wait a few more weeks? Absolutely. For you, I would wait a lifetime, I silently vowed.

Our connection blossomed into a serious relationship from that point forward. Within six months, I moved in with him and had dinner ready on the table each night. We played house very well and gave each other healthy space. I adapted quickly to his high-paced lifestyle of running a business and athletic outlets and did my best to be seen as his equal. Since I didn't have to pay for rent anymore, I indulged more in hobbies like painting, yoga, and running, which gave me a sense of purpose and balance. I also had more money for pills, and living in a predictable euphoria blinded me to the red flags in our dynamic.

I appreciated our life together, but I was also conditioned to believe that the rug could be pulled out from under me at any moment. Thus, I became defensive when my existence was threatened. In those times, I resorted to fighting dirty and targeting his insecurities just to balance the power dynamic since I relied on him more than he relied on me. I kept myself in check by letting him steer our relationship as he saw fit. Together, we surpassed my highest expectations of what a healthy relationship could be.

The sun was hot, and the turquoise Lake Tahoe water was calling us. We set off on another adventure in Lucas's Hyundai manual-shift silver chariot with Pearl Jam blasting through the speakers, Lucas maneuvering the gears and air-drumming and singing along, all while sipping on steaming hot tea from a mug that barely fit into the cupholder. It was a display of multitasking mastery. Maybe it was the morphine, but I felt like the luckiest girl alive riding shotgun in his car. I had everything I could ever want: a Bachelor of Arts degree in Psychology and Biology, a devoted partner, world travel adventures ahead, a fit runner's body, long flowing blonde hair, and the anticipation of someday starting a family with my dependable man of two years. Life was perfect.

2

THE TASK (MAY 2014)

"To be, or not to be, that is the question." *Great, thanks, Shakespeare. Easier asked than answered,* I thought. Anyone can pose the question, but how many can truly make the decision? I sat on our back kitchen concrete steps, soaking in their warmth like a lizard and pondering over a question that weighed on my heart: *How do I save our relationship?*

Like most summer nights in the high desert Sierra Nevada mountains, it was windy. I loved the fluctuating temperatures in Reno: hot days and cool nights. The wind brought with it the mercy we depended on to cool down our cozy, 1940s, two-bed, one-bath, nine-hundred-eighty-square-foot home without an AC. There was, however, an uncertainty in the air that evening. Every gust of wind beat the elm tree branches along the fence of the detached garage, testing their strength at the Forest Drive house, and carried messages from the unknown.

I concentrated on the whispers of the wind, hoping they might carry the answer to my question. As the Desert Dwellers *Museum of Consciousness* mix played in my earbuds, I replayed in my mind the fight Lucas and I had just had over dinner. Sure, the air between us had been thick since we'd got back from Southeast Asia just two weeks ago—but how had I suddenly become labeled as "playing victim to my past" and being "not worldly enough" and "not hard-working" and "not grateful," and why was I told I "shouldn't depend on a man"?

He knew my traumatic history very well, from my days in Alaska to modeling in LA, and he knew I was actively addressing it with two antidepressant prescriptions. He had met with my mother on two separate occasions and experienced her toxicity firsthand. He had met my entire family in Ukraine, for that matter. I spoke two other languages. I ran a marathon in just over four hours. I had been responsible for myself and my mother before I reached puberty. I gave up my career goals for our traveling lifestyle. Yet now, after four years of him taking care of us, I wasn't deemed woman enough to rely on a man. He had made it clear to me that he needed me to be more.

The only thing I kept from Lucas was my opioid addiction, and I managed it the best I could. The down days did make me shout "FUCK YOU" across the aisle on an airplane, but this type of disrespect was not aimed at men despite him saying I had "no respect" for them; it was aimed at me for lacking self-control. The yells came from inmate Kateryna, resurfacing when Katya failed to numb her up properly. I couldn't show him all my weaknesses, and as much as I wanted to confide in him for help, I felt it wasn't fair to keep him in the dark about my addiction. I was afraid he would leave me for good. I had been taught by my mother to never show weakness, and this addiction was my weakest attribute.

With Lucas being the most constant and stable person in my life, I was determined to do whatever it took to make him happy. We lived a comfortable middle-class life. We had student loans, ski passes, and salmon dinners with a mix of foreign friends on Saturdays. We painted our front door red and planted a shaggy Joshua tree in the front yard. This was a luxury for me, as growing up, nothing had ever been painted, planted, or promised. Mining for stability was like searching for gold, a scarce commodity, but Lucas seemed to have tapped into the source. With a six-figure income from his seasonal remodeling business, Lucas provided us the means to travel six months out of the year, fulfilling my dream of exploring the world. Oh, did we explore! Twenty-two countries in total.

Yet, over the past two years, living up to his success had become challenging, and it gradually wore down my self-esteem. I wasn't sure if I could achieve as much as he had in business or handle paying a mortgage because I lacked a clear sense of direction in my personal life. I took on restaurant and bartending jobs to support our traveling lifestyle, but I longed for a career and to continue my education. The interview invitation from the Institute of Cognitive Neuroscience at University College London was the closest I had come to realizing my dream. Lucas was reluctant to move to London —that would hurt his business, and I couldn't bear the thought of losing him. Thus, I made sacrifices for the greater good and put my dreams on hold to prioritize our relationship.

With the lost hope of a fulfilling career, I tactfully pressured him to start a family with me. After all, he possessed all the necessary resources. I found myself caught between showing my appreciation for our adventurous lifestyle and pressing for more. "Do you want children?" I asked, overlooking the Mediterranean Sea in Dubrovnik, Croatia.

"Maybe I'll have those fuckers one day. Imagine having kids now. We wouldn't be able to do any of this," he responded.

"Yes, you are right. It would be nice to have a little son or a daughter, though. You'd be a great father," I answered, swallowing my wants once again.

I believed that pregnancy might be the only thing that could motivate me to break my codeine habit. I hated taking birth control more than opioids, and while I sought opioids (aka 'tampons') from pharmacies in Spain, he reminded me to ask about NuvaRing. I purposely hadn't ordered enough birth control for our travels, but his Type-A personality got in the way of my plans.

His personality also kept getting in the way of the affection, attention, and any sense of a real connection between us. His mind was constantly ticking, very removed, and more preoccupied with getting to know foreigners on the streets than our emotional wellbeing. He kept saying I wasn't grateful, but I got tired of looking at his back, following it aimlessly around the globe. I simply wanted his embrace at nights, but even that turned into a thing I "always complained" about.

I couldn't understand what more I needed to do to prove I was wife material. My family in Ukraine began questioning our intentions as a couple because being twenty-five years old with no promises of marriage and childless was abnormal by their standards. In Ukraine, being called *bez-detnaya*, childless, is an actual insult. Living in America, I knew the rules and expectations were different, but like Lucas, or perhaps even more than him, I was cultured.

Then I snapped.

I left him in paradise in El Nido, Palawan Island, in the middle of the night, just two months prior to that windy summer night in Reno. Somewhere between Bangkok and El Nido, Philippines, I planted a stake in the ground that cracked our foundation. We soloed the last two countries on our itinerary and reunited at the airline check-in in Jakarta, Indonesia. Honestly, I wanted a ring made out of straw on my finger and a glimmer of hope for a life together. After all, I had given up my career ambitions and adhered to a birth control regime. Wasn't this what he'd wanted? But as I'd lain there in our El Nido bungalow, watching him sleep peacefully under the mosquito net, I'd known it wouldn't happen. I'd left him not because I didn't want him but because I wanted him to long for me; I'd left to convey that I felt uncertain in our direction. I'd been attentive, asking about his goals, but his responses had contained little mention of "us" and more of "my future business."

Of course, he hadn't followed me, and my insecurity had eaten me alive as I'd roamed various islands of Philippines and Indonesia alone, fasting, meditating, sleeping under the stars on deserted beaches, and visiting temples of worship. *Did he just abandon me like my mother did?* I journaled all my emotions during this time, and my thought train circled right back to, "You are the broken one" who "shouldn't have been born," and, "You are not needed." Not Lucas—he had a loving mother and had grown up in a nuclear family.

I have gone to great lengths for the people I love. Like my mother—she could beat me, use me, and abuse me, but I still stood by her side. I gladly weathered storms with her, desperately awaiting redemption for my devotion.

'I want you to be free of your mother's ways,' Lucas reminded me in an email.

"I want you to love me for my courage to confront them," I said aloud to a heron as I walked the rice paddies in Ubud, Bali.

'It's like there's this other person inside you,' his email continued; he clearly sensed the hurt Kateryna inside me.

"Then hold me, talk to me, give me space, and earn my trust so I can let her out," I released into the holy water at Tirta Empul Temple, as if the temple itself could hold what he never could.

I couldn't teach a thirty-seven-year-old man how to love, appreciate, or make sacrifices for a woman. What did I know about love as a vulnerable, wanderlust-stricken twenty-five-year-old? I was only certain of what love was not. I couldn't defend our love, not because it didn't need saving but because I didn't know how to defend it. But, as I was able to bear the emotional rollercoaster that is my mother and was loyal to the love I had for her, this pattern naturally continued with Lucas.

That night in Reno, I swallowed my pride, the fight we'd just had, and all the labels he'd put on me and decided to make one last attempt at pleasing him. I would show my independence and strength in ways only he could truly appreciate.

After watching the wind dance with the elm trees for an hour and a half, I found the answer to my question: move to Cairo, Egypt, the largest city in the Arab world. As crazy as it sounded, that decision would be the ultimate way I could show my devotion to our relationship and in a language only he would understand.

Lucas and I coined Cairo one of the "motliest places on Earth" when we visited it in early December 2012. Middle Eastern culture was the most romantic, chaotic, and mysterious concept to me. The crying violins and the sharp notes of their music spoke to my soul. The pain in the pleasure seen in everyday Cairo life reflected my Slavic upbringing. People who sought peace in the self-inflicted struggle mirrored my post-USSR Ukrainian mentality. Arabic spirituality saturated each grain of the Sahara sand and found its way into every nook and cranny of the population's sweaty existence. Female suppression hid behind black hijabs yet moved with so much freedom in the dry wind. In a few words, Cairo was a city of double standards in beliefs and expectations, secrets, deep family bonds, and hidden treasures for all to discover. Cairo, in my understanding of it, would be a place I could strengthen my character in ways only Lucas would deem worthy.

When Lucas was my age, he, too, had lived abroad. And since the day I'd met him, I had wanted to be his equal. I was following his footsteps, in the physical and metaphorical meaning, in hopes of being enough of a woman for him. I believed that living abroad like he had, teaching English in Cambodia, would be enough to convince him of my ultimate transformation. I looked up to him and his experience of living abroad, as that had given him the deep character traits I admired in him. Could living abroad be the secret ingredient that made a person as dynamic as him? To this day, he advocates for living life outside one's comfort zone, and my loyalty to please him, or anyone really, was hardwired into my subconscious.

If I couldn't prove my self-worth to my mother, I would prove it to Lucas.

I ran into our house scared shitless and with my heart racing, as though I was carrying a ticking time bomb for us to disarm.

"I just had this idea. What if I move to Cairo? You know, so I can work on myself. Maybe this is what our relationship needs, this time apart," I said. That proclamation and what my heart was feeling were on two different planes of reality.

"Really?" he said and paused. "Fuck yeah, Muffy, go get it! You loved Egypt, I'm sure you'll do great there." He beamed as he turned from his laptop to face me.

"I think this is the city that will help me overcome all those things you just mentioned. Maybe I will get out of this victimhood—like you say. I mean, it is difficult there to be a woman, and I want to build that stronger character. You know, I will be independent and be forced to survive. I know I can. I can overcome my hurts, spend time alone," I kept on reasoning, more with myself, as he was already on board with the decision.

"That is so cool, Muffy! There's lots of growth to take from that motley country. I think you should go—go and do something amazing."

What I wanted him to say was, "No, don't go, it's too dangerous!" or, "Focus on finding yourself here; what about the career you wanted?" or better yet, "You don't need to leave to prove yourself, you are enough." He let the thought bomb go off, filling the room once again with silence and routine; he blogged away on his MacBook. I sat there silently watching his back as he hunched over his little desk, waiting for a better answer than, "I'm sure you'll do great there." But he hadn't chased me in the Philippines, and he surely would not chase me now that I'd made a more permanent decision to leave.

The silence around me stirred a familiar anger, yet it also fueled my determination to stand firm in my decision to live abroad. I believed Lucas wanted this move for us even more than I did. I felt that in the pit of my knotted stomach like the feeling of just having received cold-hearted life advice from a father. Lucas was, after all, more mature than me. I blew steam out of my ears, not wanting to start another argument. Maybe this was what he needed to miss me, worry about me, and remember the good times from our adventurous four-year relationship.

I didn't sleep that night; I just lay next to the man I wanted to marry after my solo adventures. I pictured our amazing wedding day —barefooted on some beach somewhere, eloping and dancing like we did in our living room, naked and to Russian pop. I lost myself in future memories of us after my glorious transformation, imagining our green-eyed kids, hearing their patters on our hardwood floor. If I came back a more independent woman, I truly thought we could make my family dream a reality.

But this was what I wanted. What did Lucas want? I was not sure —was I just a four-year fling? I was the first girl he had lived with like this, and as roommates, we actually got along well. I knew what he didn't want, and that was my lack of experience, appreciation, and respect. Did he want kids or marriage? I prayed he did, and a part of me felt I could open his mind about having them but only after proving my worth.

Lucas had always stood tall, holding a mirror that reflected a broken image of myself. My task was to accept and process the broken pieces inside me. I was not sure how I'd accomplish this, but to "stop playing victim to my past" would mean I'd have to confront Kateryna. Terrified of what was on the other side of my past, I had very little confidence that I was able to make peace with it, especially not without my drugs. I had a sliver of understanding that maybe my drug abuse contributed to our relationship problems.

Don't even think about it, Katya, I thought, *quitting pills is out of the question. Your drug abuse is not the problem in your relationship.*

Forget the excuses I fabricated for locating pharmacies in numerous foreign countries during our many trips; Lucas had never noticed or been bothered that I always had a reason to visit a pharmacy alone. Like the time in Hanoi, Vietnam, when he was busy talking to our server, inquiring about locations to visit for a day trip. I excused myself upon seeing that there was a pharmacy across the street. I limped into my chlorine-smelling, white-walled sanctuary, telling them, "I got run over by a moped." The pharmacists were excited to see a White, blonde foreigner and were all smiles while practicing their English. A prior Google search had informed me that there were no prescription-only medications in that country, and I was pleased to get some good old Vicodin.

I lay in our bed, remembering the ease of getting my fix in foreign lands and feeling confident that I would have no problem finding my crutch in Cairo. I was also planning on stopping birth control. I had wanted to stop taking it for years, and I was excited to be in control of at least one substance while being away from Reno.

Staring at the painted Chinese character on our bedroom wall that read 'soul,' I thought, *Lucas, you have a good soul; I just need to strengthen mine a bit.* I poured out beautiful memories of all our adventures, filling the small bedroom with them. Finally, I drifted off to sleep, fantasizing about how it would feel to be a woman Lucas deserved, to be worthy of having and holding him. The butterflies in my stomach were no greater than any codeine high I'd had, so I managed to ignore my anxiety.

In a nerve-racking two weeks, I sold my 1994 Subaru Legacy, Blue Magoo, which had an unnecessary muffler, for two thousand dollars. Then I purchased a ticket to Ukraine to attend my aunt's wedding followed by a one-way ticket to Cairo International Airport (CAI).

It was a longshot, and one I wasn't totally comfortable with, as from what I remembered, men in Egypt were a little too ambitious in the presence of a woman, but Lucas and I agreed that maybe I should have Lemo meet me upon my arrival to Cairo. I was happy to get Lucas's token of concern this early in the journey. If Lucas felt he could trust Lemo, I did as well.

Lemo was a local man Lucas and I had met on our first trip to Cairo back in early December 2012. This was right in the middle of the country's most recent and violent revolutions of overthrowing President Mubarak's thirty-year rule. Not the best time for a vacation, as streets had been blocked off and bombed, and dozens of violent protestors had been gunned down in mass shootings, but we never listened to mainstream media. And meeting a good friend like

Lemo just confirmed that the world was not as bad as the masses made it out to be.

My itinerary was finalized, leaving no room for turning back. I was unemployed and had no responsibilities, so my only task was to follow through on moving to Cairo.

There are moments in life that etch themselves into the cerebral cortex; one such moment was June 12, 2014, the day I selfishly (or, perhaps, unselfishly, or foolishly—who knows) left Reno. Lucas drove me to Reno-Tahoe International Airport for the last time. As we backed out of our driveway, he made a comment that would take me nine months to process...

"...And, Sonichka, if you find someone who makes you happy, be with him," he said.

"What? I don't even want to think about that, Lucas. What are you saying?" I exclaimed, my voice edged with hostility and panic. His offer of a 'hall pass' only heightened my insecurity, not so much about myself, but about his perception of my self-worth. I wasn't sure what would come of this trip, but seeking out another partner was certainly not part of my agenda. "Are you breaking up with me?"

"No, we are not breaking up. I guess it's more of a break. I'm just saying things can happen, we don't know where life can lead us," he replied, putting on his glasses and searching for a CD to play.

After a lifetime devoted to making my mother happy and still feeling abandoned, I believed I had earned some good karma. Karma that those I loved would stick with me. Refusing to entertain the idea that my trip to Cairo would end in disaster or a lover, I decided not to argue during our last hour. So, I stayed quiet, physically biting my tongue inside my mouth. The idea of him being with someone else, especially someone better than me—someone who was less broken than me—made me feel sick to my stomach. I was really scared of losing him, and I felt that fear for the first time during that car ride to the airport.

I checked in for my flight and tagged my two bags. Living out of suitcases for six months at a time had become so routine that I wasn't bothered by not having many belongings. Lucas bought the hardcover of *How Successful People Think: Change Your Thinking, Change Your Life* by John C. Maxwell as a farewell gift and left an encouraging message, urging me to follow my heart on this solo journey. Reading between the lines, I saw again his wish for me to build a strong female character free of my victimhood mentality: 'Dig deeper, Muffy.' I cried reading the inside cover. *I already have,* I thought. I was upset that Lucas had failed to see all the experiences I already possessed at my ripe age of twenty-five, the hardships I'd already overcome, the independence throughout my childhood and teen years that had gotten me to this point.

We said our last goodbyes. Salty tears kissed my full lips as I shook, hoping to prolong his safe embrace, wishing this was all a bad dream. I wanted nothing more than to belong to Lucas, yet I was letting him go with nothing but tears staining his green t-shirt. I was emotionally numb, unable to understand the risk of my solo move to Cairo because I was still high on the freedom from reality that one only experiences when traveling for months around the world. Stepping into the unknown was like mainlining adrenaline.

When would I know when to come back? In a couple of months? A year? When I was 'better,' 'stronger,' 'motlier'? None of those logistics were discussed, and I was somehow okay with that because I understood the unknown could not be predicted.

I turned the corner and headed toward the TSA then stopped to wipe my tears. Peering around the corner, I saw Lucas confidently walking away, and I couldn't help but tremble. Was this the end for us? It couldn't be. Fear gripped me—I was terrified of abandonment. Part of me longed for a movie-like scene where he'd run back, drop to one knee, and plead, "Baby, don't run away. Stay with us. I need you." But we'd had plenty of those moments, and my 'movie moment' cards were all used up. So, I just watched him go. Did he not fear losing me? Was this how love played out, with the universe following its own agenda? I never got the answers to those questions.

Over the years, Lucas had been my guiding father figure. As long as I had his support through this experience, I was ready to fight my demons and strive to be the woman he deserved. I was ready to exchange my bravery for stability, a family of my own, and the chance to finally plant roots at our Forest Drive house. If achieving all of that required surviving in a foreign country without any plans, I was prepared to do it for us.

My soul yearned to see Katya's transformation after her Muslim baptism. Watching the aircraft fill with determined souls, I realized my journey was unmatched. They had homes to return to, but I faced uncertainty. Still, I refused to vanish without a trace; I'd overcome challenges before. Embracing my unconventional life path and growing pains, I said goodbye to Reno, knowing this was just the beginning—the beginning of a story that, looking back now, I wish wasn't mine to tell.

3
AHRAMAAT AL-JIZAH
(JULY 2014)

The hope and excitement I brought from Reno quickly turned into gut-wrenching anxiety when I left Kyiv for Cairo. My brief visit with family in Kyiv didn't offer much reassurance about my move, leaving me with a deep fear of loneliness as I flew over the Black Sea. I simply felt exhausted from already having traveled alone for six months that year and now facing the task of proving my resilience, so I lied to my concerned family that Lucas and I had it all planned out. It all felt fucked up, but my toes were already wet. The thought of all the work ahead of me, mentally and spiritually, had me spinning, so I snorted the last of my painkillers in the lavatory. I suddenly had zero confidence in my ability to thrive in a foreign country without any plans. Deep down, I already knew I would disappoint Lucas; I wasn't like him. I was an addict, and I shouldn't have been on my own.

The metal bird took a sharp turn toward the setting sun, and the cabin flooded with vibrant oranges and pinks. Two girls beside me chatted about life in Cairo. I drifted off in a daydream, sensing the gravitational pull as we descended, overhearing their muffled conversation about Maadi and shisha cafes. At least someone was eager to disembark the plane.

I reached for a motivating memory and teleported back to my Reno home. It was February 2011, and there was almost two feet of snow outside. Lucas and I played *I Will Possess Your Heart* by Death Cab for Cutie on repeat from his small black laptop speakers. It was nearly 3 a.m., and moonlight streamed through the living room windows. We were mere silhouettes, swaying and grinding to the music, holding each other with cups of beer in hand.

We decided to bundle up in our snow gear and take a seat at the metal table in the quiet, snow-covered tea garden. We kept playing this track on repeat, cranking up the volume, opening the doors so the neighbors could enjoy it, too. I set my beer in the snow then straddled him, kissing his frozen lips and tasting the saltiness of his runny nose. It was a perfect moment.

He softly sang the chorus of *I Will Possess Your Heart*, his breath warm despite the snow around us. I let myself believe him.

I wish you saw the potential in me, Lucas, I thought, as the plane landed with a hard thud, slapping me back to the present. *And I will prove myself to you, in a language that you can read.*

From the shuttle bus on the airport tarmac, I saw them—the number one wonder of the world, the massive piles of granite, their construction shrouded in mystery that only God could explain. The Ahramat Al-Jizah, the Giza Pyramids, were truly sublime. The three giants of mystery stood proud and stable in the Sahara sand. They embodied the essence of secrecy, radiating wonder and luring human worshippers fascinated by the unknown. Looking at the pyramids reminded me of what Lucas had taught me: *Thrive in the power of the unknown.*

Dragging my luggage toward the sliding exit doors, I encountered a group of restless Egyptian men blocking my way. "Oh shit, here come the catcalls," I muttered, taking a deep breath. I had forgotten how much attention I'd attracted here when Lucas and I had traveled together; it was easier then, but now I was fending for myself. *I hope Lemo is here,* I prayed with shaking hands and wide-pupil eyes.

"Kateryna!" a familiar voice yelled from the edge of the swarm.

I rushed toward the voice and met Lemo with a warm hug and smile.

"Let's get you off the street," he ordered, steering me by my shoulder toward the curb. We got into the cab he'd reserved.

I finally let out my breath. "I promised you I would be back," I said.

"You promised yourself. Welcome to Egypt!" he answered, smiling. "There is an Egyptian saying that says, 'Once you drink from the Nile, you will come back again.'"

"Wow, it is so true. Here I am!" I smiled to myself from the back seat of the taxi, looking at the endless sea of traffic on the 6th of October Bridge.

It felt good to be under someone's wing for now and off the streets; landing in a third-world country is hard on the senses. I was glad it was Lemo, as it brought back the sense of security Lucas and I had felt when we'd first met Lemo in December 2012. Meeting Lemo had been like a breath of fresh air amid the crowded graffitied streets around Tahrir Square. He stood taller than the average 5'8" Egyptian man. He was in his mid-thirties with a light skin tone, a shiny bald head, and greenish-brown eyes. His wide, hooked nose and his contagious smile made him look more Italian than Arab. The way he walked, as though he was floating, and the calmness in his voice, gave away that he was a hopeless romantic and an artist at heart even though he worked as an accountant at an offshore oil company.

"It's so nice to see you again, Lemo! Really. Lucas says hello, too."

"Oh, Lucas! He still thinks I look like his dad, huh?" He laughed.

"Yes, yes, he does. I still can't believe you sang his dad's favorite Frank Sinatra song to us in the cab that last time we saw you before our flight out. The two of us cried to sleep that night. Lucas swears his dad's soul lives on through you," I reminded him.

"Allah works in very mysterious ways, Kat," he said, reaching out to hold my hand. Despite his thoughtfulness, this gesture immediately reinforced the stereotype of 'overly ambitious Egyptian males.' I hoped he wouldn't proceed any further, as men touching women in public was not the norm, or at least, that was what I remembered about street etiquette in any Muslim country.

It was past midnight when we finally dove into the maddening traffic of downtown Cairo. It was July 21, and the end of Ramadan was just a week away. Antsy young boys filled the streets with their tight jeans and brightly colored knockoff designer shirts. They celebrated by screaming, sounding air horns, and hurling firecrackers at passing cars, displaying a restless energy that matched my own aimlessness. Cairo was louder than I remembered; constantly blaring car horns echoed painfully inside my already-mushy brain. I trembled with overstimulation, already exhausted from Cairo, even from the backseat of the cab.

I checked into my 2.5-star hotel just around the corner of the main Tahrir Square and followed the bellboy up the echoey spiral staircase to the third floor.

"Are you hungry for dinner?" Lemo asked in the hotel lobby when I came back down to say goodbye. I was about to decline the midnight dinner proposal when Lemo grabbed my shoulder again and led me outside to hail a cab. It was another instance of uncalled-for physical touch, leaving me without a choice but to go along.

"Oh, sure, okay. Thank you." I forced a smile. To him, having a visitor from the States during such a big Muslim holiday was probably an honor. I felt obligated to keep him company, especially since he had just paid for the cab and tipped the bellboy for my bags.

Lemo escorted me to El Prince, the same place he had taken Lucas and me before. El Prince, pronounced 'El Brince' because there is no letter or sound of *P* in Arabic, is an iconic outdoor restaurant/grill on the side of the road in a poorer neighborhood of the Nile front. It had been around for thirty-plus years and was famous among travelers, too. We navigated through the maze of thin metal chairs and rickety butcher-style tables, passing through the grill smoke, relying solely on the stringed lights to guide us to the back table.

To my surprise, Lemo's friends were waiting for us. After we formally introduced ourselves and I shook hands with the five other men around the table, the other local diners' necks finally kinked, and the crowd minded their own business. I was glad to feel that the novelty of my presence—with blonde hair and white skin—had worn off.

"Okay, Kat, here's what we ordered: molokheya, a traditional thick green soup with rabbit, various salads, rice, grilled chicken, grilled beef tongue, beef calf tendon stew, and, well...you'll see!" Lemo said.

I didn't feel hungry. Even amidst the smoke from the grill, the noise of the traffic, and the Arabic chatter, it was hard to keep my eyes open. I'd forgotten how foreign and chaotic Cairo felt and how much it affected me despite my experiences in third-world countries like India and Myanmar. I nibbled on everything, stayed silent, and absorbed this entirely different reality that I was now calling 'home.'

I remembered Lucas's Travels Abroad 101: *The first twenty-four hours in a foreign place are the best! Take it all in and embrace that feeling because soon it will become the new normal.* I got a second gust of energy from that thought.

"What's that?" I asked, pointing to what looked like cut-up strips of calamari. Even before getting an answer, I forked a piece and chewed it up.

"That's umm...." Lemo began to laugh. "Do you like it?" he asked, looking concerned.

"What is it? It's very chewy, is it calamari?" I gave him a squinty-faced look.

"No, dear, that's...cow penis," he replied.

The men broke out in laughter.

My stomach turned inside out, and I gagged the remains out of my mouth onto the ground, just barely missing Lemo's shoe.

After the eventful dinner, Lemo took me to the Nile island of Zamalek for shisha. The cow penis ordeal had jolted me awake—I was ready to embrace the night in Cairo.

We sat at a crowded local cafe called L.S. I thought, *How appropriate, Lucas's initials*. The small alley was packed with plastic white chairs and tables. Groups of young-adult boys and a few couples sat drinking from tall Coke cans with straws. The shisha man walked around with large metal tongs, clicking them every few seconds while twirling the burning amber coals in a giant ladle. Most of the eyes were on me.

Fuck, I thought. *I don't know what it feels like to live as a minority*. Egypt seemed like the perfect place to toughen up and learn that lesson. This was unlike any other trip I'd taken; there was no return flight booked this time, which made everything feel more intense. I reminded myself of Lucas's teachings about the first twenty-four hours in a new place: *Feel all the newness and be a spectator of reality; don't question it, don't fight it, just exist*.

I took my first drag of grape shisha, and, wow...this was what Arabic nights would forever taste like: sweet, musky, and served at 2 a.m..

I stared down the alley of black-haired locals and imagined what my life would look like here. It felt innocent spending the early hours of the morning with Coke on ice and hookah pipes; it was nothing like the West, where beer and vodka would be in hand. I imagined my almost-pious, quiet life, where I'd sit by the window and journal my thoughts, perhaps digging to the roots of my little addiction. I thought about the Turkish coffee I would be drinking on the streets in the early mornings. I wondered if I could find a gym or a park in which to walk daily.

I hadn't planned for a job here, but naturally I knew I'd find something using the skill most of the people here—and in most third-world countries—wanted: I spoke the English language well enough to teach it. I'd be a teacher somewhere, like Lucas had been.

After I'd spent some time letting my thoughts fill with rich and colorful future memories of being an expat in the heart of the Middle East, Lemo interrupted my dream state: "Hey, I want to show you my art. Can I?"

Lemo showed me a few pictures of his paintings of women's figures and flowers on his Samsung phone, treating it like he was showing me something taboo by cupping the screen's side with his palm. I gathered that he likely hadn't shown his art to many people, and as a foreigner, I could appreciate it even more.

"They are beautiful—very nice," I said with a soft smile.

The chatter of unfamiliar language around us grew louder, overloading my senses. I strained my ears to at least make out different words, even without knowing their meaning, but it all sounded like one long, undivided sound. *Arabic will be hard to learn,* I thought, but it all felt ironically comfortable. I noticed I was okay with being the outsider; I was totally present sitting on that plastic white chair in an unmarked alley on an island in the Nile.

I suddenly realized that the ease of being truly present stemmed from not knowing myself well enough—my sense of belonging, my kin, and my purpose. All I had was that present moment and a mission to fulfill without an operating guide. A darker thought crossed my mind: opioids had numbed me to the point where what felt normal was actually a lack of awareness and plans. As long as I had a supply of pills, the uncertainty of tomorrow didn't cause me anxiety. I enjoyed simply drifting along in the present moment, experiencing ultimate peace without judgment or expectation. Being in an opioid haze shielded me from diving into my deep thoughts and the traumas of childhood abuse and neglect.

"A journey like this, Lemo, is not for the faint of heart," I said.

"Sorry, I couldn't catch that," Lemo said, leaning in.

"You see, Lemo, I am here to learn something about myself.

Lucas and I are figuring things out, you know, for our future. Our relationship is up and down. We travel well together, we have fun together, but there is something missing; we fight, I fight more with him. I don't know—I want more. But I need to overcome a few things away from him. Cairo was my idea. We have so many experiences together here, so many memories. He's taught me so much about life. I really hope to overcome my shit so maybe we can get married one day," I replied with my head down.

What I really wanted to say was, *I'm a closet pill addict with a cocktail of traumas, anxiety, and depression. I lie to people every day, pretending to be something I am not, when in reality I am probably worthless. I want to be good enough for the man I love, but he would leave if he knew I was an addict.*

"Well, do you have a ticket back? When are you leaving?" he asked.

"I don't have one. I guess until I earn the money to come back. I must find a job," I replied. I really didn't have any money in savings or gold to sell. I could maybe ask my mother for help, but that always made me feel bad and as though I looked weak in her eyes.

"Do you think you will eventually get married to Lucas?" Lemo pried. I felt he asked me this for his own benefit. I instantly regretted discussing my relationship problems with Lemo. Maybe in Lemo's eyes, I was a free woman; maybe he thought this was a date.

Not wanting Lemo to get the wrong idea, I fabricated an answer that I hoped would prove to be true. "Of course. After four years, we should be, right? We just want to live separately for a little bit. I want to travel more, he has his business to run at home."

"How could he let you go just like that? And alone to Egypt?" Lemo asked the question I didn't want to answer. How *had* he just let me go like that? "Do you love him?"

"Yes, I love him. Very much. Maybe I'm not good enough to be loved back," I replied.

"You? Not good enough? Ha! You are smart, beautiful, and interesting. You have lots of courage. I only met you twice, but you have this way with people. So many talents. I mean, you have to love your-self. Don't you see that?" he preached from the edge of his seat.

"Anyways...should we go for a walk?" I asked, changing the subject.

He signaled to the waiter to come over. Instead of having his palm open toward him with his fingers folding in a flutter, his palm was facing toward the waiter, resembling a Western gesture for 'goodbye.' Everything seemed reversed here.

We strolled under the Zamalek bridge, weaving through the steady stream of cars, heading toward the Nile then down the Cornish Road by central Cairo, Tahrir Square, all the while listening to Lemo's playlist from his Samsung. I sat by the Egyptian museum near Tahrir Square, surrounded by tanks and barricades. I took out my iPhone and snapped some photos of the stray black cats, capturing their shadows cast by the dark yellow lampposts and the dried palm branches along the concrete roadblocks, aiming to convey the emotion of that moment. To me, the cats were a poignant represen-tation of life amidst chaos and instability. They didn't care if they were on a five-star resort beach in Hawaii or at an Islamic military-controlled historic tourist attraction; they simply wanted to survive. I felt like a homeless cat, searching for shelter and food, unsure of where to find either or if they would come tomorrow.

Lemo played Nina Simone's *Wild is the Wind* on repeat, as though on a movie set, in complete silence.

Once again, I was searching for answers in the wind. It was the same wind that had made me think of moving to Cairo when I was in Reno, a wind that could bring a storm or clear skies. I didn't know what changes were coming my way. I had a little hope that there would be better days, but it wasn't strong. I was scared of what my flawed character could wreak if unleashed.

I thought, *I'd rather be here with Lucas.* My heart ached. He could make the unknown less scary and turn any foreign land into a home.

I used to believe I thrived on the unknown, but that moment gave me a new perspective on what 'unknown' really meant. I usually entrusted the responsibility of navigating the unknown to Lucas as I indulged in my codeine high, filled with self-loathing and negative thoughts.

At that moment, I felt alienated and uncomfortable in my own dark presence. The hungry stray cats and a strange man sitting next to me reflected the turmoil within myself. Jobless, without a career or home, and possibly without a boyfriend, I sat in the heart of Cairo, Egypt. Despite the fear of losing my identity as a traveler/girlfriend to a successful man/survivor and fighter/graduate/artist, I felt like I belonged amidst the armored tanks. My inner Kateryna, neglected and filled with despair and hatred for life's unfair ways, silently comforted me on that bench. *We deserve this,* she said.

We don't, but you do, Katya answered. *Your mother doesn't love you, remember? You think some man can? Any man can?*

Katya was on her high horse, rebelling and basking in self-loathing. She really did feel superior while hiding behind her pill cravings. She didn't need her past to define her—just to keep her numb to the present; she was in a constant state of limbo, trusting that the world around her would have her back.

They were exhausting to make sense of. Not today. I was beyond ready for sleep.

The night finally ended around 3 a.m. Lemo walked me back to my hotel, a few blocks from Tahrir Square, wanting to chat more, but I couldn't keep my eyes open. In my room, I was pleased to discover there was a functioning AC. Sleep didn't come easily, even after I'd been up for over twenty-four hours. Thus, I journaled a rough plan.

FIND A JOB BY END OF THIS WEEK!!!

Keep pushing forward, you have six days.

I fell asleep on that productive note.

. . .

The next morning, I made the decision to change my hotel room because forty dollars a night was too expensive. While enjoying a Turkish coffee and a cigarette at the downstairs cafe, I searched for new accommodations. I had three hundred American dollars and roughly the same amount in Egyptian pounds left from selling my Subaru. All the money I had earned over the last two years in Reno had been spent on travels with Lucas. I'd saved the tips in a jar on the living room bookshelf and used them for tickets and food abroad.

By third-world-country standards, this amount should techni-cally have gotten me through two months. However, during my pharmacy patrol before breakfast, I'd found Solpadeine capsules priced at roughly twelve dollars a box. These 500mg capsules contained only 8mg of codeine along with paracetamol and caffeine —a disappointing find. Yet, they were the strongest I could find, and I could purchase them without a doctor's note.

"How exactly do you expect me to get a doctor's note? He is all the way in America!" I argued with the young pharmacist. I had been sober for almost twenty-four hours by then and could feel the with-drawals coming on.

"I am sorry, ma'am, we don't have anything stronger. Not allowed in Egypt," he and the assistant pharmacists told me.

The Solpadeine box contained thirty-two capsules, and every red-and-yellow box had a warning stating, "Can cause addiction, use only for three days." It was too late for me; I had to take three capsules at a time to feel any effect and do so two to three times a day. I needed at least 72mg of codeine daily just to function. There-fore, one box would only last me two and a half days. I really needed a job; I'd blow through my six hundred dollars in no time.

The idea of not being able to support my addiction caused me more anxiety than the uncertainty of where I would be living next week or how I would get a ticket back to Reno. This was the first time I honestly felt disgusted by the control these pills had over me. My lack of pills was a bigger concern than being homeless in the heart of the Arab world. "Great job, Katya! You've really got a good head on your shoulders," I said under my breath.

My new place, Dahab Hostel, was closer to downtown Tahrir and advertised as 'Your Oasis in the City.' It featured a tile-floored rooftop terrace, affordable single-bed rooms with straw-thatched walls, and a common kitchen area equipped with two portable stove tops and a large gas tank. A sign reminded guests to 'Turn gas OFF when not using the stove.' The space was adorned with potted plants, palm trees, a few water features, two orange cats, and plenty of small tables and chairs filling the empty areas.

Compared to the red Sahara and stone buildings below, Dahab Hostel truly lived up to its name as an oasis. Despite the scorching temperatures of about 110°F during the day, each room had its own bathroom with a showerhead. And at just thirteen dollars per night, it was an incredible deal.

Lack of sleep, poor diet, terrible air quality, and stress gave me a severe fever, leaving me miserable. I sat on the toilet with stomach issues, cold water running above me, battling the flu and food poisoning. I must have gotten sick from the street food I'd eaten at the end of an alley on my first night in Dahab Hostel. The desk boy had recommended it, praising Mama Nadine's homemade meals and even drawing directions on a piece of paper. The thought of those rice-stuffed grape leaves made me nauseous.

I only paid for three nights at a time, so when the desk guy knocked on my door that morning, I was shocked to learn that three nights had already passed.

"I'll stay for three more nights, if you have space," I told him, peeking through the straw door. "I've been so sick, I can't even get out of bed."

"Okay, three more nights," he replied. "You pay at check out!"

I had everything I needed: Solpadeine and cigarettes in my pocket. Being high truly alleviated stress. Lucas wrote, inquiring about my arrival and Lemo's wellbeing. I responded, imitating his writing style and punctuation, attempting to sound less terrified and pissed off at my situation and more like, 'I'm having the time of my life without you.'

By some Islamic miracle, I snapped out of my sickness at sundown. A crowd had gathered behind the brick wall on the neighboring rooftop, an extension of the hostel that I hadn't noticed before. Sounds of loud American rock music and clinking glass bottles drifted into my room, making me crave company.

"Hi, everyone, I'm...Kat!" I shyly introduced myself to the dim-lit crowd of mostly young men. Codeine helped me feel a bit more open.

It was only then that I realized I struggled with choosing which name to use when introducing myself. I noticed that *Katya* was for friends and Facebook friends from my Alaska days, *Kat* was for the hipsters in Reno and 'new-age' travelers, and *Kateryna* was for passport controls, doctor's appointments, or if I wanted to showcase my Ukrainian heritage. However, all three identities were those of a closet pill addict. That thought filled me with disgust once again. It was the second time this week that I had consciously identified as a druggy.

"Welcome, Kitty-Kat!" a bubbly, New-York-accented voice replied. "Want a beer?"

"Sure, thanks!" I took it and sat on the sunburned floor pillow.

"I'm Sherif! Or Anthony back in the States!" the 6'4", slender, and perfectly bald guy answered.

Oh good, I thought. *Another person who uses many names.*

Sherif, who was twenty-seven, spoke Moroccan Arabic fluently and had previously lived in Marrakech. I had also been to Marrakech, so we had plenty to chat about. His mother was Moroccan, and his father was from Spain. They'd grown up in Hell's Kitchen in New York City, and Sherif used to work as a male model. A few years ago, he discovered he had alopecia areata, a condition where the immune system attacks hair follicles, leading to hair loss and resulting in his perfectly bald head. He showed me old photos of himself, and he looked incredibly hairy and handsome.

Unfortunately, now he resembled a cancer patient without eyelashes or eyebrows. However, his upbeat personality quickly overshadowed the initial shock of his appearance, and by the end of the night, I didn't even notice his lack of body hair.

We talked about where we were from and why we had chosen to live in Cairo. I fibbed, saying I wanted to learn about culture and life outside the US and that my boyfriend was waiting for me back home. It was hard to say and felt fake, but that was the story I had decided on, and I stuck to it. I was still struggling to grasp the idea of a "strengthening journey to become a better woman," and I knew others wouldn't understand it, either.

"Why am I living in Cairo, you ask?" Sherif said. "Well, just like you, Kitty-Kat, I'm working on healing. This disease really knocked me on my ass. I'm reconnecting with my Arab roots, and Cairo is more fun than Marrakech."

Fair enough, I thought. A big part of me liked that he, too, was struggling; we were trauma bonding. I also appreciated that he could see through my bullshit coverup story. His Cairo alias story seemed more believable and relatable than mine. The uncomfortable silence that followed showed that we both understood each other's inner struggles.

Another Islamic miracle: Sherif was looking for work in Cairo, too!

"There is this language academy school here, and they take anyone who speaks in an American accent. I am going to see them tomorrow. You should come, too!" Sherif suggested.

That was easy, I thought. In my view, finding employment in Reno or in Cairo was equally simple. I'd even argue that it's easier to secure a job in a foreign country since many high-end businesses require English-speaking-and-writing individuals. I had known this already, having traveled to twenty countries and meeting expats along the way. After all, I'd earned a high honors bachelor's degree from a top-tier university in the States and had been accepted into one of the top institutes for neuroscience in the world. I could find employment. I wasn't a dud; I simply wasn't applying my education and instead was traveling around the world with a noncommittal thirty-seven-year-old man, hoping to prove to him that I was wife material.

My approach to work had remained the same since my early days working with my mother in Alaska: I could figure out how to earn money anywhere. I wasn't afraid of hard work. What mattered wasn't how much I made but rather how much I spent. Over the years, I'd cleaned homes and toilets, made sushi and pizza, worked at gas stations, coffee shops, spas, bars, and restaurants, cooked meals for families after college classes, and detailed cars. I always kept a copy of my resume in my email account, prepared to submit it for a new position.

"Oh my God, really, are you sure? I would love to! Thank you!" I said, certain I would get the job and might even be chosen over Sherif if it came to that. Besides, teaching English was the number one position I wanted to find in Cairo, as it would get me the closest to experiencing what Lucas had while living abroad years ago.

Later that evening, another traveler joined us. Teo was a short, skinny Italian journalist with dark curls, a full beard, and far too much chest hair. He produced short films for an alternative media company in Naples. In 2012, he had been shot in the liver during one of the many anti-military-rule protests while filming the chaos. He'd spent a month in the ICU and lost seventy percent of his blood. Two years later, he'd returned to Cairo because "seventy percent of my blood was from Egyptian donors. I am here to make peace with my near-death experience before retiring from seeking stories."

Cairo attracted interesting people and changed their destinies. Maybe my story here would end in a serendipitous and fulfilling way.

We concluded our night at the Dahab oasis by watching fireworks explode along the Nile below us. It was the last day of

Ramadan, and the city was going off in celebration. I was thrilled to have met a couple of interesting travelers and made friends. The three broken amigos. All of us were here to use Cairo to overcome some hardship in life. I hoped Cairo wouldn't mind if we used her chaos, uncertainty, struggle, history, and dusty magic as the stage for our ultimate transformation. Deep down, we felt better about our lost selves when we compared ourselves to those living in the dirty streets and poverty of Cairo. Our lives weren't as terrible; we didn't have to live here permanently.

I ignored Lemo's calls. I felt he was courting me with lines like, "You are made of love," and "Your soul is so precious," which he had said just four days ago as we'd sat drinking tea after a three-hour Egyptian museum tour. Egyptian men were known for being flirtatious and sexually deprived, as their culture and religion didn't allow premarital sex, but I didn't owe Lemo anything and decided not to even tell Lucas about it, if he ever came around to asking.

It's a known fact that Egypt has the highest rate of sexual harassment in the world. Some ninety-eight percent of females have experienced a form of harassment in public. I knew this prior to coming to Egypt on this trip, as I'd experienced it firsthand. Lucas knew this, having seen me being hissed at as soon as he'd taken a step away from my direction back on our trip in 2012.

Not only did this attention make me feel disgust toward the local men, but it also made me disgusted with myself. My junkie thoughts asked, *Maybe you should let them use and abuse you? You've already let others down.* The louder the catcall, the emptier I felt.

The following morning, in Cairo's tradition of starting the day around noon, Sherif and I boarded the subway to Dokki Station. From there, it was another ten-minute walk to Reach Out Language Academy. Although businesses were operational, people were slow to fill the streets due to their typical nightlife habits and preference to avoid the scorching heat of the day.

The subway stations in Cairo surprised me; they were clean! There was no smell of urine, vomit, or homeless individuals. Surprisingly, homeless people didn't sleep on the streets, either. Instead, they gathered in abandoned housing projects. They were the ones who approached your taxi window during endless traffic jams, hoping to sell you a rose. Toddlers and children rummaged through trash while their hijab-wearing mothers sat on broken road dividers cradling another baby in their henna-tattooed hands.

Petty crimes, theft, and murder were not very common. I appreciated this about the Muslims. They would take up any job, sell various trinkets, or use verbal persuasion to ask for money rather than resorting to robbery or violence. Ironically, it was the poorest people who most strictly adhered to Islamic morals. Therefore, poverty-stricken citizens of Cairo were not a threat. Although there may have been a dark side to their world, such as human trafficking, organ sales on the black market, and child prostitution, I chose to focus on the positives. I felt more fear walking on casino floors in Reno at 3 a.m. than I ever did in Cairo. Though there were catcalls, Egyptians rarely used force to harm others, especially White foreigners.

Sherif and I walked to the academy. Having him with me helped to ward off some of the catcalls. Similar to many buildings in Cairo, the ones on Dokki Street stood between three to six floors and were made of concrete and covered in red-textured stucco. The entire street looked as if it had been hit by a bomb, with trash, debris from buildings, and broken cars scattered along the tightly packed structures. I never had the desire to learn their construction year; if I were to guess, it would be in the 1930s. A sun-bleached blue-and-red sign jutted out from the third-floor window and read, 'Reach O_t Acad__m_ 6th floor.'

"Looks like on the top floor," Sherif said.

The building was somehow still intact despite missing corner bricks and a few cement stairs. We proceeded to the mid-century elevator, slid the metal accordion door shut, and pressed the top black unmarked button.

"I'm terrified of elevators," I said, closing my eyes and holding onto the walls.

We reached the sixth floor where the Reach Out Group (ROG) sign hung outside the heavy wooden door. Surprisingly, the interior of the academy looked very modern. The reception room had many black foldout chairs in rows, shiny parquet floors, clean blinds on the windows, two flat-screen TVs, and a roll-up standing banner advertising the 'Best Language Program in Cairo: Lessons in English, Spanish, German, French, and Russian.'

Two receptionists greeted us from behind a rounded counter. One introduced herself as Mona and quickly jumped up to help us. She gave Sherif and me each a Welcome Package. She asked us to take a seat until the CEO was ready for our interview. Mona wore a lot of makeup, including bright pink lipstick that made her teeth look yellow. She had straight eyebrows (a popular style in Egypt that reminded me of the ancient Pharaohs) and wore a bright pink headscarf with a matching tunic and black leggings. Her movements and English were a bit erratic, matching her bubbly personality. I asked for a glass of water, and she brought me a whole bottle.

"Mr. Mina Raafat will see you now. Come this way, please." She smiled with her yellow teeth.

Mr. Raafat sat behind a large oak desk in a small room that was painted mostly black, with one wall accented in Christmas green. There was a black leather loveseat and a small table right by the entrance.

"Come in, have a seat," he said, pointing to the chairs in front of his desk. I closed the door behind us. A moment later, a younger Egyptian man slipped in and nodded at us. He stood behind Mr. Raafat as if on guard duty. The room was filled with the scent of his Armani cologne. A great-smelling man was my weakness. He was cute and muscular.

Mr. Raafat acted strangely. He began talking about the Reach Out

Academy's history but avoided eye contact and kept looking behind us. *Maybe he's nervous*, I thought.

Sherif did his interview first. Surprisingly, they didn't ask about resumes or credentials. Instead, the CEO asked about Sherif's school performance, what he had studied, and where he had grown up.

"Ah, I really like your accent, Sherif. Never been to New York, but it's on my list!" he said.

Then the interview shifted to me. I answered the same questions.

"Thank you, I think both of you will do well here. If you can complete the paperwork in the Welcome Package, we can start right away," Mr. Raafat said.

This was not what I was used to from interviews back in the Western world. I had many questions and felt the need to interview the employer because so much information had not been disclosed.

"Um...I have questions," I said in a low tone. "What are the work hours? What is the pay? How are the classrooms structured? I have many questions about the job. Will I be teaching one student or many?"

"Mr. Samir," Mr. Raafat said to the man who had entered the room after us.

"Ah, yes, I am Samir, I'm the teacher's manager here," he said with an almost perfect American accent. "All very valid questions, and that is something we will discuss with each of you, one on one. Salary does depend on your level of knowledge, work experience, and availability. But we are looking for full-time teachers."

"Okay, what does full-time mean? I'm sorry, I just came to Egypt, this would be my first job experience here," I said, smiling at him. Codeine helped me not to blush.

"Well, we are open seven days a week here at Reach Out Academy to accommodate all our students' schedules. We have school-age teens, young adults, and business professionals—all age groups. But anywhere from five to six full days. Or double shift on day five, and that would give you two days off. We can work out a deal that is right for you, Kateryna," he said, looking too deeply into my eyes. He licked his lips and cocked his head to the side, looking up and down my legs.

"Sounds good, Samir. Thank you," I replied with a smile. I needed him to like me so I could ask for higher pay in case my perfect American accent and education background were not enough.

Sherif and I shook hands with everyone and left with a, "We'll bring the teacher enrollment paperwork and sample lesson exercises on Sunday, thank you for your time!"

On the way down the dreaded elevator, Sherif broke the ice. "Well, Samir likes you. I think you'll get good pay, no problem. It's me I'm worried about. If only I was blonde and female like you!"

"I won't work there without you, Sherif! You better be there with me!" I said, playfully angry. "Your journalism background is impressive. I don't have any certified English teaching background. He did say 'based on your education.'"

"Yeah, but you are cuter. You'll get the top dollar. I'm sure of it," Sherif replied, as we stepped onto the hot sidewalk. I followed close behind him so as not to lose him in the army of pedestrians.

There was some truth in his observations; being a blonde, female foreigner with a nice figure gave me an advantage in Egypt. I'd picked up on this concept in just an hour of sitting in a room of men deciding my hire. Perhaps I could become popular with the male students and improve the school's rating numbers. Sex sells—that is known everywhere in the world. In Egypt, they are candid about it, but only toward foreigners.

"Mina Rafaat is blind anyways, so maybe my lack of good looks didn't offend him," Sherif said.

"What? How do you know he's blind? I didn't notice it," I replied.

"Kitty-Kat, you really need to learn to read the room, Ms. Psychology Major! He never made eye contact with us. He is blind. Samir had to click things for him on the computer. And the weird handshake. He let me grab his hand and not the other way around," Sherif explained.

"I thought something was off. Wow, he really is blind," I said in astonishment. How had I missed that? Damn codeine pills. By that point, I was feeling pretty high. The pills had kicked in while we were in the lobby, and I thanked God for Mona bringing me the whole bottle of water to ease my cottonmouth. If it hadn't been for the pills, I wouldn't have had the guts to ask about the pay or give a sly smile to my future manager as a means of coercing a higher wage.

I spent the weekend looking for places to rent and brushing up on my English grammar as part of the Reach Out Language Academy onboarding. *I have been taking opiates for nine years now.* That's in present-perfect continuous tense, easy enough to remember.

During a follow-up call, Samir informed me of my working schedule. As in all Islamic countries, workdays were from Sunday to Thursday, with Friday reserved for family and prayer and Saturday designated for sleeping. I was scheduled to work from 9 a.m. until 7:30 p.m. on weekdays, teaching five classes with an hour for lunch break. Despite clenching my teeth, I accepted my workload politely.

It was harder for me to accept my starting pay. Samir stated that the best he could offer was $314 a month, with no room for negotiations. He also mentioned during his long explanation that all teachers have their own salaries and that discussing pay amongst ourselves was not allowed. This didn't seem fair, but again, I realized it wasn't my place to step in and change things in this country.

"That's not enough. That wouldn't even cover rent! I saw a few places on the expat forum going for a minimum of eight hundred dollars," I whined into the phone as I popped another codeine capsule.

"That's probably somewhere in Maadi or Zamalek. You can find a cheaper room right by the school in Dokki," Samir replied, unfazed.

"How do I find that?" I asked.

"Craigslist. You don't know Craigslist?" Samir asked.

"Of course, I know Craigslist," I replied in a bratty tone. I had never spoken to my managers in the past as though they were ex-boyfriends, but something told me that Samir—being only five years older than me and having lived in the States before, plus having been married to a woman from New Jersey for a hot second—was going to be the sexual harasser at work. I could feel his sexual attraction to me through the phone.

"Okay, I'll look right now," I said. "I guess I can't complain. It's a job. You think that's good pay for Cairo?"

"It's good enough. You seem like a smart girl who knows how to handle situations," he said, again in a sultry voice.

"Okay, thanks, I have to–"

"Do you want to get dinner with me tonight as a celebration for your new position?" Samir interrupted.

"No, thanks, I have to look for housing. See you on Sunday," I replied and hung up the phone.

Isn't it ironic how the man you desperately want usually doesn't want you, and the ones you wouldn't give the time of day are constantly chasing you? Samir's desperation made me swallow my nerves and brush off his advancements. Besides, I'd missed my goal of finding employment by a week, and I had planned to write an email to Lucas with news of my new job. I considered this teaching position to be the best option for now, but I intended to continue looking for better opportunities.

Samir's suggestion about Craigslist paid off, as I found a more affordable rental option there. I applied to two listings within a five-mile radius of Reach Out Language Academy with the hope of securing a room advertised for a female roommate in a large three-bedroom apartment near the metro station. I received a response later that evening and arranged for a viewing at 10 a.m. with Mr. Harish, the landlord.

The next day, I went to the apartment building. A door on the first floor was ajar, so I entered with a polite knock. Inside, a short man in his late sixties was arguing loudly on the phone. He motioned for me to go toward the balcony where the room was located.

To my surprise, the room was spacious and equipped with a queen bed, clothing shelves, and a small plastic desk. Mr. Harish continued yelling into the phone. I peeked out of the room and nodded in agreement. He promptly took out a pen and paper from his pocket and wrote down the monthly rental price of 2000 LE. I crossed out his number and wrote my negotiating price: 1,500 LE. After biting his lip and scanning my body three times, he reached into his pocket for two keys. He rubbed his fingers together in the 'money' gesture. I paid him, and without a goodbye, he stormed out of the door, still screaming into his Nokia phone.

'Hi Lucas,

I found a great teaching job and an awesome room for rent just twenty minutes away by foot! It came with its struggles, but I did it! Super excited. I miss talking to you, but I know this is going to be short-lived, so I will make the best of my time here. I'll send you some pictures later if you want of the space. Hope you are well. Love, Muffy.'

I was relieved that in just seventeen days, I'd settled into some normality. I was proud of my place at 20 El Sad El Aaly St, first floor, apartment number 2, right on the outskirts of the Dokki district. I'm sure Lucas would have settled in within ten days and his place would have been overlooking the pyramids, unlike mine, which was in a poor neighborhood. However, he didn't have to deal with sexual objectification; that isn't part of any man's normal existence in Cairo. As women, we always have to keep our wits about us and be constantly on the lookout for someone ruining our day or using us. That makes any task harder to accomplish, forcing us to accept things as 'good enough' just to avoid being on the streets or making extra trips on public transport.

4
WHITE POWDER
(AUGUST 2014)

One morning, while walking to the language academy, I wondered if my mother had ever fought to keep my father around. He didn't seem like a bad guy, though I had only really known my dad since I was eighteen. In the six years since, he had been a constant email and text companion, offering the best advice and lending an ear whenever I needed to talk. So, that evening, I called him and finally asked him why he left; I asked his side of the fallout story.

"I don't want you to think badly of your mother, but she was cheating on me. And not with one but many partners," my father confessed on the phone.

Honestly, it didn't surprise me—but how did she live with her mistakes? I realized that my childhood was a lie and that she had manipulated me into believing that my father was the problem. She wasn't strong enough to take the blame for her mistakes. That was why my prayers and wishes for her happiness as a child had never come true; she was at fault, too. With each passing day, after that conversation, I grew more and more bitter with my newfound truth, and that bitterness tainted my reality, leaving me desperate to find someone—anyone—in this world to trust.

I needed a close friend to make me feel like there was someone I could safely share my burdens with. I had Sherif and the three other foreign teachers at work, but I didn't want to mix my personal life with work. I had only my roommates left to befriend, but that wasn't easy.

Even after living in my new apartment for a week, I hadn't had the opportunity to meet my roommates. Our working schedules were different; I worked in the mornings while the Ukrainian girl didn't get back home until around 1 or 2 a.m. I heard the front door slam in the early morning hours and her phone calls in Ukrainian at the reception. The other occupied room was locked; all I knew about her was that she read an Asian magazine, *Vivi*, which she left out on the reception table.

"Put the teapot on," a stern, female, Ukrainian voice called from the west hall of the dark apartment.

Startled, I put out my cigarette as if I'd been caught and chastised for smoking. It was Thursday night, the start of the weekend, and I'd thought I was home alone.

"I wanted to inform you that I have guests coming," I said in formal Russian. There was no reply, just a return to the usual eerie silence.

My local Nokia cellphone—which I used in Cairo because my iPhone 4 was not jailbroken and couldn't take foreign sim cards—rang. It was Sherif.

"We are almost there, I think. Brandon is with me. So, how do we do this? Do you want us to come up, or you'll come down, or what, Kitty-Kat?" Sherif's bubbly New York accent echoed off the empty apartment walls.

"Hey, okay, let me check if the beweb is sitting there, hang on, I'll come down. Stay on the phone," I replied.

We lived on the first floor although, technically, it was the second, but they counted the ground floor as zero. I left the apartment and walked down the concrete spiral staircase, skipping steps three and twelve, as they were missing. The plastic white chair where the beweb usually sat was empty, but I knew he was close by.

The beweb, also known as the doorman, played a crucial role in every building in Cairo, whether it was a hospital, local business, or an apartment. Typically, the beweb—who was usually a man from a village in Upper Egypt—served as the unofficial manager of the apartment building. He wore an off-white galabeya and a full-bodied robe, smoked frequently, and was well-informed about everyone in the building.

His responsibilities included washing the floors, repairing the elevator, assisting with grocery deliveries, and locking the entrance doors at 3 a.m. He was familiar with every family and tenant in the building. One of his most important tasks was ensuring that unmarried couples did not enter the building together, in line with Muslim moral conduct. Since we were the only foreigners renting in that building, he was particularly vigilant about any unauthorized visitors. I learned about this from my Egyptian students when a lesson came up on 'community etiquettes in Egypt vs. United States.' Sadly, my students also informed me that foreign girls living together without husbands were often labeled as running a 'haram house' (sin house). I reassured my class that this wasn't the case where I lived.

My first beweb had strong connections. I observed him closely as I smoked my cigarettes from the balcony; he gathered information about residents and their activities. He had numerous police friends who would visit and smoke shisha by the door. He was not someone you wanted to piss off; if we were caught sneaking boys into our place, we would be evicted.

"Kitty-Kat, you still there?" Sherif called into the phone. "Dude, we are right on the corner, do you see us?"

"Yeah, I do. Don't look at me, I'll get water from the kiosk and meet you by my door," I said.

"You are so paranoid. Don't worry so much, worry-butt," Sherif replied.

"I'll go into the kiosk, and you go inside, use the elevator, and it's the first floor. If someone else comes in, go up to another floor and just take the stairs back down," I ordered.

"Okay, okay, calm down, it's not my first rodeo," he laughed into the phone.

The boys followed my instructions, aware that someone was always watching on the streets of Cairo. They must have also known that the neighbors watched their visitor activity because they stood hidden behind the elevator doorway when I came to meet them by my door. We stayed silent to prevent the neighbors from getting suspicious and peeking through their spyholes to report us. It didn't help that Sherif and Brandon—who were tall and dressed expensively compared to the local area—were carrying three black plastic bags of glass beer bottles that clanked loudly.

"Oh my God, that was scary!" I exclaimed, releasing a breath of relief and hugging my two friends as we finally entered the apartment. "Hi, hey, thanks for coming!"

"We made it! Get a beer opener," ordered Sherif as they settled down in the living area on the beat-up black leather couches.

"Sorry for the shithole. And, yes, you can smoke inside. Oh, and sorry it's so dark in here, I can't find where to buy more lightbulbs," I apologized.

"We're in Egypt, Kat. Everywhere is shitty, don't worry," reassured Brandon.

The boys and I were three beers deep when I finally met my roommate for the first time. She stood at 5'1" with medium-length, dyed blonde hair, broad shoulders relative to her body size, and a doll-like face featuring big green eyes and petite bowtie lips.

"I asked you to put the teapot on. Did you?" Her stern, annoying, Russian-accented voice startled me, instantly dampening the party mood. The twenty-something woman stood at the kitchen entrance, her eyes moving between the flickering light inside the living area and the empty beer bottles on the coffee table.

"Sorry, I thought you were joking. Hi, these are my friends, Sherif and Brandon. I'm Katya."

"Dasha," she answered quickly. "You should have asked if you can have company over," Dasha continued in broken English so that everyone would understand.

"I told you I had company coming. Have a beer with us, calm down. I didn't know we had these rules," I answered her in my most serious Russian voice.

"I don't drink. Next time ask," the dragon hissed in English before stomping back into her dungeon.

"What was that about? Should we leave?" Sherif broke my stunned silence.

"I'm sorry, dude, I have been here for over a week, and I never met her," I whispered back. "Fuck it. She's rude, I'll talk to her later."

Dasha didn't come out of her room again for the rest of the evening. The guys stayed until 1 a.m. The three of us took turns picking our favorite jams from high school and had a dance-off. It was a fun, innocent night, and I was happy to finally release some energy in a Western way.

ALLAHHHUU AKBAR!

ALLLAAAAAAHHHHHHHUU AKBAR!

Every single morning, I woke up to the male voice on a live intercom leading the adhan, or call to prayer. His voice served as my alarm clock. The adhan could be heard five times a day throughout the city. The dawn announcement was thankfully quieter, and I typically slept through it. I considered myself lucky, or rather blessed, to live one street over from the mosque. The loudspeaker was positioned perfectly, pointing through the building across the street and directly into my corner room.

The man's voice continued to forcefully remind me: *God is Great! God is Great!*

I barely opened my eyes that Friday morning. Fridays were the extra-long prayer days, and the loudspeaker would be blasting Islamic prayers for an hour or so. It was so loud that I couldn't think.

I rolled out of bed and dreaded going into the reception area. There was no way around it; I had to go to the toilet. Dasha was already sitting on the couch, staring into space and smoking an L&M Light. I passed by her, and no words were exchanged. Upon entering the kitchen, I fumbled to turn on the light.

"It doesn't work," she broke the silence.

It was already 10 a.m., yet the concrete house remained dark and gloomy, forcing us to continue using the kitchen light.

"Where can we buy lightbulbs around here?" I asked, forcing a cheerful tone.

"I don't know. We should ask Mr. Harish to fix it. He needs to do that and change the keys anyway," she said in Russian.

I returned to my room to grab my water bottle and was shocked to discover that the water inside was a brownish color.

"Oh my God! I must have gotten water from the faucet last night, and I don't remember," I complained to Dasha, showing her the contents of my plastic bottle. "I am going to be sick!"

"Ha, it's better to get the shits over with. I do that every time I come back to Cairo; I just drink from the faucet to get used to the bugs in there faster," she said in a non-amused manner.

Not only did I not have any clean water to drink, I was hungover, and Dasha was smoking my cigarettes. "These are mine, right?" I asked.

"Yeah, I took one since you guys kept me up half the night," she informed me.

Great, a thief. I later discovered that this was her style—taking what she wanted while believing she was justified. First impressions are everything, but Dasha didn't care about making good ones; she was cold and blunt, she overexaggerated any comment, and she only talked about things she deemed important.

Hours later, my Asian roommate came flying into the apartment. With an "Oh, hi!" she quickly disappeared into her room. Dasha gave me the rundown of her. She was a Japanese belly dancer and went by Dolly. She was always dropped off in a blackened BMW around noon, when I was usually at work, and would leave again before dark.

"You know, she barely sleeps in her bed," Dasha continued. I thought nothing of that comment. Dolly, like Dasha and myself, was a young adult capable of making her own decisions. "Never mind, Katya, you don't get it yet," Dasha said, and left me alone on the reception couch.

"Hey, come in here for a second," Dolly called out to me as she peeked out around the corner. "Do you want any of this stuff?" she asked, escorting me to her room quietly so as not to disturb Dasha in her room. Showing me a pile of clothes on her bed, she said, "I want you to have the first choice. Take all you want."

I had only spoken to Dolly once before this encounter. We had met by the front door last Friday afternoon when she had been scrambling to get out of the apartment. "Boyfriends! You know!" She rolled her eyes at me while her phone was blowing up. "*Ana gaya, habibi, khamas dei.*" Her perfect Arabic rolled off her tongue. I was learning numbers and beginning phrases those days; 'khamas,' I knew, meant 'five,' and 'ana gaya' meant 'I'm coming!'

As she rushed to pack up miscellaneous items around her room, I looked through the clothes she had laid out on the bed. "I have to be out now; I don't want to pay rent for next month," Dolly said, as though reading my thoughts.

"Oh yeah, I have to change dollars to pay for rent. How much do you pay, if I may ask?" I responded.

"Well, I can't be sure because I help Mr. Harish with some things, so it's one thousand or two thousand pounds. It depends," she frantically answered. I was a bit confused and annoyed by the lack of formality and clear-cut lines on rent values, but this was their world, and I was the newcomer. It was similar to how my work operated; everyone was on different salaries but no one knew the qualifications.

"That Dasha is scary. Be careful," she whispered.

I felt like Dolly and I had been good friends for years, and she was looking out for me. "Yeah, she seems pissed all the time at something. I can't understand her," I complained.

"Here, do you need an iron or hair dryer?"

Dolly's frantic packing suggested she wasn't content with her moving-out situation. Her phone kept ringing constantly. She finally answered it. "Basam, almost done! Please, ten minutes." The atmosphere grew heavy after that call, and a small voice inside me suggested she was leaving under bad circumstances.

"Are you going back to Japan?" I asked.

"One day, yes. I need to make money before I go back. I have a daughter there that needs me to work."

I found this strange but didn't comment, just nodded my head in understanding.

Why would a Japanese woman rather be belly dancing at shows in Cairo and making chump change in the useless Egyptian pound than somewhere near her daughter in Japan making better money? The situation seemed off. I wondered whether she had been forced to leave, perhaps as a fugitive, or if she had been shamed and disowned by her family—or, worse yet, trafficked for sex work.

I realized then, as I politely declined Dolly's hand-me-downs, that I was in the same category as people like Dolly and Dasha. While I didn't know Dasha's full story yet, I suspected it was a tie-dye lie. This realization made me question if something was off with me, too, given that I was living here as an expat.

Had Sherif also lied to me about why he was in Egypt? And why had I willingly left the comfort of a first-world country? If I were to say it was to become a better woman for my boyfriend, people probably wouldn't believe me. They might think I was crazy, or worse, envy me for having a passport that allowed easy travel. They might see me as careless and ungrateful, like one of those Instagram travel influencers leaving the US just to create content. But that was far from my truth—I didn't have a place to call my own like them, and my boyfriend had supported my decision to move here, a concept that would likely seem crazy to anyone else.

Dolly threw the duffel bag over her shoulder and left with a "Good luck to you, I like you," and a "Bye, Dasha."

I lit up a cigarette at the reception. Dasha helped herself to another L&M Light without asking and perched in her signature squat position on the cushions. Even on furniture meant for relaxation, she always seemed tense.

"Don't pay attention to her. Many girls here tell lies," she said, responding to my unspoken thoughts.

"What is she lying about?" I asked.

"Don't be so stupid, Katya. Why else would we be in Egypt? We earn money here in any way we can."

"Well, I'm not here just to make money. How could you think that? My school only pays me three hundred fourteen dollars a month, and you see how long I work," I replied.

She grinned creepily. "Yeah, I've worked at a school before."

"Exactly, so you know it's tough, and we're so underpaid," I continued.

"This isn't America, Katya. You're just in the wrong school. There are better ones," Dasha said.

She described the different social classes and how the wealthiest A-class children attended exclusive daycares and schools where only English, French, or German were spoken. She bragged about her past experiences, the places she had visited, the jobs she had held, and the influential people she knew in Cairo and Ukraine. I suspected she wanted to make me jealous, but her lavish stories meant little to me. Her story and demeanor reminded me of Dolly's—they didn't add up. If she had such a glamorous past, why were we sitting in this dusty ghetto apartment, smoking our lives away under a single light bulb in an ancient chandelier? I had many questions about her current situation, but I didn't want to delve into them just yet. Lost in my thoughts, I reminisced about the places I had been and wondered, *Yes, Katya, how and why did we end up here?*

"I need to do something. I can't just sit here all day," I said. Listening to Dasha was exhausting; everything she said was a one-up game with no room for a reciprocal conversation. I dreaded going out in the heat, but I needed it for my sanity.

"Go," she said, her pale face bug-eyed. "Bring me some cigarettes. I'll give you the money later."

I dressed in my usual conservative outfit: a chevron-patterned maxi skirt and a loose, white, long-sleeve blouse. I was tired of eating cheap, greasy street food on the way home from work and leftovers on the weekends and needed to get groceries and make a meal, maybe a salad. I decided to explore the local neighborhood of Dokki. There must be an outdoor market nearby. I also planned to scout out more pharmacies for Solpadeine.

Walking the backstreets of Cairo is challenging and requires guts and a thick skin. I usually walked alone on the main roads to avoid large pedestrian crowds, facing only car traffic as a danger. In busy areas, I prepared for groups of children following me and beggars attempting to sell me items as well as more sexual harassment, such as constant whistles and comments from men. Just the other day, two boys on a moped had lunged to pull off my skirt as I'd walked home from school. I'd screamed, and they'd laughed, circling back for another go, but I'd quickly slipped into the standstill traffic, finding a tight spot between cars.

I couldn't Google specific places because the roads weren't mapped, forcing me to rely on landmarks and memory.

Stepping onto the makeshift curb outside our corner apartment building, I met the beweb perched on his plastic chair. "You go where?" he asked.

"I go market," I replied without smiling.

"You go end street, right, left, another left, and you have market," he instructed, waving his hands in specific Egyptian gestures.

"Shukran," I said, meaning *thank you.*

"Oh, you speak Arabic!" His face lit up.

"Not yet," I replied, ending the small talk as a crowd began to gather.

The curb ended past the kiosk with boxes of Lay's chips and Molto croissants. I stepped onto the Sahara sand, keeping my head down to avoid eye contact. The streets were busy but less so than on weekdays. People yelled across the street, car horns blared every forty-five seconds, and Arabic pop music blasted from street cafes, overwhelming my senses. Crossing the street was an art form. I quickly learned that in Egypt, you don't wait for cars to stop. It's like the game Frogger; you cross one lane at a time, stopping in the middle until the next lane clears. Walking in a diagonal line at a steady pace usually allowed me to cross without waiting.

In the fifteen long minutes it took to reach the outdoor market entrance, I was sexually harassed three times. Just past my building, two sweaty middle-aged men exiting a gym followed me, one making kissing sounds and calling me "Mouza! Mouza!" The other asked in broken English, "Habibti, what your name?"

A few steps later, a teenaged boy on a moped shouted, "I love you!" and honked repeatedly, making a whole crowd in white plastic chairs stare at me. I consciously forced myself not to sway my hips too much and held my shirt taut so the wind wouldn't draw my silhouette. Spotting a pharmacy across the road, I quickly ran inside to escape the forty-eight lustful eyes staring at me. I was relieved to be away from the attention and even more grateful to have found another source for Solpadeine capsules.

I asked for my pills in my most respectful voice and made the mistake of asking for tampons, thinking it would justify buying narcotics. The male pharmacist understood 'SOLPADEINE' but not tampons, Tampax, or 'menstrual cycle.' He looked confused and scratched his head. The man behind me, dressed in slacks and a baby blue button-down, said something in Arabic that made the pharmacist blush. I smiled slightly at the customer in thanks, my face burning with embarrassment. The pharmacist made me wait then returned with a small, dusty six-pack of light tampons. I threw the box in my bag, gave him a two-hundred note, and ran out without waiting for change, mortified.

The customer from the pharmacy, a stage-five clinger, followed me, asking where I was from, how long I was staying in Cairo, and if I lived nearby. I walked faster to get away from him. Was he following me because I had smiled at him? Frustrated with his persistence, I turned around and screamed, "FUCK OFF! GO AWAY!" Distressed and flustered, I realized his interest wasn't because I'd smiled at him. The tampons had been brought from the back of the pharmacy as if they were contraband. It hit me: only non-virgins used tampons, so asking for them signaled, *I'm deflowered and free game.* These men were sick.

I felt violated, dirty, and infuriated after realizing how sexually deprived and at the same time sexually motivated and utterly obsessed with the thin layer of flesh covering the vaginal opening these men were—this whole culture was! These thoughts squished my face, activating my stoic Slavic genes and producing the meanest expression for miles around. I felt my heart pounding in my ears and wanted to attack the next man who looked at me. But fighting back would be counterintuitive because showing anger would further encourage their persistence. Showing any kind of reaction would translate into interest. There is no winning with uneducated, desperate men.

Ignore and suck it up, Katya, I thought. *You're out here alone without protection, attracting attention with your long blonde hair, white skin, and broken hymen. And your father, brother, or husband is allowing you to be on the streets unprotected—it really is your fault.* That was exactly what the male population was thinking: it was my fault for attracting attention.

Even with my travel experience, navigating Cairo would remain challenging, especially without a male presence nearby. I was fighting to prove my independence as a single woman in a country where doing so was counterintuitive, practically impossible, and downright absurd; the irony hit me like a ton of bricks. A free country like the United States allowed women to prove their independence. I must have been so struck with wanderlust and clearly dumb enough to take the road less traveled to not realize that Cairo was a bad idea a month ago. Pausing to process this, I hid in an alley, pulled out a cigarette, and felt the weight of many eyes judging a White woman smoking in public. I took my drags, damming up the river of tears forming behind my eyeballs.

I had two choices: let this country destroy me or prove to Lucas that I could handle myself in a hostile world. I already wanted out, not even having managed to buy groceries for myself yet. I wasn't the only woman struggling on these streets; maybe I was just weak in character, too dependent on a man, or not worldly enough, or I complained more than I needed to like Lucas had suggested.

I refused to let Egypt strip away my dignity. I needed to survive, work, and save for a ticket home in the next few months. Finishing my cigarette, I vowed to turn each hardship into a lesson. I calculated that with my three-hundred-sixteen-dollar salary, minus two hundred dollars for rent, it would take ten months to save nine hundred dollars for a ticket back. However, quitting pills, which cost twelve dollars a box, was necessary. It was a catch-22; I needed the pills for sanity but needed to quit them to escape Cairo's insanity. So, I opened a new box of my favorite yellow-and-red capsules and swallowed three without water.

My high kicked in faster on my empty stomach, and once again, the world appeared as if I were viewing it through a glass door. Thoughts of Lucas drifted through my mind, and I imagined our reunion at the airport. I kept my head down, focusing on the market goods spread out on the ground. Women in full black hijabs with henna-tattooed hands and fingernails sat selling homemade cheese, bundles of herbs, cucumbers, eggs, soap, and bags of beladi (whole wheat and barley flatbread). The market scene held a lot of beauty, complex culture, deep history, and rawness that I wouldn't have appreciated if I were still sober and distressed from the harassment. This experience at the market showed me that I had a lot of work ahead of me before I could comfortably exist in my sober state.

"God, it's hard to leave the house. I feel I am in a far worse mood than before I left. How do you handle all the harassment? What does 'mouza' mean?" I complained behind my codeine veil of bliss to Dasha as I unpacked my groceries in our dark kitchen.

"It means sexy, pretty girl," Dasha answered. "Well, I have been here three years and still can't handle the harassment. That's why I don't go outside. Just don't pay attention. Did you get my cigarettes?"

I threw her the pack of L&M Blues, and she lit one up.

"You know, we have delivery for everything here. Even groceries. Pharmacy. Everything."

"Wow, well, I'm not leaving the house then. Fuck, I still have to walk to work, though."

"You see, if you don't know anyone here, it's hard to survive. It's all about who you know and not what you do," Dasha said, confirming the exact thought I'd had after the stage-five clinger encounter: you can't survive here without a man's protection.

"Well, I am not here for long. My boyfriend is waiting for me back in Reno. I think I'll stay a couple more months, then I'm leaving and never looking back!" I said without analyzing that my situation was probably far better than hers; if she had been here for three years, her situation must have been more complex than mine.

That comment changed something in Dasha. She switched back to her compulsive lying and fluff, claiming she liked it here, made

76

good money at different jobs, and didn't plan on returning to Ukraine soon. She contradicted herself by complaining about 'stupid Egyptians' and professing her love for Cairo in the same breath.

These contradictions made it clear she was torn between doing the right thing and the Cairo thing, just like I was. I struggled with the choice of returning home or using my money to sustain my nine-years-strong addiction. Neither option felt fair or achievable; I didn't want these to be my only choices.

We talked and browsed social media until late that night. Dasha finally shared her family background and told me about her engagement in Egypt. She described how her fiancé had taken care of her financially, hadn't wanted her to work, had vacationed with her at beach resorts, and had supported her family in Ukraine. She painted a picture of an Egypt I couldn't believe—a utopia every woman, even in the States, dreamt of. It was the ideal I had been raised with, like Dasha had, in Ukraine: a supportive man handling the bills while the woman did the dishes, barefoot and pregnant.

Here I was, struggling to prove just half of my womanhood to Lucas, to earn my right of passage of splitting rent, bills, and chores. All the while, there were some men who didn't expect their wives to share these responsibilities; they were just to be women. Was it better this way? Was I worthy of that?

I dismissed Dasha's story of a utopian marriage as exaggeration and lies. I didn't need a tale from a lost Ukrainian roommate to cloud my purpose and beliefs.

Eventually, Dasha's fiancé had left her, as his family didn't accept her being a foreigner and because he was actually already engaged to an Egyptian girl. He married within a month after their breakup, most likely playing Dasha as his mistress and guilty pleasure. Despite the heartbreak I could see on her face, she remained hopeful of finding another husband. It was difficult to fathom that the same men who had harassed us on the streets could also be providers and protectors.

"Wait, you have a son in Ukraine?" I asked.

"Yes, he's six. You know, I was a virgin when I married. Then I had my son, and he left us. A Ukrainian guy. Now my mom watches him, and I am here to send them money," she said.

"I'm sorry, but your English is great, and you can teach English in Ukraine for good money. Why Egypt?" I asked.

"I'm just used to it here," she replied coldly. "I'm off to bed," she added, leaving me with even more questions than before.

"Good night," I said, unsure of what to make of our conversation.

She left me sitting on the couch feeling a deepened sense of unfairness about my situation. I decided to contact Lucas. That day had been a wild ride of emotions—from dealing with broken lights to facing harassment and feeling undervalued as a woman. Dasha's situation and the idea of an ideal relationship with a Muslim man added to my frustration. I was mad that Lucas hadn't checked in or asked for my local number or my address. He seemed like he didn't care at all. I wanted to tell him off, write a bitchy message about how I felt, and complain about the men on the streets. But Lucas was my only hope out of this mess; I was especially aware of this after seeing Dasha stuck without plans. So, I killed the pity-party and wrote a positive update to Lucas, about the market goods and lack of tourists in my neighborhood.

'I'm happy to hear you are getting totally immersed with the culture, Muffy!' was the gist of his reply.

For the past three weeks, I'd been working at Reach Out Academy, teaching conversational English, grammar, and vocabulary to adult Egyptians six days a week for ten hours a day. It had been exhausting, to say the least. My voice was nearly gone, and I had little time to look for more suitable employment. Before leaving Reno, I hadn't given much thought to what to expect, but it wasn't working two hundred and forty hours for chump change. Subconsciously, I'd expected to be paid Western salaries from Western-funded companies. I hadn't anticipated the high cost of living in a third-world country. As payday and rent day approached, I felt anxious about giving away all my hard-earned money for nothing.

It had been almost three months since I'd left Reno and the Sierra Nevada mountains. I longed for the beautiful open sky and red sunsets. Fall in Reno was magical, with leaves changing colors and crisp evening air. I missed the feeling of being in public without hiding. I missed drinking from the faucet and the shade of our elm trees in the tea garden.

Cairo was the same grind every day: hot, dusty, polluted, lifeless, and monotonous. There was nothing beautiful about it and not a plant in sight—only trash, dust, and concrete. The congestion of cars, shops, and people put me in a bad mood before I even got to work. As I walked, holding the students' corrected homework, I felt eyes staring at me from every angle.

I had become skilled at weaving around people, keeping my head down, and avoiding the street cafes where men sat in broken plastic chairs, drinking tea and smoking shisha pipes. My neck constantly hurt from always looking down. I wished I could look up and meet the eyes of my fellow Egyptians, but I couldn't. In the most populated city of twenty-two million, I struggled to hide. My posture, which had always been slumped in disappointment, only intensified my sense of vulnerability.

In theory, this harsh conditioning was supposed to make me not care what people thought of my image. My psychology degree told me that exposure therapy worked well to treat anxiety. By exposing myself to my fear stimulus repeatedly, the stimulus should eventually have stopped producing the same response, and I should no longer have seen it as a threat. But the fear stimulus evolved from only ruthless young men to the random child, woman, cat, and car approaching me. By the end of the first month in Cairo, my fear stimulus had become generalized to anywhere outdoors. I became a walking anxious mess, constantly aware of my every move, and my social anxiety grew directly with my fears. I had to double my daily codeine dose from 72mg to 144mg just to make it to class.

Where was my therapist when I needed her? I emailed Linda a heartfelt message about my drug abuse and told her that I'd lied to her all this time. An hour later, I got a 'delivery failure' message, which meant she probably didn't work at the same office anymore.

Why don't you tell Lucas? my subconscious whispered at the peak of my codeine high.

"And tell him what? 'I'm sorry you think I have unharnessed potential, but I'm suffering. I know you don't like me playing the victim, but honestly, I am a victim—to this disease, or is it my past? Who the fuck knows anymore?'" I answered aloud.

I didn't necessarily want to quit pills completely, I just wanted to find a way out of my financial problems. Codeine helped me keep going and cope with my tough reality. I thought about using my addiction as a reason to leave Cairo and find peace in rehab. But then I pictured Lucas's disappointment as I signed papers at the admin office, admitting to my illness. It was hard to imagine him seeing me so vulnerable. For now, I planned to just get through another month.

Why don't you tell your parents? my subconscious continued to pry.

That will be unnecessary, so stop right there, Katya answered. *When have they ever cared about who or what you were doing? Your father left you and has never given you a single dollar in support, and your mother is a liar and actually got you hooked on the pills, remember? You think at twenty-five it's time to start asking for parental guidance? They have their own families to worry about. Your time has passed.* She shut down that conversation quickly. I hung my head in shame.

After finishing my tenth cigarette of the day, I sought refuge under the AC in my room as the last call to prayer sounded. It was late August, and the new regime under President El Sisi conserved energy by shutting off power every few hours, sometimes as much as six times a day. I took this moment to decompress from the long day at work and the 95°F heat outside. Soon after, I heard chatter and the front door slamming at the entrance.

"Hi! I'm Alina." A skinny brunette waved at me as I peeked around the corner to the front door. She turned her attention to the door as our beweb entered the apartment threshold, carrying more suitcases. She conversed with him in fluent Arabic and gave him a ten-pound bill as tip.

"I'm Katya, nice to meet you," I replied in Russian.

"Oh, Katya, my best friend growing up was Katya, too!" she beamed.

I sat on the couch, smoking another cigarette while listening to Alina and Dasha talk. From their conversation, it was clear they knew each other.

They entered the reception area laughing, and Alina took a seat on the leather chair across from me. As someone who enjoyed observing people, I sat quietly, assessing Alina's demeanor.

Her movements were confident, from her perfect walk and steady head to the slight swaying of her small hips. Even her choice of words in Russian showed confidence. She seemed agile, like a former gymnast. She stood about 5'6" with a small frame, long legs, filler lips, and tattooed eyebrows. She was in her early thirties, wore a long brown faux hair braid, and dressed in brand-name clothes. She smelled of expensive perfume. She confidently pulled a square box of Virginia Slims from her Louis Vuitton bag, lit a cigarette with a fancy black lighter, and swiped her finger across the glass coffee table to check for dust. Her movements were quick and jerky.

"Where did you get those?" I asked, pointing at the cigarettes.

"From Dubai, so, no, you can't smoke them," she said, chuckling. "It's so dusty here, do you girls clean? We need to get a cleaning routine going."

"It's impossible to keep this place clean! I clean every day, and still, there's dust. The balcony door doesn't close," Dasha lied; she hadn't cleaned once since I'd lived with her.

Alina was friendlier than the other expats I'd met; I liked her right away. She carried herself with a carefree yet confident demeanor and was accepting and quickly adaptive. With a motherly persona, she asked the right questions to keep a good conversation going. She seemed mysterious and wealthy, yet here she was, living in a poor neighborhood of Cairo in a shitty apartment. I was thrilled she was rooming with us. I felt we could become close friends; she seemed like someone I could trust, unlike Dasha.

"You know her?" I asked Dasha after Alina finally went to bed.

"We did a promo together for Heineken in Sahel last summer, but it's a coincidence we are living together," Dasha replied. "She is a model, you know."

"Oh, that's nice! I assume she's been here for a while, because her Arabic is perfect," I replied.

"I think like eleven years or something," Dasha said as she gathered her dirty dishes and walked them to the kitchen, obeying Alina's request to keep the house tidy and clean.

The following day, I received my long-awaited first paycheck from Reach Out Language Academy, and it was eight hundred LE short of what my contract promised. The school director, Mina, explained why I was underpaid. He had deducted from my pay because I had started a week into the semester, which was counted as a probation week. Also, we'd had four days off due to power outages, and I had taken a sick day, which I could not recall.

My expected three-hundred-fourteen-dollar monthly salary fell short by one hundred fourteen dollars, leaving me with two hundred dollars despite working close to two hundred and forty hours that month. Teaching over seventy-five students how to write resumes, business terminology, American slang, and accents, as well as grading homework, had earned me a mere eighty-three cents per hour. What made it worse was the mental toll I had endured just surviving each day. Even if Mina wasn't blind, I probably still would have cried in front of him. I'm sure he could hear the disappointment in my voice. Quietly, I left, feeling underappreciated and defeated and longing to go home.

That was the straw that broke the camel's back. Tears and snot dripped down my face onto my Samsung Notepad as I wrote to Lucas. I demanded to know why he hadn't even asked me for my local number in case of emergency or why he wasn't even curious to know which street I lived on. I complained about not having had my period for three months and feared that the birth control he had forced me to take had left me infertile. I asked why, despite seeing his online status on Skype, he had failed to call me. I also complained about my unjustified paycheck and having only two hundred dollars left. Sitting in my cockroach-infested apartment, I felt utterly abandoned and disgusted, asking myself, *Why me? What did I do wrong?*

"I don't fucking deserve this, God!" I screamed into the pillow. I jumped out of bed and frantically searched my backpack to check my supply of pills. I was thankful I had three more, enough to get me through half the day.

The girls must have heard me sobbing because I could hear whispers in the reception room. I gathered myself for my nightly cigarette and joined them. Their expressions didn't offer comfort or permission to vent. Instead, they showed their familiarity with such breakdowns, rendering any questions pointless. Alina simply nodded and handed me her prized Virginia Slim cigarette. That made me feel less alone. We sat quietly, each absorbed in our phones, until a key turning in the lock startled us.

"Who is that?" Dasha asked, curled up into a ball on the couch.

Alina left the cigarette in her mouth.

"Hello, girls! Salaam alaikum," Mr. Harish, our landlord, announced himself as he peeked around the front door.

I jumped up and went into my room to cover myself, as I was wearing a tank top with no bra. The last thing I needed this evening was for a man to look at my provocative nipples and fantasize about me.

"I am here to collect rent!" he said in a cheerful voice when I returned.

As Dasha got up and went to her room to fetch her share, he stood by the door, watching her ass as she passed him. I went back to my room and grabbed my first paycheck. Coming out, I noticed him whispering something into Alina's ear, but she held a stone-cold face and didn't flinch.

"Here you go," I said coldly, handing him the Reach Out Academy envelope then sitting down on the couch.

Dasha angrily threw her money on the table and sat on the couch with a sour face, turning away from him.

"Thank you, habibti." The sixty-something-year-old smiled at me. "Oh, you smoke. Cigarettes are not good. Do you smoke hashish?"

The girls turned to look at me.

"Um, no, Mr. Harish, I do not smoke hashish," I answered.

He fell into a sinister laughter before he said, "I smoke a lot of hash. It makes me fuck a lot. Do you like to fuck a lot?" He was looking me dead in the eyes.

My face turned beet red, and I opened my mouth to say something, but nothing came out.

"Oh, you are shy, so, yes, you do like to fuck a lot."

How has the day gotten worse? I thought. The men at Reno bars had never approached me, as my resting-bitch face repulsed them. I alone ruined girls' night and my friends' chances of having prospects approach our group. The girls would tell me, "Please smile, you're scaring everyone away."

"This is not nice to ask," I finally said, standing up to leave. My roommates sat motionless with helpless expressions, offering no protection or support.

"No, wait, sit, I am joke, relax. Look, I bring something." Mr. Harish reached for my hand to pull me back onto the couch.

"I will stand, thank you," I hissed back, now standing behind the couch, arms folded, feeling embarrassed that I was embarrassed.

"I bring lots of money!" he announced again in a cheerful voice. *Un-fucking-real, this guy.* Mr. Harish set a black leather bag on the table and unzipped it. The bag was filled with stacks of two-hundred and one-hundred-Egyptian-pound notes. He looked around the room for our reaction, leaned back into the couch, and with a swift motion, proceeded to unbuckle his belt.

"What are you doing, man? Stop. Please, stop!" Dasha shouted, as if drawing a verbal pistol.

I couldn't believe what I was witnessing; the smoky room and the single, lonely lightbulb illuminating our stage created a brothel's dingy atmosphere; it felt like we were in a scene straight out of a horror film, in which one of the prostitutes would soon slit the sweaty man's throat. I squinted my eyes and turned my head, bracing myself as if to avoid the inevitable blood fountain.

Meanwhile, Alina stood up with her hand raised, ready to slap him.

"Okay, okay, just calm down," he said, raising his hands away from his groin as if a real gun were pointed at him. "This is a lot of money. This is one hundred thousand pounds." He took out the cash from the envelopes that both Dasha and I had brought him. "Oh, yes, you said you would pay me later." He pointed at Alina with the stack of two-hundred-Egyptian-pound notes from my paycheck. "And, Dasha, this is not enough; you know the price." He threw the money into his black duffle.

I wanted to run to my room and send an email to Lucas saying, *GET ME THE FUCK OUT OF HERE, PLEASE!* But part of me knew Lucas wouldn't believe what was unfolding.

I couldn't leave these girls alone to fight this; I had to stand my ground as Mr. Harish put on his show. After all, he had the power to kick me out or demand more pay. Going to the police or complaining to a housing authority board wasn't an option; those didn't exist in Egypt, and the lack of any women's protection laws would favor Mr. Harish. The whole country seemed misogynistic, and somehow, we girls would be blamed for our landlord's abuse.

The room fell quiet, and us girls gave him our best Slav stares in defense, hoping they would deter him. I felt like I was standing on a landmine, and if I even flinched, the whole place would implode.

He looked straight at me as he asked, "How much for you to be my bride?" His natural tone of voice and relaxed body language made it seem like everything he was doing and saying was just a normal part of doing business. We were being abused, bribed, insulted, and manipulated in our only safe place away from the streets; this monster of a man had come bearing all the negativity we battled daily, presenting it on a silver platter with mint tea. What was more disturbing was his gentle smile and clear look in his eyes —he was a true master of deception, a true walking evil.

"Mr. Harish. I am priceless. No money in the world can buy me. Don't you have a wife already?" I attacked back with confidence.

"Yes, I have a wife. She is old and doesn't give sex. I have my second wife, and she is from Slovakia," he replied.

"Okay, so two wives are enough. This is crazy, what are you asking?" I rolled my head back, hoping Allah would come to help.

"Okay, habibti, next time I will bring more money, and I will find a price. We all have a price," he said, zipping his bag and his pants and leaving as fast as he'd come in.

"Bitch!" Dasha yelled at the top of her lungs as he slammed the door. "I said he needs to change locks and he can't come in using his own key." She was so frantic and angry that she took one of Alina's Virginia Slims without even asking.

"I will get him to do that, don't worry," Alina said, returning to her phone chat, calm and collected as if nothing had happened.

"What the fuck was that? Is this normal?" I asked, still staring at the front door.

"Happens a lot. You will get used to it. Better to find a woman landlord or a foreigner. But that is hard to find," Alina said. Dasha just nodded and grinned at me.

I tossed and turned all night. The anger and fear of that night's attempted bride bribe just wouldn't metabolize out of my system. I had flashbacks of that Russian man in Los Angeles attempting to rape me when I was fourteen. The men in my life seemed to always be taking advantage of me. Why did I fall victim to men's abuse? Was it a reflection of my choosing?

Crying, I swore that I was done with navigating men and their desires. I cursed Lucas for never seeing the good in me—I had given up my career and put hormones in my body for his pleasures, his goals, and his motives! And after four years of taking and taking from me, he wasn't here to protect me when I needed him the most.

The following Saturday morning, Alina was busy making her fresh-squeezed OJ in the lightless kitchen. This was her thing: OJ and fresh garlic. When those two foods came out, that meant she wasn't going out for the night. I knew her schedule by that point, and it was one week on for partying and three days off. She would sleep for most of her down days and only surface to eat, get groceries delivered to her, and watch Facebook videos while chain-smoking on the couch.

Alina was very predictable in her mealtimes, smoke breaks, laundry days, and party times. And she loved to clean. Dust was always off the couches and the coffee table. The floors were always wet from her mopping. *Whatever she is on,* I thought, *thank God for her OCD in keeping this home a bit in order.*

"Eeek!" she squealed from the kitchen.

"Those roaches, fuck! I can't anymore—fucking disgusting!" I yelled back.

"I don't even have an appetite anymore," she said, as she threw her dishes in the sink and walked out for a smoke with me.

Alina made me feel safe. She seemed to have Cairo figured out, and her manicured toes only reinforced that feeling. I liked how she quickly adapted to threatening situations; she didn't care about the food or if cockroaches were all around. She had a survivor mentality that drew me in, as she reflected the qualities within me.

Moments later, her phone rang. She jumped up, ran to her room to talk, then called for me.

"Do you want one?" she asked, pointing to the small pile of white powder on her bedside table. "I was going to stay in tonight and clean, but my plans changed," she added, bubbling with energy as she searched her closet for an outfit.

Alina was testing me to see what level of haram (sin) I was on, and I knew it. In a world where men ran the show and provided for our comfort while we sought to escape their manipulation, maybe crossing a moral line opened a door of freedom. It was clear someone took care of Alina, and whatever that meant lay on the other side of this cocaine line. It felt like an invitation to a lifestyle that part of me knew was wrong, but it had its benefits in this backward country. After all, we were single White women, living alone without a man's protection. I had to see what her reality looked like, especially after seeing how unbothered she was by our landlord's harassment.

"It's 10:20 a.m., Alina, are you serious?" I said, looking at the cocaine on her side table.

"I need to wake up, long night ahead. You're coming with, by the way. Thank God I didn't eat garlic," she replied as she pulled her hair extensions from the vanity table.

We stared at each other for an extended awkward pause. The pitying look in her eyes spoke to me, saying, 'Please let me save you from all this grief.'

"I mean... I guess. It's not that much."

"That's my girl!" she replied and began to split the tiny pile into two pinstripe lines.

At 10 a.m., with the second call to prayer blasting over the street intercom for all the believers to hear, I sniffed Charlie with my new Ukrainian friend. This marked the beginning of a new lifestyle and a gateway to the Cairo scene I had never imagined could exist in a Muslim country. I was regressing, consumed by my hatred for this city, the harassment, the constant fear, and my own self-loathing.

The toxic people around me were dragging me down even further, and, to be honest, I was letting them.

5
TRUST GAMES
(SEPTEMBER 2014)

J ust three short months ago, I believed the Cairo experiment would transform me into a stronger woman—a woman with superhuman powers despite her rotten past. My hopes of finding that strong woman within me had disintegrated down to a pile of white numbing powder I sought out daily. My mission to come to Cairo, prove my independence and worldliness, stop playing the victim to my past, and become a more stable woman had taken on an entirely different trajectory of self-destruction and co-dependence to the wrong people.

The girl I found at the end of that first cocaine line from Alina was brilliant—far exceeding Lucas's expectations. She was free to be weak, and I hated being strong. She was hurt, and I hated treating my wounds. She didn't want to figure out her life nor did she care about anything or anyone, and I was exhausted from figuring anything out or caring about anyone.

It felt like I had removed my full black hijab, revealing who I was behind the veil: a product of pain. I finally met the Kateryna within me, the inmate I had been avoiding for years. Kateryna was ruthless and reckless, like a train on the verge of derailing. She was that muddy little girl running through the puddles in Ukraine, but instead of smiling, she was disrespectful and destructive. She yelled out her needs and demands, no longer silenced by her mother's expectations. She played the rightful victim to her childhood traumas, seeking answers to why her parents had given up on her and why she wasn't loved. She wanted to know why they were so weak and irresponsible. She cried out for her mother, who had never been there for her emotionally. She blamed her father for leaving her so early in life, reasoning that his actions had instilled in her the belief that she deserved to be used and disposed of, which made her fall victim to men and their abuse.

Kateryna needed to rebel after being locked up at the age of twelve, when she was forced to become a woman. I never had the luxury to rebel and be a child, an adolescent, or a moody teen; I was always figuring life out for my mother, ensuring my sister's safety, or dealing with Lucas's noncommittal, adventurous lifestyle. Rebelling against everyone felt wonderful; for the first time, I was free from expectations. I finally asked, *What do you need, Kateryna?* She answered, *More drugs.*

As any brilliant engineer would advise, you must disassemble the machine into its pieces, study them, and understand their interactions to grasp how the machine functions as a whole. Before attempting to fix it, you must understand how a machine operates. So, I began Kateryna's much-needed deconstruction, piece by piece. I had to explore this other side of me, study it, befriend it, make all the necessary mistakes, and hopefully avoid ending up dead in a ditch somewhere. I knew this was a dangerous game to play, but to fix myself, I first had to allow myself to break down completely.

In the month after I entered Alina's drug world, I learned a lot in my Cairo playground. In Egypt, you could be two people at the same time—a sinner and a saint. A pious Muslim might snort cocaine, or an educated foreigner might have low morals. The male harasser on the street who commented on your ass might also walk his sister to school to protect her from other males. I fit right in as the closeted drug addict who wanted to use a man for her own pleasures all while wishing the man she loved back home would come and save her.

"Do as I say, not as I do" really summed up life in Egypt. My roommates and I enjoyed picking apart the double standards. We questioned and judged the wealthy, 'come from good families,' A+ class people, knowing their hidden drug and alcohol use. We were not, however, superior in any way. Myself especially. I became the double standard I mocked all day, and I loved it! This new party environment was perfect for my inmate Kateryna to flourish in. She pushed me aside and set out to become the hero of the day. I let her be free to do as she pleased.

Everyone had their own social currency on the streets of Cairo, exploiting their desired traits for a cost. Watching my roommate's lifestyle, I quickly learned my social currency was that of a non-virgin foreigner who could take advantage of Muslim men for a meal at minimum and drugs at maximum. My survival power was as easy as being me—a White, blonde, Western woman who said Egyptian words like 'Inshallah' and 'Mashi.' My local boy-toy would do anything for me: take me on trips to the Red and Mediterranean Seas and to any party and nightclub I wanted, buy me any food (including groceries), and most importantly, provide me protection from harassers. In return, he got to raise his social currency by hanging out with a foreign girl.

Egyptian couples had to wait until marriage to have sex, so courting rituals between Muslim boys and local girls could last for years during which the boyfriends provided for everything. While some marriages were arranged, wealthy parents often planned their daughters' futures by sending them to affluent schools, ensuring their only options for partners were other wealthy boys from wealthy families. This followed Islamic traditions; even though Prophet Mohamed married women from all 'castes,' money still married into money, and the classes couldn't cross.

We knew this and demanded much more from the men we allowed to court us: more experiences, better outings in forms of trips, and, in my and Alina's cases, more drugs. Honestly, we were selling ourselves short, but since our end goal wasn't to marry (unlike the local women), we took what was given. These men knew we were deflowered just based on our skin tone, and their chances for consensual sex could come at any moment.

At the core of my degradation, and between doses of drugs, an ember of hope still burned. Hope that maybe someone would notice my fall and rescue me. I didn't want to completely lose myself in the desert or overdose at some random house party; I simply wanted someone to care enough to notice that Katya was not well. Not just anyone—I wanted Lucas to notice.

More and more time passed between my check-ins with Lucas. I had nothing good to report, and I did not want to tell him the truth of what I was doing most weekends. I knew the right thing would be to tell him everything, to confide in him and ask for help, to let him know I was afraid and wanted out, but then I remembered how he'd told me to let go of my victimhood mentality. His beliefs about me were set in stone: no matter what I said or did, I would be playing victim to my past when I should have been working on fixing that character flaw. Complaining and asking for help would only backfire, rendering me even weaker in his eyes.

"Who are you?" I asked my bathroom mirror one morning as I got ready for work. "No, really—what the fuck do you want?" I directed this question to my codeine-constricted pupils after taking six pills to recover from a cocaine hangover from the night before.

There was no reply. I couldn't see into my soul through my pinhole pupils. I took another drag of my cigarette and blew smoke onto the mirror. After slicking my oily hair back into a low ponytail, I flushed the toilet without noticing that it might clog. The addiction took a toll on my body; my stool was dark, rock-like, and came only every ten-to-twelve days.

I decided today would be my last day at Reach Out Academy.

Samir, the manager, had crossed too many lines, making it harder to show up each day. At first, he'd persistently invited me to dinner after almost every shift; I'd quickly shut down those advances. The occasional inappropriate body scans and side winks were something I could ignore, as I faced similar attention daily on the streets below. But last Monday, he'd called me into his office for my monthly review and locked the door behind him. He'd approached me and grabbed my chin for a kiss; I'd ducked and told him to stop. "I like that you play hard to get," he'd said. I'd reminded him that I would not go out with him and warned him to leave me alone or I would report him to Mina. "You think he'll believe you or me?" Samir had asked.

My phone rang; it was Ahmed, my current boy-toy.

"Yella, I'll pick you up after work today, and we're heading to my friend Ashraf's house. Plan to stay the weekend. Bring a change of clothes and a swimsuit," he said in his usual cold, sultry voice.

"Sounds good. I'll be ready at 4 p.m. downstairs from Reach Out Academy," I replied.

Ahmed often picked me up from work to grab food, go dancing while high on ecstasy at prestigious nightclubs, or take road trips on weekends. We had already been to Taba and Ras Shetan, small Bedouin towns on the narrowest part of the Red Sea and near the border with Israel. We rode camels, slept in bungalows, and snorkeled in the Red Sea, halfway to Saudi Arabia. We had stayed with many of his friends at the Mediterranean Sea development for elite Egyptians called Sahel, in villas right in front of the clear turquoise sea. My favorite outing with him had been the prior week, when he'd taken me horseback riding among the pyramids at sunset.

I'd met Ahmed through Dasha about a month ago. He'd taken us to Cairo Jazz Club—a place that didn't play any jazz, only electronic music, and served Heinekens in glass bottles and Johnny Walker on ice. Ahmed looked like an Arab version of a young Robert De Niro, right down to the mole on his face. We both liked Metallica. His cold, mysterious demeanor and lack of emotions somehow turned me on.

His English was almost accent-free, and he dressed in luxury-brand clothing. Like me, he did blow three-to-four nights a week and always had some on hand. He offered me a line as soon as I sat in his black KIA the first time I met him.

Our relationship was very sexual. I'd broken Alina's rule of waiting as long as possible to sleep with someone because I couldn't control my impulses. Ahmed was into BDSM, and I hadn't realized how much I would crave that. He needed to tie me up and spank me, and I needed to feel used and contained. We had a symbiotic relationship, and with the cocktail of drugs in my system, I didn't care what happened or how it happened.

He had a sweet side, too. The first night I'd stayed at his apartment, which resembled a vampire den—cold and dusty—I hadn't been prepared with any toiletries. He'd woken up and, without saying a word, gone out to buy me supplies. He'd returned with two bags, one filled with three different kinds of toothbrushes, Panadol, Dove shampoo, and body wash, and the other with a variety of breakfast options. He'd also brought me my first latte from Starbucks in almost six months.

Did I feel guilty for being with Ahmed? Of course, I did. Did I care what would happen? Not really. Did I love Lucas? Absolutely. With Lucas, I'd always had to show my strengths because I was afraid that he would leave me if he saw my weaknesses. I'd pretended to be okay just to be good enough for him, and the pills had helped me maintain that facade. I wished he would stop worrying about what was good for him and give me the space to be vulnerable, hug and pity me, and love me for my weaknesses, too.

Throughout most of our relationship, Lucas was fixated on creating a travel blog where he could share his insights about different countries and their people. Yet, he'd never let me reveal my truth—the addict I was, the girl who would give him anything, the fighter with high expectations for herself. He'd overshadowed me completely.

Emerging from a troubled youth, I hadn't been prepared to run the marathon with him. He had life figured out while I was still searching for the reason my mom had never given me unconditional love. Growing up, I had been expected to be strong, working early in my teens to support my mom and help raise my sister. Now, it was my turn to hurt and be vulnerable.

If you find someone who makes you happy, be with him. Lucas's words echoed in my mind. That memory pushed me to take another shot of cheap vodka, swallow a fourth pill of codeine, stay out until sunrise, and seek out a lover to fulfill my needs.

With Ahmed, I craved the attention Lucas never gave me. The difference was, I felt free to be weak with Ahmed. He only needed me to be his submissive sex slave while Lucas wanted me to be like his successful entrepreneur mother. With Ahmed, I didn't have to be my best self. I could be the victim—the same victim Lucas had told me not to be but with whom I deeply identified. This path to self-discovery was dark and twisted, and I hadn't hit rock bottom yet. But guilt was creeping in faster than my drugs could numb it.

Ahmed arrived on schedule that Thursday and picked me up from Reach Out Academy. I received my last paycheck of three hundred sixteen dollars, with two hundred dollars going toward next week's rent. After two months of working, I had only managed to save around one hundred ten dollars toward my ticket back to Reno.

"I quit," I told Ahmed as I slammed the door of his freezing KIA shut.

"Why?" he asked. He accelerated to fifty miles an hour and took an illegal U-turn.

"Because," I mumbled with a cigarette between my lips, "they are rude. Nothing else. Let's go to Ashraf's house!" I changed the subject.

If I told Ahmed about the sexual harassment I'd experienced from Manager Samir, I wasn't sure Ahmed would believe me; he might think I provoked Samir or that my tight clothes had invited such behavior. I'd decided to handle the situation myself. After Samir had grabbed and smacked my ass, I'd elbowed him away and stormed into Mina's office, demanding my final paycheck by the end of the day. "Why don't you ask Samir why I'm leaving, sir?" I said as I exited his office for the last time.

I also had to end it with Ahmed after the weekend. I was numbed and in a constant state of drug withdrawal. I was spiraling faster and faster out of control, and I couldn't keep this up much longer. "Fuck work, and fuck this boyfriend; I'll figure it out later," Kateryna rebelled. Maybe she'd had enough of this lifestyle and had a better plan for getting out of Cairo. I followed her instincts, hoping they would lead to a better outcome.

September 25 marked a very special day for me; it was Lucas's birthday. I promised myself I would leave Ahmed before then as a way to lower my guilt for being such a monster. Our 'girlfriend experience' relationship, in which I used my 'boyfriend' for a wallet, meals, parties, and drugs, had to come to an end just thirty-two days into our whirlwind summer. Ahmed was getting too close by introducing me to his parents and staring too long into my eyes. Perhaps he was even falling in love. That was uncomfortable, as I didn't have any feelings toward him.

I felt guilty that Lucas and I weren't communicating often, and when we did communicate, I lied to him and said I was working hard to save money. Since I was technically cheating on him, I wondered if Lucas was seeing someone else, too. Even if he was, he wasn't out sniffing cocaine and popping ecstasy pills with random women.

'Hi Lucas, how are you? Any plans for your birthday? I hope we can Skype soon. I have a lot to tell you about Egypt! I miss you. Hope all is well! Love, Katya.'

I wrote him that email from my iPhone 4 as I rolled out of a double-king bed at Ashraf's house in Katameya Heights, New Cairo —a very affluent part of town. Ashraf was a famous shaabi (Egyptian rap) artist. His home featured a double, spiraling, marble staircase around a Greek statue in the foyer, just like what you'd see in the movies, and a huge outdoor pool surrounded by palm trees and a vine wall.

I got up to leave the cocaine den, stepping over other men passed out on the floor. Ahmed was still asleep, snoring loudly, with two other girls lying next to him and a guy on the edge of the bed. The closed curtains created complete darkness, with only the large digital clock on the headboard providing light. It was already 3:45 p.m.

"Ahmed, wake up! I have to go home. I want to go home." I shook him. We'd been up until probably 10 a.m., snorting mountain ranges of cocaine and jumping in the heated pool. I ran to the bathroom to check for a nosebleed.

He drove me home in Ashraf's jeep since his KIA was nowhere to be found. We had probably misplaced it at a neighbor's house that night, too drunk and yakked out to remember.

"I can't be with you anymore," I said, blowing smoke out of the cracked window. We were just one street away from my apartment.

"What the hell are you saying, Katya? What?" He glared at me.

"I can't, and I don't want to. You know, I can't fall in love, I feel you are falling in love. I have to figure out how to get home, Ahmed. This is just fucked up. Where the hell is your car? We got so fucked up last night."

Katya liked blaming others for all my problems. It was Ahmed's fault I'd put almost two grams of cocaine in my nose.

"You're a bitch. You used me. You're a fucking slut! A washed-up coke-whore!" he continued.

True, I thought, *I can't argue with that.*

"Oh, you love me! I know that's not true," I said, unbuckling from the car. "I warned you! Don't date a girl who travels."

"Wow...okay. Fine, you're no one to me," he said, and there was a long pause. "Happy fucking birthday to me."

"It's your birthday today?" I asked.

"Yes, September twenty-fifth. Get the fuck out of the car. Bye!" he yelled, almost pushing me out of the passenger's side.

The coincidence of Ahmed's birthday also being Lucas's birthday felt like a sign that I needed to focus on Lucas. I didn't feel bad for dumping Ahmed on his birthday and felt zero remorse stepping out of the Jeep. I ran straight up to my room to check my tablet to see if Lucas had responded. With the time difference, it was the morning of September 25 back in Reno.

His response came later. He said we should catch up another day, as he was heading to Downieville to ride mountain bikes and have dinner and beers with his friends. Great. I didn't fully trust him to sleep alone, given that he'd jumped into bed with me on our first date and a few times thereafter while he was dating another woman. My post-cocaine-binge anxiety was no fun. I popped three codeine pills and opened a fresh pack of cigarettes. It was at this time that Alina, the storm, blew into our home.

"Oh, thank God you are home! Bitch! We're going out to a house party!" she announced in Russian, running up to me and hugging me.

"Alina, I literally just came from a two-day house party. I don't want to go," I said diplomatically.

"Don't be dumb, it's going to be so much fun! These guys, oh my God, these guys are so popular in Egypt. I've been wanting to go to their house parties for months now," she insisted.

"Okay. I'll go." I gave in so easily. Alina was in luck; my now five codeine pills had kicked in at the perfect moment. Plus, I was full of guilt and nerves, convinced that Lucas was out cheating on me just like I was cheating on him. Not talking to him on his birthday broke my heart. What was I going to do, stay at home crying? No. He was the one who was supposed to be missing me.

I never thought that going out to party with Alina, as I usually did, would lead me into the hands of a monster. The decision I made in my vulnerable state completely changed the course of my trip.

. . .

It was easy to spot our ride for the party among the low-end sedans of our poor neighborhood. Just the walk to the car felt ominous as we made our way toward the halogen lights with emergency blinkers on—a predator signaling in the dark, luring its prey with Western luxury.

"Habibi!" Alina cried as we took our positions in the red sports car with plates that looked out of place. I took my usual seat in the back as the guest.

"Amla-eh?" a higher-pitched male voice answered her.

"Rami, this is Katya. Katya, this is my good friend Rami," she introduced us.

He stretched his hand over his head toward the back seat for a shake. I touched his ultra-smooth, long fingers and gave the customary slight shake. In the Arab world, gripping hard on first introductions is rude. I once asked Dasha why, as in the West, a stronger grip shows respect. She told me that a slight handshake is more customary, less assertive, and shows humility, unlike the Western style, which can be interpreted as too aggressive.

Soft hands, I thought; *he hasn't worked a day in his life*. This was a trait of the wealthy I'd learned to notice. Right away, I could see he came from one of those privileged circles where money seemed to shield people from consequences. The watch on his wrist, the expensive scent of his cologne, the flashy car, and the little party box he slid from under the seat all signaled his status.

"Let's party?" he asked, reaching for the box.

"Yella!" Alina squealed.

Rami watched me through the rearview mirror, holding my gaze longer than I found comfortable, and I studied him back as he spoke with Alina. He had a boyish, almost nerdy look, even with a full beard. He could have passed for mixed European, his amused, mischievous stare giving him away. I sensed that he liked me.

We drove for an hour and a half in traffic to a wealthy suburb on the edge of Cairo. Rami's phone constantly buzzed with calls and WhatsApp messages, but he didn't seem bothered to check them. We finally arrived at a three-story villa with more men than women. Someone was blasting Trey Songz.

A group of five men came to meet us as Rami held Alina's hand and walked us into the living area. I followed, holding Alina's hand. The men greeted us with double air kisses on each cheek and full-body scans. Feeling uncomfortable, I took a seat on the couch. Alina floated away with a couple of strangers, leaving me alone. I yelled for her, but she just motioned the "OK" hand gesture and went out to the balcony.

"Are you having a good time?" Rami asked as he sat down next to me. He had been watching me from across the room. We were the only two on the couch.

"Yeah, it's okay," I replied, forcing a smile that didn't quite reach my eyes.

"Here, try this," he said, holding up his drink.

"What's this?" I asked.

"It's vodka soda... with a little something to make you feel happy," he hinted with a sneaky smile.

"Is it MDMA?" I asked.

"Kind of like that, yes," he said, pushing the glass toward me with a big smile.

"Look, just take a gulp and let me know. Do I seem really unhappy to you?" he asked.

"You seem fine," I answered.

"It's okay—I promise. I'll take care of you. Do you trust me?" he insisted.

I glanced at his friends watching us from across the room. My choice was to either spend the night in Rami's company or be hit on by all of them one by one. Under my fidgety codeine and cocaine high, I used my best intoxicated judgment and chose my driver, Rami.

I drew in a large mouthful of his drink from the straw. He said it was something called GHB—a name I barely recognized at the time, but one I would later come to understand all too well.

"That's my girl." He took my hand and squeezed it hard. "Come, let me introduce you to the people you need to know. But the most important person in the room you already know—it's me," he said, and winked at me as he pulled me off the couch.

Rami introduced himself with a kind of arrogance and confidence that came from old money. He carried himself as though his family name alone could open doors. His circle was made up of men from similarly connected families. As I spoke with them, Rami seemed to admire my easy social manner, occasionally giggling and squeezing my hand.

The GHB kicked in within thirty minutes. My body started to feel limp, light, and tingly. Unlike being high on codeine or cocaine, where I was more in control of my body and mind, I couldn't snap out of this trance even if I focused. While cocaine made me antsy, this liquid took all my anxiety away. I felt euphoric and dizzy; my limbs felt heavier, and colors looked brighter. I could feel the music in my body. The euphoric feelings came in waves, as though following my breath. Breathing in felt good, and breathing out recharged me for the next wave. I had a huge smile and stood closer to Rami, leaning on him as I started to lose my balance and feel the pull of gravity. The world around me felt heavier as we chatted with more of his friends. I worried I would get sucked into the ground from the weight of reality. Suddenly, I had the urge to dance, so I left the conversation abruptly and floated around the room, letting the euphoric energy move through my body. The more I danced, the higher I felt.

Rami watched me dance for a while, sitting alone on the stairs to the third floor. From my perspective, he was just a dark human figure in a light blue T-shirt. My vision was blurred, and the world was spinning faster. I was sinking deeper into what I could only describe as the Gumby stage. I lost track of time; what felt like minutes was probably hours. I noticed the lights around the house were off, and the number of people seemed smaller. A group of blurry, melted men sat on the couches, watching me, too.

"Why did you take the drugs, Katya?" Rami asked me, jerking me down by my bicep while still sitting on the stairs. His force snapped me a little closer to reality.

"What?" I asked, confused in my drug stupor. I plopped down next to him. I couldn't understand the question, and for a few seconds, I couldn't recognize him. I forgot how I'd got there and what I was doing.

"Everyone is watching you right now. You can't handle the drugs or what? Stop shaking your ass so much," he scolded me. His eyes were black.

I couldn't comprehend what was happening or how to answer his question. The GHB made me happy, but my heart raced faster, alarmed by Rami's comment. "You told me to take them," I slurred back.

"You didn't have to. But you did anyway. And now you look like a bitch! You're turning all these men on," he said.

I was getting higher by the minute, spinning out of control. I ignored his comment, hung my head, and cradled it in my arms, fighting to slow down the spins.

"You trusted me, that's why you took them. But you need to learn how to act around others, especially when you are with me," Rami continued, now speaking directly into my ear. I was nodding in and out of consciousness.

"I'm not with you. I'm here because of Alina—where is Alina?— but, yeah, I trusted you," I slurred. All I could focus on was how distant my voice sounded. By this point, I was leaning on his shoulder, barely able to keep myself sitting up on the stairs; my eyelids were glued shut.

"Yes, you are with me. And it looks like if I wasn't here, you'd be hit on by those other guys. I'm doing you a favor." His logic seemed reasonable through my distorted reality. I felt guilty for being so high while everyone around me seemed normal. I was more scared of how high I would get from the GHB than of what Rami was ranting about.

My eyes rolled to the back of my head every time I opened them, so I kept them shut.

"Okay," I agreed, unwilling to even engage with what he was saying. *But I thought you were all friends,* my mind broadcast its last rational thought. "Can I have some water?" I managed to say with my thousand-pound tongue.

Rami squeezed my hand hard and forcefully held my face up until I met his eyes.

"See, you even need me for water," he said.

"Okay, I need you. Yes." I squinted at him, still too scared to open my eyes fully so they didn't roll back. Then my memory went blank.

When I woke up, I found myself on the L-shaped couch in the main living room. It was dawn. Rami was lounging on the chaise across from me, on his phone. Music was still quietly playing, and a handful of people were still stumbling around the kitchen nearby.

"Where is Alina?" I asked him. My head was pounding. He was ignoring me, but I kept staring at him as I sat up fully on the couch. "Hello? Where is Alina?" I asked again.

Rami giggled while looking at his phone, typing a message. He locked his iPhone and quickly turned to me, his eyes filled with disappointment. He pursed his lips, bit the inside of them, and glared at me.

"Katya, you disrespected me last night," he finally said, breaking the awkward silence. His stare was dark, a complete 180-degree change from his giggling just seconds ago. "You shouldn't have taken the drugs. You passed out, and we had to stay over here. I was supposed to pick up a friend last night, and now all the plans are ruined." He folded his hands across his stomach and cocked his head to the side. I didn't know what to do with this information.

"Dude, sorry, I didn't know how high I'd get. I need to go home," I replied. "Where is Alina?" I felt uncomfortable and annoyed.

Rami didn't answer. He just picked up his phone again and giggled in response to the message on the screen.

My heart pounded with anxiety. I felt he wasn't sane with his sudden emotional shifts, his emphasis on being "disrespected" by an almost complete stranger, and his blatant ignoring of my simple questions. My mind replayed the last memories I had of last night. I couldn't remember how I'd got to the couch, at what time, or if I'd ever got my water. I forgot why Rami was angry at me and what I had done to "disrespect" him. I started to think that maybe I had done something embarrassing—maybe I had thrown up, maybe I had fallen down and someone had moved me to the couch. I was spinning in fear, unable to remember anything other than asking for water.

Looking down at my wrist, I noticed a silver bracelet. I couldn't remember how I had gotten it or whose it was.

"Nice, isn't it?" Rami asked, noticing me staring at it.

"I don't remember. I don't remember much from last night. It's not mine," I replied honestly.

Rami clicked his tongue in disappointment and shook his head. He stood up and walked away.

"Can you take me home, please?" I pleaded in his direction. I couldn't afford to take a cab since I had to conserve all the money I had left, and the drive back was at least an hour in Cairo traffic.

"Let's go," he said, his back turned to me as he pulled the keys out of his pants pocket. I ran to follow him out the door.

Why was I trusting random strangers to take me home? Trust was a concept I'd never had to question before. I was accustomed to English-speaking Egyptian men like my previous "boyfriend," Ahmed, and his friends, who always accompanied me to parties with respect and protectiveness. I felt safe in their presence, no matter the circumstances. They seemed honored to have a foreigner in their care and company. Rami, on the other hand, seemed annoyed by the responsibility of having to drive me home.

The ride home was quiet. Rami drove recklessly and seemed very angry. I was glad the streets of Cairo were empty so the drive wouldn't take hours. He played *"Like I Love You"* by Justin Timberlake on repeat—one that circled around the idea of being a "good girl" and how that earns trust.

Trust—that word was central to Rami's conversations, as he constantly emphasized how much he wanted me to establish that trust between us.

But was I a "good girl"? His disappointment made me doubt it. I must have done something so terrible that this stranger was completely appalled and disappointed in me. Had I embarrassed him or acted spiteful toward someone else? I felt utterly guilty and ashamed, but I didn't know why. Was it the GHB and cocaine hangover, or was I overlooking a real, terrible mistake? Had we slept together last night?

"Did we do anything last night?" I finally broke the silence, strategically a few streets from my place. Parties like this—with too many drugs and sleepovers—almost always ended up in one-night stands. I'd been blackout drunk before without having memories of sex, but I'd never been this out of my mind on a new drug like GHB. Even if something sexual had happened between me and Rami, the cold way he was treating me—unlike the sweet and gentle way any other guy would have treated me after getting laid—convinced me that whatever had happened after I blacked out was unthinkable.

Rami turned off his music and abruptly pulled over and turned off his car. He did the same long, lip-biting stare before he spoke. "I thought you were different. From the moment I saw you, you didn't look like the other bitches that usually come to our parties. And after I put that bracelet on you—it's mine, and it means something to me —and you don't even remember. You think I will disrespect you like that and sleep with you when all those people are around? I'm not that kind of guy, Katya!" He was almost yelling.

I was initially very confused, too hungover to decipher his twisted statement. Was the bracelet a gift from him? I guessed I was somehow ungrateful after he'd given me something sentimental, but everything he said still sounded distorted to me, even in my own head. Was I missing something?

106

Instead of calling him out on how crazy he sounded, I felt scared. By the look in Rami's eyes, he was seriously hurt, and his hurt was somehow caused by me not remembering what had happened last night.

"I'm sorry, Rami. I—I didn't know that I would pass out. I've never taken this drug. You gave me this bracelet? It's very nice. Thank you. Of course, you wouldn't touch me. I trust you," I said, reaching out to hold his hand. I wanted to defuse the bomb quickly and get the fuck out of that car, but he jerked his hand back and continued his speech.

"That bracelet, I mean it. It's a sign that I trust you. And I told you last night and will tell you again: you being here alone in Egypt without someone watching you can get you in trouble. I will protect you. But you have to trust me. And, honestly, you are a bit weak and not very smart with men giving you drugs. That was a test, and you failed—but that's okay, because I can teach you how to have fun and still be classy," he said with a warm, kind smile on his face.

I appreciated that he wanted to look out for me, something I wished Lucas was doing. I liked how Rami recognized my weakness for drugs and wanted to protect me from myself. He had either figured me out or was completely out of his mind.

He instructed me to go to sleep and think about what he had just told me. When I left his sports car, he made no move to kiss or hug me. He just ordered me to make sure my phone was charged when he called around 5 p.m. to set up dinner plans.

Our relationship unfolded in the same toxic way it had begun. The next six weeks felt like Kateryna's bootcamp, with Rami as the program leader. We started with long phone calls discussing "open-mindedness," "classiness," and "moral standards." According to Rami, me being "open-minded" meant I was too liberal with drinking and premarital sex. He believed Western women lacked proper impulse control and abused their freedoms without rigorous religious standards. Sometimes, he said, these standards were necessary to avoid committing the "full sin." For him, morality was always a gray area; nothing was black and white.

Rami told me he could teach me the correct and classy way to gracefully ride the haram (sin) line, as moral standards could be tailored to each situation. For example, a local Egyptian girl shouldn't engage in premarital sex according to Islamic standards. Rami believed that unless the ultimate sin of premarital sex was committed, everything else leading up to the act—including partying, drinking, and doing drugs—could be disregarded. This approach allowed someone to bend the rules without completely breaking them, maintaining a sense of moral flexibility while avoiding the ultimate sin.

His interpretation reminded me of a couple I had met while with Ahmed in Sahel on the Mediterranean Sea. Selma and Rahim, after doing ecstasy all night with us at Selma's house, ended up having sex in her room. They asked me to come in and speak to them privately as their psychotherapist in the aftermath, as both were traumatized that they had taken each other's virginity. Selma was distraught, fearing she would forever be shamed by her parents and that Allah would never forgive her. Rahim was ashamed that he hadn't been able to control his impulse. They vowed to stay silent, blaming the drugs rather than taking responsibility, picking which sin to acknowledge. It was a clear example of how society's double standards allowed people to rationalize their actions, just as Rami had argued.

I did like how Rami questioned some of his own Islamic ways, saying that men are only as good as their women, not the other way around. He claimed that a good woman had the power to control her man, especially his anger. She "held the remote," as he put it. Thus, I learned that I should be good first, and a man would follow. He also believed that good people attract good people, which is how Allah wanted it to be, while bad people attract lessons. I found myself aligning with his views and couldn't imagine that I was bad because

Rami didn't seem to be. He was helping me understand my deep internal flaws.

What I didn't know then was that he was grooming me, just like a good narcissist does, with selective morality, inconsistency, and self-justification. I had never met men like Rami and didn't know the warning signs to watch out for. He hypnotized me, slowly stripping me of my will, brainwashing me, and preying on my vulnerabilities. All the while, I believed his actions toward me to be a deep form of respect, adoration, and maybe even love.

He asked questions about my deepest fears, my childhood, my dreams, and my pains. He never replied but just listened. Looking back, it's hard to remember exactly when and how he pried my self-esteem open; he'd find an entry point and keep picking at the scab until he fully infected me. I couldn't understand why I felt so guilty, so shameful, and like such a loser, and I constantly sought Rami's approval to even read an article or share a post on Facebook. If he saw I shared an old photo of my travels, he would quickly call and say, "Delete that now. That is the past, and you are just stuck in it. No one wants to see you in tight leggings doing yoga on a beach. Do you need more attention? Call me, we can hang out." He always had a solution for everything.

My roommates started to notice things, too. They wondered why I stopped talking to them, spent my days talking on the phone with Rami, and accompanied him to all his outings at night. I told them to stay out of it and assured them that I was fine. I also stopped writing to or caring about Lucas and my family. I lost track of time and any sight of goals—past or future. If Rami didn't ask me to do something, I didn't do it. If he told me to stay and wait, I stayed and waited.

On one hand, Rami made sense. On the other hand, his actions never aligned with his words. He told me how terrible it was that I wanted drugs, yet we took drugs together. Why was it okay for me to take drugs only under his supervision and never outside of it? With episodes like the night that we'd met becoming biweekly events, I lost track of what was real and what my brain was piecing together to fill in lost memories. I had strong feelings for Rami, but they were the product of intense codependency.

Slowly but surely, Rami picked out a role and a daily agenda for me. I couldn't ask for much because he dismissed my needs with, "No, habibti, I know how to make you happy." Since I was no longer working at Reach Out Academy, I complained to Rami that I needed to focus on finding an income. He set up interviews at his friends' companies for positions I never knew the details of, only to have me fail and not get the job. Looking back, I realize those interviews were never real; they were just another way to keep me dependent on him. He helped with rent, food, and everything else.

He slowly stripped away my free will. I couldn't see it then, because he had become the hand that fed me. Our contact was rarely sexual, apart from him asking me to pose for risqué photos while on a GHB roll, and the handful of advances I made at parties that he would stop before committing what he called the ultimate sin. It was a darker, more twisted relationship of power and control. "Stop turning me on!" he would say after taking photos of me. "That was a test to see if you finally got it. You failed. Stop being a bitch!" I felt ashamed, yet again falling for his trap. It was always a game between us. I couldn't fully understand why he didn't want any sexual favors in return for all he was doing for me. But I quickly shut down those thoughts, blaming my unclean, faithless mind. *He's a good Muslim man.*

Rami taught me how to have class and earn respect among the elite partiers: be well-dressed, do as the man asks, and never talk much about myself. He knew how to navigate the double standards of the Egyptian lifestyle. I began to idolize him because it felt good doing just the right amount of bad. Since he was grading my demeanor by his standards, I started to think of myself as a good enough woman. I questioned even more why Lucas never saw the good things in me and wondered if it was Lucas who didn't lead by the right example.

Rami and I attended many parties around Cairo and along the

Red Sea coast, some of which he helped organize. These events drew club owners, actors, and celebrities, often held in private villas with built-in elevators. Some parties featured cocaine rocks the size of golf balls on marble coffee tables, ecstasy pills, ketamine bumps off exotic car keys, and, of course, GHB, which was always held in a brown bottle with a black pipette top. I barely remember the parties —just swallowing the laced drinks and waking up on a couch or bed with Rami sitting next to me, watching me. Some weekends started out sober, when I attended the most extravagant Egyptian weddings in gowns he picked out and borrowed from his wealthy female friends. I spent only one or two days at home each week. I began to think my roommates were jealous of the pampering I received with their concerned statements of, "Katya, do you really think Rami is a good man for you?" But in hindsight, I see they were really just worried I was going down the wrong rabbit hole.

I feared disappointing him. He had an impulsive side, which I had seen a couple of times. At a two-day private villa party by the Red Sea, I made the mistake of dancing too closely with his friend. We had been awake for two days, sipping the GHB Rami gave us, and I completely lost my mind. He came up, squeezed my hand very hard, and told me he would cut off his caretaking if I ever did that again. "Katya, you have the remote to my temper. Don't regret holding it!" From that day on, I never dared to leave his side.

I couldn't do much in my free time. If I left my apartment and he called, God forbid he heard the street noises or people's chatter. "You went down from your place? It's dangerous outside! You like being harassed. Go home now," he would scold me. "If you need anything, call my driver, and he will get it for you." I had his driver's phone number and would order groceries to be delivered, which Rami would pay for.

Rami followed the social media accounts of me and all my family members. He created a Skype account just to check when I was last online. Sometimes, he would call me on Skype when he saw I was online, and if I didn't answer, he would rant about how I didn't appreciate everything he was doing for me. Skype was how I kept in contact with Lucas and my sister. I spoke with Lucas a few times, but the conversations weren't memorable since I was usually recovering from a party and sleeping the day away. I probably just told lies to keep Lucas thinking that I was doing fine. I hadn't told Rami about Lucas and feared what would happen if he found out about him. I didn't expect him to physically hurt me, but I wanted to avoid another moral lesson and the tests that could follow.

My codeine abuse was heavier than ever. I could go through a box of twenty-four Solpadeine pills a day to cope with the constant withdrawals from a cocktail of drugs. I was irritable, irrational, and confused about how five weeks had already gone by. Rami's lifestyle amplified my addiction. The more drugs I took with him, the more codeine pills I needed to feel "normal" again. To help me swallow the GHB and the tenth opioid of the day, I thought about all the people who hurt me. I thought about the old, paralyzed man who had masturbated for me to hear, my attempted suicide at fourteen, and my mother telling me she hated the day I was born. These thoughts generated anger, and the anger gave me the excuse to alter my world and put myself in dangerous situations. I was embodying the very victim Lucas had constantly accused me of being.

In that state of mind, everything started to feel like confirmation. The only truth I knew was that everyone I had ever loved had abandoned me. Those I hoped would protect me had let me down. I was never good enough for anyone. To match my internal world, the external one needed to be just as dirty. I wanted the worst to happen to me, just to prove the point that no one cared about me. I fantasized about my near-death, and that maybe, just maybe, someone would come to rescue me. I wanted someone to listen to my thoughts without expecting anything in return.

Some part of me knew this couldn't continue, so in a codeine-fueled attempt to get Rami off my back, I finally decided to tell him about Lucas.

"I have to tell you something, Rami," I said to him over the phone, interrupting his speech about how messed up society was.

"I'm listening," he said softly.

"So, I have a... boyfriend, sort of, I guess, back home. Back in Reno. I'm not sure if we are still together or not, but yeah. We talk," I said, pinching my eyes closed.

There was a long pause on the other end.

"What kind of boyfriend lets their girl go to a country like Egypt, and by herself? Unprotected, unsupervised! You don't have a boyfriend. Besides, would he still love you knowing that you party and go on dates with me? You need to leave him. Trust me, he's not a good man." Then he added, somewhat calmly, "What's his name?"

I actually agreed with Rami, and as he had shown me how to avoid personal consequences, I blamed Lucas for the mess I was in.

"Wait, call me on Skype, I want to see your face when you're talking to me," he continued before I could answer.

I restated the same thing, but now on video.

"You do not love him. I can see your face. You fear him," he said.

What I really feared was Rami. "I don't fear him—"

"Look at your face. You do. Don't lie to me. What's his name?" he asked again.

"Stephen," I lied. I knew if I told him the truth, he would find Lucas on every social media account and probably send compromising photos of me to shame me or blackmail me, which Rami had threatened to do before.

"Are you sure it's Stephen?" he asked. He could see that I was lying; I wasn't making eye contact with him. Rami always wanted me to look him in the eye.

"Yes, Rami. It's Stephen. Steve. I've been with him for four years now." I made an effort not to raise my voice, to sound normal, and to look him in the eyes.

"Well, if you are, and I know inside you do have a decent side to you, you would stop talking to him. You don't deserve someone who neglects you. You can be better, but I still have so much to teach you, Katya," he said, biting the inside of his lip again.

"Okay, I'll tell him later," I said.

"Tell him now. Call me on your cell, I want to hear you talking to him," he instructed.

I called Rami on my cell, then Skyped Lucas, and the moment he picked up, I said, "Hi. Why do you never write first? Why are you so distant and don't even care to ask if I have enough money for living here?"

"Katya—whoa, wait, wait. I sent you that two hundred dollars like you asked when you wanted to see the gynecologist. How am I not helping you?" Lucas replied.

A month back, I had asked Lucas for help because I'd stopped menstruating and needed to see a specialist. He sent me the money and sympathized with my situation. I'd forgotten his help entirely until he just mentioned it, and I was embarrassed that Rami had heard this.

"Yes, that was on you because I told you for years that I didn't want to take birth control. That's beside the point. You don't care about me. You don't. You don't care what I do all day, who I'm with, none of it!" I said, my body shaking. I was fishing for excuses to break up with him.

"Listen, Katya, I'm giving you the space you wanted. Hurry up and come home, then—I don't understand. You're working, you don't have money? Get a better job! Figure it out, I'm not sure how to help you," Lucas said.

"No. You have to figure it out for me. I am your woman, aren't I? Men are supposed to be protective of their women, and you just left me out here alone!" I said, sounding foreign and too Egyptian to myself.

"Who are you? Egypt is really getting under your skin," he replied.

Yes, yes, Lucas, it is, I wanted to say. *But you are doing nothing about it!*

"You know what, I don't want you anymore. We are done," I said, almost throwing up.

"Are you seeing anyone else?" he asked, sounding defeated.

I paused before answering. "Yes, I am. And you know what? He cares about me! He cares about what I do every day, and what I eat, and fucking everything you don't care about!" I yelled into the phone.

"Fuck you! Really?" Lucas said. "Okay, we are done. You've gone off into a world I do not care about anymore. I hope you're happy and he treats you with all the care that you need! You're dumb to not see reality, and it looks like Egypt maybe was the right decision for you." With that, he hung up.

I was in a cold sweat and curled up on the couch. I couldn't believe this was how our four-year relationship had ended: over Skype, in less than ten minutes, while Rami listened. This is how low a drug addict will go for another box of pills and another line of cocaine. Rami was my world now; he controlled my next dose, my rent, and now my personal decisions.

"You did good. But you should have told him you don't love him. Do you love him?" Rami asked through the speakerphone, breaking the silence.

"I don't," I said, doing my best to keep the sobbing out of my voice.

"You don't what?" he asked.

"I don't love him," I managed to say firmly. I wanted to hear myself say it and to believe that this was the right decision. But I still loved Lucas, and I didn't want this to be my reality.

"Okay. Good. Now, tomorrow we have the grand opening party of ALURE club. We are honored guests. Yella, get some sleep, and tomorrow I'll come for you at 8 p.m.," he said and hung up the phone.

I cried myself to sleep, looking over photos of Lucas and me. My plan to tell Rami about Lucas had backfired. I felt trapped, confused, and angry—angry that I was in this situation where a controlling

Egyptian cared more about my daily life than the man for whom I'd taken a leap of faith and come to Cairo to impress.

Maybe I really wasn't good enough yet, like Rami had said. At the core of my identity, I was just a drug addict. And who wanted to be with a drug addict who ruined everything and played the victim? I popped my last pill and prayed to the Christian God to get me out of that mess.

I had a purpose as Rami's arm candy. I didn't have to be mentally strong, say the right things, fulfill a future purpose, or work to support myself. All that mattered to me was finding pharmacies for my next codeine dose. Running low on the pills brought me more anxiety and fear than the thought of never getting out of Cairo.

The following night, at the grand opening of ALURE with Rami, God finally answered my prayers and showed me a way out of this situation.

"I really want to go home. I don't feel good," I shouted into Rami's ear at the club.

We were sitting at a VIP table with a group of eight of his friends. Alina had come, too, but with a different crowd. I'd only seen her walking by as we'd entered and waved to her.

Rami shook his head no, took the dark brown dropper vial of GHB, and squeezed two full droppers into my vodka soda. I didn't pick up my drink. He held it up to my face and glared. Out of anger, I took three large pulls from the cocktail straw.

"I'll be right back," I told him. "Bathroom!" Rami followed. In the bathroom, I put two fingers down my throat and threw up the contents. I was sick of being high all the time and furious with him for forcing me to break up with Lucas.

For my second attempt at leaving, I waited until the boys' drugs kicked in and they stood up around the couch dancing. Rami never seemed high, but he kept sipping his drink and watching everyone. Maybe drugs don't work on the devil.

"Okay, I really am going. Sorry, you don't have to drive. I'll take a cab. I don't feel good—I think I'm sick," I shouted into his ear again.

I stood up and began giving hugs and goodbyes to his friends. I leaned down to do the same with motionless Rami on the couch. His eyes were black. With one swift motion, he grabbed my arm and pulled me down to the couch.

"You're not going anywhere! You hear me? I'll tell you when you can go!" he hissed into my face.

Then, with full force, he slapped me across the face, knocking me down to the floor. This was the first time he had laid a hand on me, but I wasn't surprised. For the first time in a long time, I remembered I had free will—to leave, to not take drugs, to take care of what I needed. That realization was more surprising than the pain on my face. I was almost relieved by the slap because he had just handed me the reason to take back my control and get the fuck away from him on a silver platter. But I did hope that this would be the end of Rami's reaction.

He stood again, grabbed a handful of my hair, and pulled me back up. Then he slapped me again, and I fell on my ass, missing the couch. My dress slipped up to my waist, exposing my panties. His friends looked back to see the commotion and, as though on cue, stood around us in a wall, blocking the beating I was about to receive.

Rami kicked me in my groin and thighs a couple of times, punched my head, and kept screaming, "Look at this bitch! Your pussy is hanging out!" It all happened so fast. I did everything I could to protect my body, curling in a fetal position on the sticky nightclub floor. The music disappeared, and all I could hear was my racing heart. I knew if I fought back, it would get worse.

He peeled me off the floor and ordered me to pull down my dress, as if my modesty was more important than the dignity he was feasting on.

"You wanna go home? I'll take you home!" he screamed.

I scanned the area and saw Alina looking over at me from the bar. She just shook her head and mouthed, "Sorry."

Rami dragged me to the elevator. He shoved me down again, and

I fell to my knees in front of the elevator. People were watching us, but no one intervened. I had never seen such public displays of abuse, but maybe this was normal to them. More likely, since I was a White woman, they assumed I had crossed some moral standard line as foreigners were known to do. Domestic disputes were never anyone's concern; these men had a religious responsibility to keep their women in line. I felt helpless.

My instinct was to calm him down before he hurt me too much. I processed that fast and stood up. I wrapped my arms around him and smiled.

"Oh, Rami, I'm sorry. I deserve that. I'm not leaving without you. Let's go somewhere else, just the two of us," I said to him.

"No! I'm taking you home," he said coldly, once again grabbing a handful of my hair and shaking my head.

On the way to my apartment, we were quiet. My body ached from the punches, but I did my best to act as though none of it had happened. I forced myself to sit properly, legs closed. We pulled up under my house, and with a "thank you," I opened the door to leave. Rami grabbed my arm and bit my hand, reached over me to shut the door, then screamed, "You're not going anywhere!"

"Please, Rami, please. This is enough. I need rest. I'm sorry," I said and started to sob.

He put the car in reverse and sped off.

I've had a handful of eye-opening experiences throughout my life, all of which were traumatic and transforming. This moment was by far the most memorable. Sitting in the passenger seat, I thought of my mother. I realized I had never wanted her more than I did in that moment, and yet she wouldn't be able to help me. Whether I was near her or thousands of miles away, she couldn't help me. No one could. I realized that I was alone and at the mercy of my twisted friend. The world outside the window suddenly became more beautiful as I contemplated how my next minute would end.

Rami screamed at me, lecturing me about how I wasn't good enough. As if reading my mind, he told me I was just like my mother and she wouldn't ever save me, just like Lucas wouldn't. The openness and carefree nature of being under the influence of GHB had made me open up to him in the past. I had told him about all my issues with my mother, not realizing I had been handing him a weapon to use against me. I didn't want to agree with him, but there was evidence that he was right, so I kept quiet. Then he struck me again, grabbing the back of my neck and slamming my brow into the dashboard. The blow made me wet myself a little.

When we got to the mansion, he raped me. As he entered me, as I lay on my stomach with my arms pinned behind my back, it felt familiar. My body recognized his sexual energy, but my mind had no recollection of it. I didn't fight back. I wanted to, but I was afraid that if I didn't comply, he could really hurt me. He had already broken my spirit; my body was just the dessert. I stared out the mansion window at the lighted pool and the lion statues around it. My tears were all drained, dried in black makeup streaks on my face.

"You'll remember me this time," he whispered into my ear. *Of course*, I thought. That's when it clicked for me: GHB erased memories, and in that moment I began to fear he might have been using it on me all along. Suddenly his shyness around sober advances felt different; I wondered if he preferred women unconscious, their bodies at his disposal, where he could feel superior without ever committing what he called the "full sin" with someone awake. The thought nauseated me. I kept asking myself how a man who could already beat a woman could then go further. What kind of darkness had to live inside him? I'd thought my mother was terrible, I'd thought Lucas was unfair, I knew I was a liar and a cheat—but here was Rami, and in my eyes he put all of our sins to shame. I lay motionless, numb; it was over in two blinks of a blackened eye.

Moments later, his friend, the son of the mansion's owner, came in nonchalantly, asking for a cigarette. He jumped on the bed and smacked my naked ass. They laughed, but I just kept my head in my pillow and my eyes closed. I lay there in shock until I fell asleep, with Rami lying close by, hoping this was just a bad trip, that it wasn't real. I thought I would wake up in the morning back in my bed. My mother would call, someone would come—they had to. I didn't even have a financial way out of this situation.

But I didn't wake up in a different place. I woke up in the same place, only with a new emotion: determination. I felt a rush not to be victim to Rami's twisted mentality. I knew I was stronger than him because I didn't need to hurt people for my own pleasure. I recognized the demons within him that he thought would destroy me.

The real problem in my situation wasn't only the abuse I had endured—it was me and my victimhood mentality. It was my self-loathing as a response to how everyone hurt me. I put pills in my mouth, I snorted cocaine, I drank designer drugs, I let men use me. This was what Lucas had been telling me all along: stop playing the victim. I had created this mess.

The only way out was to embrace all the bad choices I had made up to this point, or at least begin to, so I could escape. I vowed to take back control. Since the source of all Rami's twisted games was my weakness, I decided to turn the tables on him; to use all the strategies he had been using on me against him.

With that vow burning inside me, I stood up and undressed in front of him, staring him dead in the eyes, just as he had always taught me to do. He blushed and turned away. That was my proof: he was a powerless loser, an immature boy playing pretend with control. A spoiled, broken narcissist. I had given him power by submitting, by fearing, by trusting, by being weak.

"Do you want to fuck now?" I asked with a cold stare. He giggled and ran out the bedroom door, locking me inside. I still needed him to hand me my purse, keys, and phone, so I had to be careful with my next moves. Locked in that room, I realized escape would mean playing along until the right moment.

As part of Rami's usual weekend agenda, we were headed out again that night—this time to a birthday party at yet another club.

"How do you expect me to go out with a black eye, ya Rami?" I asked, irritated, hoping he might finally offer to take me home.

"I see what you're doing. Fine. I'll take you home—but only to grab clothes and makeup," he replied, exhaling his frustration. He treated me like contraband: afraid to be seen with my bruised face, yet unwilling to let go of his control. We drove back to my place, but before I could step out of the car, Rami handed me my phone and dialed it himself. "Stay on the line," he ordered. "Do not talk to anyone. Grab your things. You have five minutes. If you're not down, I'll come up for you. I know how."

Deep down, I had vowed to take my power back. But in that moment, survival meant obeying him long enough to stay safe. For all I knew, he could storm the apartment and strangle me on the spot. So I grabbed my dress and makeup and slipped out the door without disturbing Dasha. Still afraid of him—his power, his persuasion—I truly feared that if I didn't return to the car, he could find a way to hurt me even more.

On the ride back to the mansion, my vow hardened into a plan: I would drug him, beat him, and take all my dignity back.

Caked in makeup, I clung to his arm and walked into the club. This time I didn't wait for the offer; I asked for Ketel One, soda, and three droppers of GHB. I knew the drill. If I didn't take the drugs, Rami would force me, and I was done with any more forcing. I knew my sins, and the boat club on the Nile would be the stage to repent them. I kept an eye on which pocket he slipped the brown vial into, waiting for my chance. Then I led him by the hand onto the crowded dance floor, rehearsing my escape in my mind.

In a few hours, Rami was cemented to the VIP couch, nodding off. My next goal was to get the valet ticket in his wallet and the keys to the car, where my passport, purse, and phone were. Even in his altered state, the devil that was Rami was only concerned about losing the vial of GHB. Even in his near-blackout state, he was slurring and yelling for me to find it. I pretended to be looking for it. His friend, Arnie, was there, assuring him it would be okay with little slaps to the face. To my dismay, Arnie also gave him an antidote: a huge line of ketamine.

"Are you feeling okay? You should take some, too, Katya. Keta-mine is so you don't get GHB overdose," he said in a big-brotherly tone. Arnie had watched the beatings at ALURE, and now he was offering me help out of my drug stupor. All these people were twisted. I had been through the Balkans, Southeast Asia, parts of Europe, and India, and I had never come across such low-life, double-standard men.

Seeing that Rami was coming around and standing on his own, I also took a bump, and to my relief, I sobered up in minutes.

By then, it was almost 5 a.m., and all the boys were ready to call it a night. I could see lust in their eyes. My determination was dimin-ishing, and my plan to drug him on that couch and take my purse and run had failed. Fear crept back in, as I knew I couldn't go back to that mansion room. I hung my head and let Rami walk me out of the club, defeated.

The next thing I heard were yells and curses in Arabic coming from the parking lot, followed by Arnie running up to Rami and screaming, "Come quickly!" The group of boys ahead of us were shouting at the valet attendants. Rami quickened his pace and dragged me into the commotion. I found myself looking at Rami's smashed-up foreign car. The driver's door was bent in two, the front was crushed, exposing the engine, and the passenger windows were shattered. It looked as though someone had run into it three times. It seemed like a sign for me to finally make my escape.

Rami looked at me first. "You did this!" he screamed. "Stay here!" he ordered and plowed his way into the fight. I looked up at the heavens and thanked God. I took off my heels with one quick motion, sprinted around the back of the vehicle, and grabbed my purse from the passenger-side glovebox. Then I ran. I ran down the street along the Nile as fast as my marshmallow legs could carry me, hailing a cab around the first corner. Rami was yelling for me to stop but unable to leave his totaled car and the subsequent responsibility behind. Thank you, guardian angel, or whoever you are.

———

I slept all day and through the night. Dasha came home early Monday morning, and upon seeing my bruised face and arm, she quietly sat next to me, smoking. I cried and told her the whole story. She didn't say much, just that it was good he was finally out of my life. She reassured me that he wouldn't be able to come up here since the beweb wouldn't let him and offered to buy me some groceries and cigarettes from the kiosk. I told her I wasn't leaving the house and thanked her.

I called my fifteen-year-old sister, Masha, and finally told her the truth about Rami's abuse, leaving out all the messy details about the drugs. She was devastated and insisted we tell Mom, but I asked her not to. "It will only prove Mom's point that she was right and that I shouldn't have come to Egypt. Besides, I don't need her help; she'll use it against me one day," I told her. She agreed to let me tell whomever I wanted whenever I was ready. I also warned her that Rami might reach out to her and not to believe anything he told her. I felt bad for even letting him into her life.

Go and get it, Muffy! You loved Egypt, I'm sure you'll do great there: I remembered Lucas's words when I'd announced my plan to move. How irresponsible and naïve of me to have thought anything good would come out of the Arab world. How reckless of Lucas to have allowed me to go, knowing what he knew of Cairo and the hostile environment we'd both experienced. *You wanted to come to Cairo. That was your idea. And I am giving you the space*: I remembered his last words. I hadn't needed space; I'd wanted him to be closer. I'd wanted him to stop me and advise me on a better direction. Digesting this with a brainwashed and selfless mind, I wondered if Lucas was in on the manipulation and control from Rami. Was this a setup? A punishment of some sort? It couldn't be; that was just my paranoia talking.

. . .

I'd escaped my situation but lost my freedom to leave my own house. In the days following my escape, Rami stalked me, parking outside our balcony and calling non-stop. I finally turned off my phone and shut myself off from the world. He didn't break in and strangled me, like I feared. Just circled like a vulture.

That spark of determination had only got me this far. Now, PTSD kicked in with sleepless nights and long days of chain smoking. I couldn't believe that almost two months had passed under Rami's control. I didn't realize how much he'd controlled me until I slowly started processing each of his moves. I could only handle processing a few incidents at a time, as I would cry until my tears dried up. So, I did what any girl would do after leaving an abusive relationship: I changed my looks and reconciled with 'the good ex.'

Dasha offered to get the hair dye, and Alina offered to help me dye my hair. We bonded as friends, and it was the first time I laughed in months. For the first time in my life, I put chemicals on my hair. I felt unhealthier putting chemicals on my hair than into my body. But then again, I had never promised myself I would stop taking pills, just that I would stop letting people tell me how to run my pity party. It was my journey to self-destruction, and I wanted to be left in peace to walk my winding road, now as a dark brunette.

After five days of calling me, threatening me, and blackmailing my sister, Rami finally gave up. I knew I had to keep my mouth shut since I was still in this country without a ticket out. Even though I wanted to inform the authorities, I knew the law in Egypt didn't protect women's rights. I wouldn't be taken seriously, especially after saying, "Yes, police officer, I did know what drugs he was giving me." I chose to remain unnoticed and hoped to be forgotten by Rami.

My next step was to face the man who had allowed me to go to the unsafe Middle East on my own without a care in the world. I contemplated how to start my email introduction, aiming not to sound needy (which he hated) or weak (which he hated equally) while still being honest.

Hi Lucas, I've been lying to you and I'm a drug addict...

Too much. Too raw. If I opened that can of worms, our entire relationship would be judged as a lie. I had stood up to my abuser, but I couldn't let the man I loved see me as unworthy.

Hi Lucas, I made a terrible mistake, I am so sorry...

That sounded better. I sat down and wrote for four hours straight, pouring out my deepest desires. I reminded him of our journey, confessed the truth about Rami—the GHB, and the three-way call when I ended things. I left out only one thing: the blunt reality of my hidden painkiller addiction.

When I finished my eight-page essay, I asked him to help me leave Egypt and to give us another chance. Then I popped another codeine, lit a cigarette, and pressed send.

I hoped Lucas would pity me, as I truly was a victim now. What I wanted from Lucas was for him to appreciate the strength it had taken for me to escape. I had always wanted Lucas to be the hero in all of my stories.

6

THE PRINCE
(DECEMBER 2014)

Screaming into my pillow only provided temporary relief from the guilt I felt for getting myself into my shit situation. Crying only eased the chest pressure for a few hours. Desperation consumed me as I, again, sought a way out of Egypt, my head, my skin, my mistakes, and my past. I had failed to show anything worthwhile to Lucas. I had broken up with him under the pressure of a monster. The only report card I had to give him read, "I was beaten and raped." That realization killed me the most—not what Rami had done to me, but that I had failed Lucas, landing myself in such lowlife situations. He had believed in my abilities to come out on top, yet I had failed him. His lack of response only tightened the unbearable knot of anxiety in my stomach.

As days passed, I truly believed Rami's abuse was my fault. I became convinced that if I had just focused on my work and stopped playing the victim, I wouldn't have put myself in danger.

I kept taking codeine. I promised myself I wouldn't take any other substances, but detoxing from codeine in my current state of mind felt impossible. I had attempted to quit as a junior in college the year I'd met Lucas, but even then, with nothing to complain about, quitting pills had been too much to bear. I would commit suicide before attempting to part ways with my crutch, especially now.

I couldn't rely on my innate instinct to call Mom and Dad for help. My father lived in a small village and worked as a butcher; his life savings wouldn't cover half of my ticket back to Reno. My mother had joined a religious cult from Russia with her husband and cut off communication from everyone. I had no choice but to fend for myself alone, hoping that Lucas would eventually rescue me.

Between violent breakdowns, I applied for jobs and went to two interviews, focusing on high-paying hotel hospitality positions. My plan again was to work for a month, earn enough for a ticket, even if it was to Ukraine, and prove to Lucas that I was worthy at least of making it out of Egypt. I despised myself and needed Lucas's validation. However, with each passing day and a continuously empty inbox, my hope dwindled.

The last person I should have trusted on this planet was my roommate, Alina, who had seen Rami beating me at the club and done nothing to help. But she was the only person I had to talk to. She was just as 'morally low' as me, a fellow party girl there for the pleasure of our abusers. Neither Dasha nor Alina questioned the incident or my two-day absence. When I told them that Rami beat me, their silence spoke volumes. The look in their eyes revealed that they, too, had been victims of physical abuse at some point, the price for playing at the Cairo playground. They had the same look as they'd had when Mr. Harish, our landlord, had bribed us with marriage several months back. I had become their equal. But what they didn't have—and I hoped I did have—was an offshore boyfriend, someone I believed would rescue me. This, I felt, bred jealousy between us.

Three weeks after I'd escaped from Rami at the club, I was still hiding away at my house, only leaving for the two interviews at

Hilton and the Four Seasons. I assumed Rami had given up by then and stopped stalking me; at least, I hoped that was the case. The PTSD from my rape still lingered in the air. I'd spend my days checking my email every hour, hoping to get a response from Lucas. I longed to ride my bike on university grounds and have one of Nicole's $4.25 croissants, to feel normal again, as normal as I had felt before.

"Katya, for the last time, and don't make me come begging, please come with us!" Alina yelled down the huge hallway.

"I told you: I don't want to go anywhere but home," I yelled back. "Wherever that is..." I added quietly to myself.

Alina was busy packing to go with her new boy-toy, Omar, to Ein Sokhna, a resort town on the Red Sea, three hours west of Cairo.

"Come on! Come stay with us," she insisted. "We can wake up late and go to the beach. It will be peaceful, I promise! You might be leaving soon anyways, and you just need to get out of this depressing house and have one last good memory of Cairo!"

I tossed and turned in my cold bed, pulling the hood over my head. They didn't heat the damn concrete apartments in Egypt. Winters were brutal, and it was December 15, 2014. Alina's invitation, though imperfect, felt like a lifeline. My thoughts spun around in the cold silence, and I wanted so badly to escape the constant replaying of painful memories. Desperation ate at me, pushing me to take any chance to break free from my mental prison, even if it was just for one night.

"Fine. I'll come. But please, promise me nothing crazy. No partying, no bullshit, Alina," I said.

By the time Alina's boyfriend, Omar, arrived to pick us up, two hours late, I'd changed my mind four times. I was scared to leave, afraid of running into Rami. I felt guilty for even considering the possibility of happiness because I didn't deserve it. I deserved to stay home and be miserable.

"Why are we at the fucking hotel?" I asked Omar from the back seat when he stopped at the Fairmont Nile City Hotel.

"Quick stop for drinks in a room," he said.

Having drinks in a hotel was normal since clubs and bars were closed during the weekdays, and we couldn't have boys in our apartment. Plus, Omar most likely still lived with his parents. But something told me we were not going to wake up by the Red Sea. Alina insisted I stay, promising we would make it out there by early morning. Why was I trusting her again? I didn't know.

The three of us walked into the Fairmont Nile City Hotel, an iconic building on the bank of the Nile. Cairo didn't have many tall buildings, and I'd seen this exact hotel from across the Nile with Lemo on my first night back in Cairo, admiring the pattern of lights from the rooms. *Full circle*, I thought to myself. I had come to what my eyes had admired. I smiled, thinking this was a good closure to my Cairo adventures. To me, all the shit I'd endured were adventures and the thick skin I had grown out of this toxic environment was a souvenir... but only if I got to go back to Reno.

I sat on the couch in front of the registration counter while Omar attempted to get rooms. As standard protocol, he had to get two, because unmarried couples were not allowed to stay in one room. Watching the entrance's revolving door, I noticed an unremarkable, muscular, 5'10" man dressed in gray Nike sweats, black Nike shoes, and a distressed white V-neck briskly walking up to meet Omar. I could smell his Oud Wood cologne as he walked by; I took it in with a deep breath. Mr. Nike Pants went to the hotel registration counter and broke the ice with the staff.

This felt like a setup by Omar; he must have invited his friend since I was alone. I was sure Alina hadn't told him that I wasn't in the mood to meet anyone, so he'd genuinely thought he was doing me a favor. If they dared to touch me, it would be my chance to teach these Egyptian boys a lesson. I was ready to beat them, bite them, and scream to the hotel staff if they as much as laid a finger on me. All my pent-up anger from Rami's abuse still needed an outlet.

The boys walked up to me.

"Katya, this is Amir—Amir, Katya," Omar introduced us. "Please give him your passport, and he will get a room under your name."

Amir in Arabic means 'prince; nobleman.' He reassured me with his smiling eyes. I liked that. His demeanor made me feel like I could trust him. Little did I know then, I had just met the father of my future daughter.

"Hi," I said. "Wow, I don't even know you, and you want my passport." I rolled my eyes at Amir. I was not interested in him at this point. Checking my side pocket in my day bag, I gave him my passport. I reasoned that he couldn't do much damage with it in a crowded lobby.

"Thank you very much; I will just be a minute." Amir smiled at me, giving a slight bow and rolling his R's with respect. There was something different about him, but I could only attribute the small tickle in my stomach to his large, shiny, and perfectly dark Arab eyes. "American?" he asked, surprised.

"Yes," I said, turning to give the same confused look to Alina seated next to me on the couch.

Amir had seemed like an unremarkable Nike-clad man from a distance, but the way he'd interacted with the hotel staff reminded me of how Lucas connected with random people as though they were childhood friends. Amir's laugh was loud and contagious. His movements were deliberate and confident, just like Lucas's. There was a drive behind him that I found very attractive. The color of his dark skin, with almost a tint of gray on the fold of his soft neck, really stood out to me. He put his hand on his heart when he spoke, in a gesture of gratitude, and used the one Arabic affirmation I knew, 'gamil' (beautiful), instead of the word 'meshi' (okay) that other Arabic men used.

Despite his profound similarities to Lucas, I wasn't in the right mindset to meet anyone, entertain anyone, or talk about myself, my messed-up situation, and my plan to leave Cairo. But it looked like Amir was planning on staying. I had imagined Omar and Alina would be in their room, and I'd planned to lock myself in mine until the three-hour drive to Ein Sokhna. But now we had a fourth person, and a male at that. I was not comfortable.

Up in one of the rooms, the boys lit up cigarettes and were jittery, giggling, and clearly uncomfortable. This whole situation was taboo to them, and I could smell their adrenaline in the stuffy hotel room air. I doubted they'd had many hotel parties with non-virgins. Amir got into the mini bar and pulled out chasers for the vodka bottle Omar put on the table. And to their disappointment, my legs didn't sprawl wide open.

Out of spite, I decided to milk this situation to the fullest. I had Amir order the salmon dish from room service, an American brand of cranberry juice for my vodka, and an extra pack of Davidoff Slims. I kept my face in an expression of complete disappointment the entire night. Alina kept telling me to relax, saying in Russian that this was just a quick stop before our drive to Sokhna. I wasn't buying it.

"That's my favorite brand. Abercrombie and Fitch," Amir shared, pointing to my overnight bag.

"The bag is fake," I said, shutting him down. *Not my first rodeo, Amir*, I thought. *I know this act of flaunting wealth.* I could tell he was from a wealthy family, had attended private English schools with American teachers, and had never worked a day in his life. The polished gold Rolex on his wrist and the smoothness of his hands gave it away, just as Rami's smooth and manicured hands had given away his privilege.

"Where in America are you from?" he asked.

"I've lived in many places, but I was last in Reno, Nevada. It's next to San Francisco," I replied in a monotone voice.

"I haven't been to the West Coast yet, but I'm going on a trip to Las Vegas and New York in a couple of weeks. I love New York. I go every year," Amir bragged, proving my hunch that he was from a well-traveled family.

"The clubs must be nice there!" Omar added. They were hoping to impress me.

"Yeah! Well, my uncle owned a club in one of the Twin Towers, but 9/11 happened, and he lost it all," Amir continued. "PHD is my favorite club. One Oak isn't bad either. Do you like those, Katya?"

"I've been to New York, but not in clubs," I answered as I lit up my expensive cigarette. "Must be nice to be able to travel so much and party at nightclubs. My parents aren't rich and don't pay for my stuff. I can't afford to go there. When I travel, I stay in cheap Airbnbs and eat street food."

The room went quiet. My honesty made it clear I wasn't there to pretend to be cool or rich or to brag about being American. I had checked out of these courting games weeks ago. The knock from room service brought movement back into the frozen room.

Later, as the conversation turned to gym routines and Instagram posts, I interrupted them, addressing Amir directly, "You know what really bothers me?"

"What?" Amir locked his phone and put it down, giving me his complete, undivided attention.

"This whole open-minded mentality in Egypt and that people brag about it. Open-mindedness should be the norm and a given right for everyone, not something to brag about," I said. I was on a different wavelength than the rest of them, lost in my own thoughts while participating as a spectator in our gathering.

"I see. True," Amir answered with smiling eyes. He had such expressive eyes. But so did every man who'd ever lusted over me.

"I'm 'open-minded,' but most people think it means sitting here drinking and smoking with you. That's not the point. That's not what open-mindedness is," I continued.

Amir sat up straighter, looking more interested. "You're very deep, I can see that," he said with a smile.

He wasn't going to break me, no matter how good-looking, respectful, or kind he pretended to be. I knew this was a game to get into bed with me. I didn't want another 'situationship,' relationship, or any man for a meal—even though I needed one.

By 2 a.m., I was fed up. I bitched Alina out in Russian about not taking me to the Red Sea like she had promised then left for my room. The one thing I hate most in this world is broken promises. "Your word is so important to me," I told her. How stupid of me to trust her yet again. I realized she, like everyone else here, played persuasion games only to say 'bukra' (tomorrow). After eleven years of living here in Cairo, I couldn't really blame her. I just wished she'd kept her Ukrainian word.

I was almost asleep when I heard a knock on my door. The hairs on the back of my neck stood up, as I imagined Rami standing there.

"What are you doing? It's 6 a.m.!" I yelled at Amir through the crack of the door.

"It's 5:30 actually, and I bought the room. I need to stay here," he said. "Open up."

Jesus Christ, please leave me alone. I was too tired to get a cab and leave. That was what I should have done hours ago. But the Fairmont Nile Towers Hotel was on the other side of the Nile, and my place was about a five-dollar cab ride away. I needed to save money for cab rides to job interviews, something I wasn't used to because I'd always owned a car in America.

I rolled my eyes and opened the door. Without waiting for him to come inside, I walked back and jumped into bed, turning my back to him. He stood there for a minute before plopping down on the bed next to mine.

"That's it? You're just going to sleep?" he asked.

I blew air out of my nose like a winded horse. "Dude, you think I'm here to fuck you? You honestly think I don't see that Omar invited you here as my date? Look, I don't know you, and I don't want to know you. If you even try to put your hand on me, I'm calling the police!" I screamed. My voice was shaking. I felt the tears building up behind my eyes, as I stared out the window at the Nile.

"Whoa, what did I do? What happened? Why are you so on edge?" Amir asked.

"You really want to know what happened?" I laughed sarcastically, turning to look at him. "Okay, I'll tell you, so maybe you'll leave me alone!"

I pulled my arm out from under the blankets and showed him the bruises on my inner biceps. "See, I'm hiding from Ashraf Rami. He beat me, raped me, and has been stalking me. I'm leaving Egypt very soon, and I just wanted to go to the sea one last time. But Alina didn't tell me about this hotel room or meeting any men. I'm really over everything, and in my mind, I checked out of Cairo weeks ago." I stated all of this in one big breath.

"Oh my God, Katya. What a fucking asshole! I've heard of him, but I don't know him personally. I hear he is bad with girls," Amir said. "You seem so honest and down-to-earth, I can't imagine someone laying their hand on you. I will fuck him up if you want me to!"

He was furious now, and I sensed it was genuine. His bedroom eyes shifted to angry eyes then to shameful eyes in a moment. I had called him out on his intentions, and he felt guilty.

"So, please, the last thing I need is to get to know anyone or whatever you want from me," I replied.

"Well, it sounds like you can use a friend you can trust," he said.

"Ha! And how can I trust you?" I asked, leaning closer to his face. I wanted to get a better look at him in the dim city light filtering into the hotel room.

"Look, I got the wrong impression of you. I won't touch you, okay? I am here because Omar asked me to come. Let's just talk. I am wide awake and can't go home now. My parents think I'm at a friend's house. Maybe I can help you somehow," he insisted.

I sensed the sincerity of his concern and opened up to him completely, turning on a dime. Perhaps it was because I felt vulnerable and needed to share the weight on my chest. Part of me wanted, for once, to be open about myself to someone willing to listen. The fact that he'd offered help almost made me cry. Another part of me didn't care what he thought of me and hoped I would scare him away. I wanted to leave a bad taste in his mouth if he ever sought to manipulate girls like this again—barging into hotel rooms at 6 a.m.

As if in a therapy session, I vented about the rock-bottom situation I was in. I told him about Lucas and my life back home and showed him photos of Reno, Ukraine, and my blonde hair. I shared how hard it had been for me living in Egypt as a woman, the daily sexual harassment that imprisoned us women in our homes, and that it wasn't safe even in our own homes, as landlords looked to take advantage of us. Speaking on behalf of all Western girls who got sucked into the Egyptian double-standard world, I told Amir how twisted this 'open-minded' world really was and that I was sick of playing the game and just wanted to go home, wherever that was.

By the time I finished my emotional vomiting, the sun had risen. We talked more, covering all topics of the Eastern and Western worlds. I felt a weight lift and actually started to enjoy our conversation. He showed a lot of sympathy for my situation, never arguing or making excuses for my experiences.

"I'm sorry for all this that happened," he said. "But there are good men in Egypt. And, yes, you have met a lot of bad ones. Just like there are bad American men. I agree, being a woman here is difficult; you need protection from a man. I protect my sister and mother from those harassers all the time."

"Yeah, I'm sure there is a good side. If world travel has taught me anything, it is that there are good and bad people everywhere," I said and soon drifted off to sleep.

When I got up around 11 a.m., Amir was gone. He had left me a note on the hotel stationary pad: 'You're beautiful. It's your soul that makes you beautiful.'

I grinned at his words, pitying him for falling for the damsel in distress. Every man wants to be a hero, and he had been mine for a few hours. Regardless, it was a nice touch—one that reminded me of when Lucas would leave me sweet notes in random places around our house.

As I expected, Ein Sokhna was a bust. I got Omar and Alina up and demanded a ride home. While waiting at the hotel reception, I realized Amir had never asked for my number. However, he'd promised to help me and made me feel like he was a friend I could trust. Had my damsel-in-distress act scared him away? It would have definitely scared Lucas away; he preferred women who were more independent and self-sufficient. But Amir was Arab, and from what I'd learned, the good ones perceived vulnerability as feminine and instinctively wanted to protect us. They were more attuned to tradi- tional gender roles.

My gut told me that Amir was just waiting for the right time to engage with me. I couldn't explain why, but I felt calm and confident that he would be there if I needed him.

Back home, I slept for the rest of the day, and around 5 p.m., I got a phone call from the Four Seasons Hotel HR recruiter.

"Hello, ma'am," a voice said. "Can you come in for an interview on Thursday at 1 p.m.? We are considering you for the position of Hotel Relations Manager. Please be ready with a passport, a copy of your CV, and be prepared for a drug test."

"Yes, okay, I will come. Thank you. MaSalama (goodbye)," I replied and hung up.

Immediately, my anxiety took over with racing thoughts about the long cab rides to the hotel, haggling over inflated fares, charming the men at work as a 'Relations Manager,' the heat, and my intense hatred for this city. I sat on my bed, cradling my head, as a rat scur- ried out from under it. Fuck, I had to take this job and get out of there. I wouldn't pass the drug test, though. I was sure that the GHB, ketamine, hashish, and cocaine hadn't left my system in the three weeks since I'd taken them. Not to mention the daily opioids.

Motivated by the seven-hundred-eighty-dollar monthly salary, I was determined to use every tool I had to land this job. This was my ticket back to the Western world.

"Alina, ask Omar for Amir's number, please," I yelled down the hallway.

"Ooh, you like him, huh?" she beamed.

"He's okay. But I need his help. I need to ask him for clean pee," I replied.

"What? Pee?" She laughed.

"I don't give a shit. I need money. I just got a call back from the Four Seasons for an interview in two days. They're going to drug test me. I need to work. I'm not sure if Lucas is even coming or not. Fuck! At least I can make enough money for a ticket back," I explained to Alina.

Asking Amir for clean urine was awkward, to say the least. Especially after the venting session I had unleashed on him the night before. But we laughed it off, and that felt nice. I hadn't laughed that hard in months.

The shaved, sane, and stoic Amir arrived the very next morning, delivering a lunchbox containing a plastic container of drug-free urine wrapped in aluminum foil. I met him outside of our building and collected my package from the passenger's seat of his BMW. Before leaving, he invited me out to dinner that evening, emphasizing that we were friends. As repayment to him for the absurd favor he'd just done for me, I agreed to it. We arranged to eat at the very Four Seasons where I'd hopefully be an employee.

For the first time in a long while, I felt hope. Hope that I would soon be leaving Egypt and that my story wouldn't end like it had for my roommates, who were stuck here. I felt like the chosen one, like a first-born daughter should feel. That night, sitting with Amir, who was both asking about and contributing to my escape plans, I didn't feel alone in figuring out my next steps. I took a deep breath of the desert air, feeling empowered that Rami's abuse hadn't broken me. I had risen above my pain, and the universe had started opening the right doors.

As Amir and I finished our post-meal shisha pipe on the rooftop of the Four Seasons, a frown formed on my face. It was a bittersweet moment, as I realized I had opened up to him in such a short time more than I had to anyone else. This side of me—was it Kateryna?—was unfamiliar. I wasn't afraid of judgment, nor was I pretending to be stronger than I really was.

Riding the elevator back down to Amir's car, I felt a big wave of sadness come over me. Perhaps it was knowing that we would never see each other beyond these last few months in Egypt. For every messed-up story I shared about my childhood and my deep secrets, he reciprocated with his own hurts, needs, and desires. He would stare at me in amazement, constantly reiterating that I was the strongest woman he had ever met, the most interesting, driven, and talented person he had ever known. Yet, I was in the worst position of my young adult life: homeless and broke.

I felt torn between how Amir and Lucas saw me, as though my self-image was reflected differently in two bodies of water—one tainted, one clear. Which one was I? A strong woman or one that lacked strength? I clung to Lucas's ideas of me, as he was the one I had spent the most time with.

7
THE CONTRACT
(JANUARY 2015)

The following morning, I sat on my couch, stewing over the concept of a strong woman and reflecting on my dinner with Amir the night before. "Strongest woman I've ever met," Amir had said, and I laughed at the absurdity of that. How did Amir see any strength in me?

I recalled the cliché line that behind every successful man, there's a strong woman. *What does a strong woman look like?* I thought. *How does she sound, walk, and talk? How does she feel being the strong woman behind her successful man? What is she strong for, and why isn't she successful, too?*

Behind every successful man, there wasn't always a successful woman. She was often in the shadows. If she was successful, it was a tailored success. To feel self-worth, she molded her needs around his. It was either that one woman or many disposable ones who made the man feel worthy by letting him dip into her feminine creative energy.

Behind every successful woman, there was no man. At least, that was what I saw on social media. The successful woman was usually lonely. She probably wondered why her distinguished status, her expensive French night creams, and the ten thousand miles on her

Peloton didn't lure a suitable mate. She was probably too powerful, pragmatic, and intimidating for a man. She didn't need him but wanted him. A powerful man didn't necessarily want a successful woman in his life, but he needed her to feel worthy, needed. She was there to validate his worth on a steady basis.

Thus, there was this universal idea of the need for a strong woman in a man's life. Like how Lucas wanted me to be strong. Maybe being strong was better than being successful. I didn't know; I didn't think I was either of those in his eyes. But how was I in Amir's eyes? I didn't feel strong, as my life didn't reflect that. A directionless opioid addict, last time I checked, was not strong in any way. But maybe I was. I did know that whatever my successes were, they were intangible, yet Amir saw them.

My sober thoughts started to not make sense, so I popped four codeine pills and lit up a cigarette. That first pull of the morning cigarette, and the rush from it, was unlike anything else. I especially liked the smell of the initial spark of the chemicals on the paper. That smell always reminded me of my mother when I was growing up, and in good ways. I held the first drag the longest, feeling the nicotine rush poison my veins. It connected me to my flow, the asana, as the medicine hit my lungs, heart, head, and legs. The dizziness hit right on point. I took another drag, but the effect was lost. By the second drag, my morning breath was masked by tar and tobacco. Toxicity set in, and all was familiar in my world.

I wedged the L&M Blue between my lips and—careful not to inhale the unfiltered smoke—checked my email. There it was, the long-awaited response from Lucas. His name in bold made me forget my thoughts about Amir and strong women. My face went pale as I scanned his words, desperately searching for hope but finding only disappointment:

'You broke up with me, remember... Now you need my help...

Why should I help you? You made bad choices... You have a lot of work to do, mentally and physically.'

My heart raced faster as I finally caught sight of a glimmer of hope:

'If you really mean what you said about wanting to spend forever with me, I am willing to come and see if we can work it out... We will see, I can't promise that we will get back together, but I am willing to take another chance on us.'

His fatherly tone always triggered a nauseous feeling, but in that moment, I screamed for joy. Despite everything, the person I wanted to spend the rest of my life with was still holding on. Shaking, I typed a reply, thanking him for giving me another chance and for renewing my hope.

"Girls! He's coming!" I screamed down the hallway. "Oh, my fucking God, I can't believe it."

"Who? You're crazy, calm down!" Dasha peeked out of her room.

"Lucas! My Lucas!" I replied, shivering with excitement. I started to cry.

There was no reply from the girls, but I didn't care because my ever-so-trustworthy codeine high kicked in, putting me in a state of elevated bliss.

This was my second chance; this was *it*. I could not fuck it up again.

Re-reading and analyzing every word of Lucas's email, I could feel his anger and disappointment in his short phrases and precise punctuation. But he was willing to come for ten days and travel farther south up the Nile to Aswan. He suggested we take a trip and have some serious conversations. I had until January 10, less than a month away, to get my mental state together and—most importantly—cut down on my Solpadeine intake. Or, at least, make an effort to, so I could comprehend and thoughtfully contribute to our heavy talks.

I was terrified Lucas wouldn't recognize me, both externally and internally. I wasn't sure he would like the new me and the way I was wearing my pain on my sleeves. Cairo, the drug scene, the cockroaches, my dark brunette box-dyed hair, the wasted time—I felt embarrassed for him to see me like this. I was not the girl he had left at the Reno International Airport. Imagining him standing in front of me, I felt our vast differences already. He was stable and sane while I was barely surviving and on the edge. This was a clear indication of my weakness.

Was it my drug abuse that had changed me more, or was it confronting Kateryna? Was it Rami's hands that had finally broken me, or was I really so naive that I'd fed into his manipulations? Whatever it was, I just wanted Lucas to feel sorry for me. I needed Lucas to set aside his belief that one shouldn't play victim and support me as the victim of abuse. This rock bottom, this state of mind, was now part of my identity. It was what I had endured to transform. Maybe I was not a better woman, but it had changed me, and I would forever hold these scars. Wasn't strength measured by the hardships one could overcome?

I needed him to validate my self-worth because Cairo was not a true reflection of who I was. I was the blonde girl trusting his lead, holding on to him on the back of a moped through the jungles of Vietnam. I was the woman he had made love to on that secluded Lake Tahoe beach. I was the business partner who had supported his goals of a travel TV show. I was the one who had made all of our Thanksgiving meals to perfection. I was the model for his new camera lens, standing on the windy lookout of the Tokyo Tower.

Lucas and I exchanged more emails, and he requested that we talk on the phone. We planned for him to call me directly on my local cell phone since our internet was too slow for serious conversations via Skype. High on Lucas rather than pills, I asked Alina to take me dancing and bring the boys.

Lucas couldn't have called at a better time: 1 a.m. while I was at a nightclub with Amir, Alina, Omar, Dasha, and Dasha's boyfriend.

"Hello! Lucas?" I said, running out of the noisy Gu Bar. Stepping onto the gangway from the Nile Maxim boat, I plugged one ear with my finger to hear my man's words.

"Katya, hi. Can you hear me? Is this a good time? Are you at a party? I thought you'd be sleeping," Lucas said.

I ground my teeth. Not a good start. Even so, it was so nice to hear Lucas's voice; I hadn't heard a pure American accent in three months. "It's so good to hear your voice. I stepped out with Alina to a pub. I'm on a different schedule here. Nope, wide awake. You remember those cool Egyptian nights."

"You can talk then?" he continued, sounding annoyed.

"Yes, I'm here," I said, looking up at the sky. As I did, I saw Amir walking toward me on the gangway. He lit a cigarette and stared at me. Staring back at Amir, I continued, "I'm so happy you are coming. Thank you for giving...us...another chance."

"Did you really mean all you wrote to me? About the future you want with me? And, I mean really, that fucker, that Wolfgang-looking prick, beat you?" Lucas's voice was angry.

That took me aback. Why would I lie about being abused? I had discussed this enough in emails. I had explained to him—without too much detail so as to spare him—exactly what had happened. No ex wanted to hear about the sexual details of another lover, so I was vague. But his skeptical tone, his classic need for reiteration and validation, was not what I had expected from my hero. He sounded three beers deep; the repetition gave it away.

"Yes, I want a future with you and only you, Lucas," I said. "I wrote like eight pages on what I felt. We have so many memories together that I just can't let go of. I'm not lying. I swear I didn't know what I was getting into with that fucker. I was being manipulated. He told me to do things and controlled everything I did. He told me to break up with you because you didn't care about me. And at that time, I felt it to be true. I was scared, but I didn't know how to get out of that fucked-up situation. Yes, I took drugs with him, and he beat me."

"You sounded like you loved him when you broke up with me," Lucas continued, sounding more concerned about his own feelings than the situation I was in.

Amir kept taking pulls of his cigarette, speaking to me with his eyes. They were sad, and his energy told me he was very jealous. I kept walking farther toward land, and Amir followed five steps behind me.

"No, Lucas. That's insane. How could I let go of everything we've been through over a guy I just met weeks prior? I love *you*, Lucas," I replied desperately.

A lot of silence filled the spaces between my pleading. The energy was hostile both on the phone and on that gangway with Amir following me. He was just doing what men in Cairo did—protecting a girl alone outside.

I grinned and nodded at my bodyguard then cried into my Nokia, "I just want to go hooommeeee."

"I'll come, and we'll see. The best case is we move to San Francisco together if all works out. But I'll get you as far as Kyiv, Ukraine, for now. You need to get a job and fund your own ticket stateside. Come on, Katya, you're twenty-five. That would be the grown-up thing to do."

I hated this fatherly tone and treatment toward me; this was one of the reasons I had left him that time in the Philippines. I wanted a partner, not a life coach. Still, even though I had passed my first interview with the Four Seasons and could get out on my own if need be, I couldn't bear the thought of spending another minute in this polluted city, so I swallowed my hatred.

"Okay, I'd love that! I'll do that. Yes." I cleared my throat and hid my sobs. "I love you."

"See you on January tenth. I'll email you my flight schedule," Lucas declared and hung up.

I felt like a complete and utter disappointment. A lump formed in my throat, like the feeling you get when your father catches you sneaking back into the house at 4 a.m. What was I doing now, going to nightclubs with directionless partiers? I seesawed between blaming Lucas for not advising me against going to Cairo and regretting my own decisions to hang out with men, do drugs, and party my life away. I also struggled with the thought that I'd sacrificed my dreams of going to grad school to pursue neuroscience in London for Lucas's travel dreams. My blame game was spiraling out of control.

Anger began to boil in my chest, and my face turned bright red. I was angry at my parents for not setting me on any yellow brick roads and not giving me the tools to love and respect myself. I felt furious that I had agreed to what men had decided for me. They had used me and disposed of me when they'd got what they needed: my femininity, my caring ways, my unselfish desire to lift them up as kings.

Amir interrupted my breakdown with a cigarette offer.

"Are you happy with your conversation?" he asked, lighting the Davidoff Slim.

"I don't know. I-I need to go home. Home, home," I said.

My instinct was to take more codeine to calm my nerves, but I remembered my bargain with the universe to cut back in exchange for rekindling my relationship with Lucas. Despite this, I automatically dug through my purse, hoping to find a pill at the bottom. I did and took it with another vodka soda that I got when I returned to the club.

"Katya, I really like you. I know you don't want to hear this, but I can't help it. I have to tell you," Amir said later, when we were in his car leaving the nightclub.

"Amir, I think you're a great person," I replied. "Kind, caring, and, yes, I'm attracted to you, too. But–" I wanted to stay faithful to Lucas. After all, he was coming all the way to Cairo to give me a chance.

"Stop right there," he cut me off. "I won't bring it up again. Okay?"

The ride home was silent and jerky. I kept looking over at Amir in the driver's seat, and each time, he gave me a gentle smile. I wanted to do the right thing, I really did, but before stepping out of the car, I leaned over and kissed Amir's full, plum-colored lips.

Cracks in my future relationship with Lucas were already beginning to show. His fatherly reply had tipped me over the edge. Impulsively kissing Amir and stirring the pot even more only complicated my feelings, which were never really clear to begin with.

I decided not to return the calls from the Four Seasons because I was sure I was getting my ticket out of Cairo to Ukraine, "at the least," as Lucas had said. Twelve days following Lucas's call, my roommates and I welcomed the new year, 2015. I couldn't believe I had already been in Cairo for six months. The girls and I set the table with Ukrainian pelmeni, salads, and pickled mackerel fish. I also made homemade noodles, sauce, and Cioppino. Amir insisted on paying for the seafood and ingredients, taking me to the best imported food stores. Thus, I, of course, invited him for a tasting. For the first time in six months, I made a gourmet meal in our poorly equipped kitchen. I finally got to indulge my one true passion in life: cooking. I did my best, as three boys were coming over for dinner after midnight. The beweb had the night off, so we snuck them in without any issues.

The Champagne flowed in plastic cups, and music filled the room. We took group photos and danced in our dusty living room. It felt oddly normal, and I was the happiest I'd been in months. That evening was devoid of hardcore drugs, elite parties, and fake connections. Yet, I felt guilty when I caught my reflection in the bathroom mirror and saw the pleasure written all over my face. Lucas wouldn't want this for me; I should be grounded.

This was Amir's last night in Cairo. He was about to embark on the two-week trip to New York and Las Vegas he had mentioned when we'd first met. With every Champagne refill and beat drop, I realized I would miss him. Being in his presence made me feel calm, and his daily concern for me made me feel important. After the drinks ended, Amir didn't ask to stay in my room; he only came in to ask for a blanket so he could crash on the couch.

"I don't have an extra blanket. Why don't you come share mine?" I smiled at him.

His body was like a furnace, heating the frozen concrete room, and I threw myself into his arms. His washboard abs, round biceps, and ripped thighs seemed unreal. Amir was the most attractive man I'd ever seen or touched. Never breaking his intense eye contact, he undressed me very slowly, saying, "Oh my God," every time he removed a piece of clothing. He kissed my shoulders, forearms, palms, and neck, leaving me breathless. We didn't just have sex; we made love, over and over again, never breaking eye contact and with our foreheads touching. It was almost 8 a.m. when I finally fell asleep. He left in the morning with a soft, "I'll miss you, Kat-kuta. Please write to me," and a kiss on my forehead.

That evening with Amir validated two things for me: I was worthy of love amid my self-destruction journey, and I was still sure that my path was with Lucas. My roommates disagreed with the latter.

"Amir is so nice, Katya," Alina told me over morning coffee. "I've been in Egypt eleven years now, and I've never met anyone like him. Polite, smart, and caring. You should really think about this Lucas guy."

But being with Amir meant I had to stay in Egypt, maybe not indefinitely, but longer than I'd be comfortable with. He was still a boy in many ways—living with his parents and not having a stable career. I wasn't ready to jump into a new relationship after a one-night hookup.

As the girls and I nursed our mild hangovers on the couches with leftover Cioppino, a moment of clarity came to me. I wondered why I needed a man to feel as though I belonged. Why did I need them to validate my self-worth in the first place?

"Do you girls want a husband and kids—or, well, more kids for you, Dasha?" I asked.

"Yeah, of course, us Ukrainians are programmed that way,"

Dasha proclaimed. "What, you don't want to have a family? Let me talk to your parents!"

"Of course, I do! I want to have the right one, though. Unlike the family my parents had. I want it to last," I replied.

I was halfway to my thirties with no concrete hopes of marriage or a family. I'd wasted all this time proving to Lucas I was both wife and mother material. I had to have a child soon; that was why I was so eager to find the man to give me one. Not only had my upbringing taught me to want a child, but I physically wanted a daughter more than anything in the world. I wanted a child to feel whole and to keep me from ever being alone. I was so glad I'd stopped taking the birth control Lucas had enforced because, for once, I was starting to feel my biological clock. And it was ticking loudly. But now I was in a complete hormonal imbalance, as Aunt Flo hadn't paid a visit in four months by that point. I felt my heart rate skyrocket—a new fear was unlocked. What if birth control had permanently messed up my reproductive system?

I spent the rest of the day dwelling over that thought and despising Lucas for his selfishness. "Use a fucking condom then," I said out loud, reliving our planned Wednesday intercourse sessions. I was determined to talk to Lucas about his family goals yet again and especially make it clear that I was never taking birth control pills again.

I had high expectations for Lucas's arrival. I imagined us giggling and smiling ear-to-ear. It would be a glorious reunion of two lost souls hardened by distance and time. I missed his body, his older-man hands, and the way he held my hips up during sex. I wanted to be his again, to rekindle that feeling of lust I'd once had for him when we'd first met on campus. I wanted to look into his eyes and feel his need to have his way with me. I wrote down a list of restaurants for us to try and new places we could discover in Cairo and our trip to Aswan.

I also thought about what he might bring for me from the States. His usual gifts were handmade silver jewelry, shoes, or perfume. I could really use some boots right now; it was cold in the desert winter. Maybe even a warm hoodie; he knew my apartment was brutally cold without heating in the winter. He would be, for the first time ever, a guest in my house. Perhaps he would bring a nice bottle of Napa Valley wine for the girls and me to enjoy since there wasn't any good wine in Egypt. Perhaps a nice Petite Syrah, like he knew I loved.

But my beloved hero let me down the night he arrived in Cairo. I read his energy as he walked out of baggage claim. He seemed frantic, probably in the early stages of culture shock. This wasn't West Coast California with a laid-back vibe; this was the heart of the Arab world, a third-world country. He hadn't noticed me yet, probably still looking for a skinny, long-haired blonde girl.

"Lucas!" I yelled and waved.

His eyebrows shot up when he saw me. We hugged, and he smelled of fabric freshener, a luxury I had forgotten about. His embrace was followed by a back pat. I hated when he did that; it always conveyed his disappointment in me.

"Welcome to Cairo!" I grinned. "Wow, I can't believe you're actually here. Thank you!"

"Man, I don't remember this airport being such a dump," he said. "And, wow, you look so different without your blonde hair. Please tell me you will change it."

"Well, we came here right after spending a month in India, remember? Anything compared to India is God-sent," I explained. "Yeah, it's box-dye; it will fade in time."

Driving back in the rickety cab, I saw Cairo through Lucas's eyes. It looked like a post-apocalyptic city with few working lights, broken wires overhead, and neighborhoods of rubble. I felt embarrassed he was seeing Cairo amid another crisis—still wounded from its years of ongoing turmoil. Almost ashamed that the country, like me, hadn't cleaned up.

Egypt was still in recovery from the post-2013 instability after Morsi's ousting and the Brotherhood crackdown, under constant attack—violence in the Sinai Peninsula, military checkpoints on the streets, and the sting of inflation and high unemployment. We discussed politics, his favorite topic, as I tried to acclimate him to the poverty and unrest of my city.

"We're here?" he asked, looking out the windows at the seven-story block apartments on my poor street. Cats scurried around the parked cars as our cab approached my building.

"Yep, home away from home." I grinned.

The beweb was outside, as though awaiting our arrival. I'd already warned him of Lucas's arrival; I'd said he was my older brother visiting me. The old man believed me.

Lucas was surprised to find our three-bedroom apartment was actually very spacious.

"This is nice, Kat. Not what I expected," he said. Our place was lightly furnished with random couches, tables, and fake plants, but the living room was large enough to ride a bike around in. I showed him my room at the end of the hallway, which had two queen-sized beds pushed together, a small vanity mirror, and a huge but empty built-in closet.

I let Lucas unpack his small suitcase as I sat on the edge of my bed. He pulled out his toiletry bag and a change of clothes. I was hoping he had brought something special for me.

"Oh, I got you these—I remember you telling me it's hard to find them in Cairo," he said, holding out a gas station plastic bag. To my disappointment, inside was a box of ten tampons and a bottle of ibuprofen.

"Thanks. I'll let you shower," I said and left the room.

As if on cue, the girls came out of their rooms and followed me to the living room.

"Well, how do you feel seeing him?" Alina whispered, lighting up a cigarette.

"He's taller than I expected," Dasha added.

I shouldn't have been smoking, as that had always been a deal breaker for Lucas, but that damn box of tampons pissed me off, so I lit one up. "It feels weird. Very weird to see him in our house. He's so American."

"What did he bring you?" asked Alina.

"You won't believe it—a box of tampons," I said, embarrassed, forcing smoke out of my lungs.

"What? No, Katya, no. Is he serious?" Alina asked, leaning closer.

"And what did he bring for the house? He's our guest. You can't come to a home empty-handed," Dasha added.

"Nothing, girls. He brought nothing," I said, looking out the window.

"That's fucked up. Amir would never do that," Alina said and left the room.

Lucas knew better than to come to a home without bearing a gift. That was Ukrainian cultural etiquette, an unwritten rule in many cultures. A simple gift was always expected: chocolate, coffee, flowers, a small toy if a child was in the home. Especially when the guest was coming from foreign lands. Lucas was very much aware of this etiquette. He'd visited my family in Ukraine a few times, and he was a world traveler, having been to fifty countries, who loved nothing more than studying different cultures and rules. He was the one who had taught me not to show the bottom of my feet in Japan, as it's a sign of disrespect. By not bringing a gift to our home, as a foreigner and the first American these girls had met, he made me that much more embarrassed about my situation and left me wondering if he'd done so on purpose.

I placed the gas station box of tampons in front of Dasha. "I don't menstruate anyways. Have these for beach days," I said and retired to my room for the night.

My American prince did, however, bring an unforgettable gift. The following morning, my vagina burned when I used the bathroom. I had never felt that kind of sensation down there. Upon closer inspection, it was clear I was infected with an STD.

"Morning, can I ask you a question?" I sat next to Lucas on the bed. He was still half-asleep and vulnerable. I got straight to the point. "Why did you put a condom on then take it off midway last night?"

"Well, I'm sure you never tested yourself after Wolfgang or whoever you've been with," he said. "Plus, you're not on birth control, right?"

"You know I can't get pregnant. I told you how it works. No period, no egg. If Rami gave me something, I would have symptoms by now. So, no, no one did," I explained. "But that's not why you started with a condom."

"I just wanted to be safe," he said, now sitting up.

"Well, not safe enough. You gave me something. I'm in so much pain right now down there," I said, looking into his eyes.

"Fuck. Katya... It was a one-night fling," he confessed. "I took my last pill yesterday on the plane, and I thought six days on antibiotics would be enough. I wasn't feeling anything anymore."

It wasn't a one-time thing. I knew him better. He was an advocate of safe sex and wouldn't dare not use protection unless she had proved she was on birth control. He must have known her for some time. My stomach turned with jealousy. Did he already have another woman on the back burner?

We spent our first morning in Cairo calling pharmacies for chlamydia antibiotics. They delivered the medication, and Lucas said his doctor had told him to take it for a week, but just to be sure, he said I should do a ten-day course. I was scared by the worsening symptoms, so I agreed.

The cat was out of the bag; Lucas had been with other women. I was almost relieved, as I had been with men, too—clean men, however. The thought of him with dirty bar sluts turned me off, but I could feel his remorse and concern for infecting me, so I didn't poke the snake any further. I took my medicine in silence. Over coffee, I

packed my bag for our Aswan trip. Our overnight train was scheduled to leave later that night.

The three of us—Lucas, me, and his STD—arrived in Aswan the
following morning. I had never been more on edge and in pain, even
just sitting down. Any hopes of rekindling our romance through
emotional dinners and steamy sex had gone out the window. I
couldn't focus on anything but my abnormal vaginal discharge. I
could smell myself and wanted to puke. I felt gross, annoyed, tired,
and fat, as Lucas had pointed out that I had gained some "good
weight." Guilt weighed on me, too—guilt for being a directionless,
broke, drug-addicted loser in Egypt. But I was hoping to fix our relationship by doing what we did best: traveling together.

I couldn't appreciate the adventure with him now the way I'd
been able to in the other twenty-two countries we'd visited. The
energy was off, both from him and me. It didn't feel as though we
were walking on eggshells; it felt like we were walking through a
minefield. We both wanted to vent about our issues, but neither of
us wanted to stir the pot just yet.

I seriously contemplated telling Lucas about my opioid use
because I wanted to be open and real with him about my weak
points. It had been so liberating to show my scars to Amir, so why
was I hiding them from Lucas? If Lucas asked me directly, "Are you
on any kind of drugs?", I was ready to tell him the whole nine-year
story. But I needed to get my facts straight and understand why I
took the drugs.

Between visits to Egyptian temples and tea breaks, I researched
opioid addiction and found an article explaining what prolonged use
does to the brain. I felt relieved to learn that addiction is a disease,
not a moral failing, a choice, or a personality flaw. If Lucas asked, I
would start with that exact line: "It's not a moral failing or a personality flaw."

The damage opioids had done to my developing brain since the age of fifteen was scary. This drug changes the brain's chemistry and function. While not permanent, it can take many years for the brain to heal itself after stopping. Opioids affect a person's psychological state, causing depression, mood swings, and paranoia. They also reduce the dopamine receptors in the brain that control judgment and behavior. It's a highly complex disease to cure, and the residual effects scared me the most.

I prepared the 'I think I have a drug problem' speech in my head, but the fear of him rejecting me was stronger than my need for liberation. I dropped the rehearsals. Of course, I wanted to experience life without the shackles of opioids and fantasized about the help and support I could receive from loved ones if I opened up. I pictured Lucas holding me, rubbing my head, and saying, "We will get through this. I can help you. Thank you for telling me." But that was just a fantasy. In reality, he would most likely tell me to deal with it on my own and to get professional help.

We took a felucca boat and checked into the Nubian Farm, a colorfully mosaicked, brick-and-mud, ten-room hostel on the west bank of the Nile across from Aswan. We were given their 'honeymoon' suite, which had a king bed and a painting of the Egyptian god, Horus, above the headboard. I called Alina to check in and complain about my unbearable STD symptoms.

"Tampons and an STD, wow. I hope this ends well," she mothered me.

I also texted Amir, who had texted me multiple photos of his time in Vegas. A part of me wanted to be there with him; at least then I wouldn't have been suffering from an STD.

We were served dinner on painted wicker chairs and tables at the rooftop terrace. We ate questionable chicken, amazing rice, and refreshing cucumber salad. I didn't have much of an appetite because I could see the brewing conversation behind Lucas's eyes. We had made nothing but small talk the whole day. As the sun set over the Nile, casting sailboat silhouettes against brick-red river-banks, Lucas unleashed his calculated approach.

"So, Katya, what do you want?" he finally asked. "You wrote a lot. But I need to hear it from you."

I took a deep breath and chewed over my thoughts before answering firmly with, "I want marriage and kids." Straight to the point. That wasn't a new concept; just ten months ago, I had walked out of that bungalow for this same reason—his lack of urgency in starting a family or showing any signs of even wanting one.

"What's the difference if we are married or just living together?" Lucas asked.

"There's a big difference for me!" I said. "Marriage is a mutual commitment that we're in for the long haul. It's a promise we keep working toward. Marriage is security to me."

Saying that out loud to Lucas sounded wrong and demanding. Deep down, I still felt unworthy of being a bride because of my drug addiction. *Addiction is not a personality flaw*, I reminded myself. Yet, asking for marriage, instead of it happening organically, lowered my self-esteem.

"You don't want kids, do you?" I asked him, shaking my head slightly.

"I don't know; it's too far out to say," Lucas replied. "We still don't know if we can make it in our personal relationship. I will only bring kids into this world if I know for sure the relationship is solid."

How is he not answering directly? He's thirty-eight years old; it's about time to think about this.

"Of course, I understand and agree with having solid parents," I said. "It was a yes-or-no question. You don't want to, then...?"

Abruptly, our conversation shifted. We bickered back and forth about how we needed to communicate. I put words in his mouth and got defensive. He beat around the bush and brought up the past. He kept reminding me that I had broken up with him, and I kept reminding him that I had been under mental manipulation. We both had valid points, but in hindsight, these were molehills, not mountains.

"Let's write out what we expect of each other if we are to make it to marriage," Lucas suggested.

What? You want me to write out marriage expectations like a business contract? I was heartbroken by the lack of romance. That was the price I paid for someone with a serious case of Type-A personality.

Nonetheless, I agreed. "Okay. As I said, I will do whatever it takes to make it work between us."

Writing out our expectations felt like investing in cryptocurrency. I couldn't make a valid prediction in such a volatile market. Everyone wants to get rich quickly, and no one expects their investment to tank. Like marriage, the investment only pays off with time and holding on to the stock. You can't lose if you never sell. What I wished he had said was, "I love you; I'm willing to work through the ups and downs with you. We're still here, and that already says a lot." Instead, I had to swallow my thoughts and let him decide.

Sitting at separate tables with our backs turned, we started on our lists. I stared at the blank page for a while, unable to write anything down for two reasons: I wasn't sure what a healthy marriage looked like or what the formula for longevity was, and I was unhappy with the whole situation. For me, our conversation about marriage should have been as simple as Lucas saying, "Katya, I love you, and I will keep choosing you no matter what, every day." A woman needs kindness, softness, and some cheesy words to say along with "I do" to her groom. After all, marriage is a leap of faith; no one can honestly predict the outcome.

I managed to write down three points:

Communication

Love

Respect

This is all I ask of you.

I love you.

I folded the notepaper and brought it to him. He was already on what looked like page three, which was shocking but expected from Lucas. I left him sitting there, writing over hot tea.

"Are you done?" I asked, startling him after a good thirty minutes had passed.

"Yes. Here, read it," he said, handing me the papers.

My smile disappeared, and my heart sank as I held his seven-page contract. He had written out his expectations for me in bullet format. How selfish of him! How unfiltered of him! I thought I knew him after five years, but now I saw that what I knew was only who he was on the surface. I'd never expected him to be so demanding. This was a man whose passion was to spontaneously travel the world and meet locals, but his calculated expectations for the biggest unknown —marriage—obviously did not play by the same rules.

The list read:

- *Stop smoking*
- *Find my own way to San Francisco and focus on bettering myself with a solid work plan*
- *Find work right away in SF, take any job that becomes available to start making money*
- *Make at least $3,000 a month*
- *Help cover household expenses; rent, utilities, transportation*
- *Prioritize starting a business as to not be part of the rat race*
- *Treat him with respect and allow him to be the leader of the family*
- *Be nice, outgoing, and understanding*
- *Keep cooking great healthy meals*
- *Eat healthy and lose weight; stay in good shape*
- *Work on my past*
- *Don't be depressed*
- *Be driven*
- *Read a lot*
- *Always have goals to work toward*
- *Mend family relationships*

- *Stop finding and making excuses*
- *Do sports*
- *Allow him to do sports and not intervene when he needs to check out of the day and go on bike rides*
- *Understand that he needs to travel a lot and let him go*
- *Don't be jealous*
- *Give him space when needed*
- *Make good friends*
- *Learn how to fight fair and not use threatening and defensive approaches*
- *If we have a family, I cannot be a stay-at-home mom. I need to keep my business/job going and find a balance between family and work life*
- *Support him in his dreams of doing a travel TV show and understand that everything he will be doing is to fulfill his dream*

Selfish, selfish, even more selfish. The list infuriated me. There was no mention of "we should;" it was almost all "you should." Most points affirmed that who I was currently was not the woman he saw fit to be his lifelong partner. I opened my mouth to respond, but no words came out. If I questioned a point, I'd be violating the *stop being defensive* rule. He returned to our room, leaving me sitting there as I went over the list three more times. We were in Egypt, and he was a Muslim man seeking an arranged marriage.

After the initial shock wore off, I started to see the logic behind his expectations of me—his logic, not mine. The points were valid to a fault. This was normal; what Lucas wanted, Lucas always got with me. I felt good if Lucas felt good about me. It had been this way for many years, and it had brought us to this point. If I reacted how I wanted to—by throwing the list in his face and saying, "Are you fucking crazy? We are done!"—that would just prove his point that I was disrespectful. This list was manipulative, yes, but his approval of my image was like a covenant by which I closely abided.

I wanted to question how these contractual points would be enforced. How would I know his criteria for what classified as a good friend? There was not enough clarity, and this would most definitely lead to his disappointment. The most shocking part was that I was expected to be the selfless supporter of his dreams. What about my dreams? It was clear he didn't care if I had any.

Instead of going to meet Lucas in our room, I took a walk and called Amir. He answered after a few rings.

"I was dreaming about you. How are you? I miss you." His deep, sultry voice put a smile on my face.

"Good morning. I hope Vegas is treating you well. I'm thinking of you, too," I whispered.

"We're having a blast. Long night last night. I'm so hungover right now. I wish you were next to me. Damn, I want those silky lips of yours," he said.

"Me, too, actually," I replied. "Me, too."

"How's, uh, Lucas?" His tone changed.

"Well, you know, he wants me to move to San Francisco with him. We're working it out, I guess. There's a lot to unpack. Hey, do you want a family?" I asked.

"Of course, I do. Isn't that the goal of every couple?" he replied.

"In a different universe, seeing and knowing what you do about me now, would you want a family with me?" I asked.

"I would, even in this universe," he replied.

Amir's words made my night. I needed the reassurance that my longing for a family wasn't as far-fetched and complicated as Lucas had made it out to be. My monthly salary and business ownership shouldn't be deciding factors for starting a family or marriage. Those aspects shouldn't benchmark my worthiness. I felt torn between what I believed and what Lucas believed for me.

Setting aside the idea of contracts, sky-high expectations, and my codeine high, I returned to our room, crawled into bed with Lucas, and nestled my nose into his neck.

The rest of our trip in Upper Egypt was memorable. We drove out to see the Abu Simbel Temple, where the four giant statues carved into granite reminded me of the great power humans possessed, even in 1200 BC. I felt fortunate to see this wonder of the world yet, at the same time, insignificant in the temple's shadow. Lucas and I smoked shisha on the street with local farmers, walked along the Nile, and drank hibiscus tea while discussing politics.

Not once did he ask how I was holding up after Rami. He didn't ask if I felt safe, how I was managing with my savings, if I always had a meal, or how I was getting by. To this day, I think Lucas never truly believed that the rape and kidnapping happened to me.

In our time back in Cairo, we toured mosques, old neighborhoods, and the modern art museum—normal things that I should have experienced on my own but hadn't, as I had been too busy getting into trouble. Of course, it was easier walking the streets with a man for protection. I told this to Lucas over and over again when he expressed shock that I hadn't explored the city in which I lived.

We took Dasha and Alina out to a fancy dinner in Zamalek, the man-made island on the Nile. I could feel the girls' jealousy of my knight in shining armor coming to take me away from the depth of Cairo's despair. On his last night in Egypt, Lucas purchased me a ticket from Cairo to Kyiv, departing in two weeks' time, just as promised. I was grateful.

"I hope to see you soon, Sonichka," Lucas said, holding my shoulders as we stood outside my apartment building. The taxi driver had already loaded his bag into the trunk.

"I do, too," I replied. "Thank you for coming, I enjoyed our time together." We observed the no-PDA rule on the streets.

Honestly, I hadn't enjoyed it as much as I'd wanted to. I wished it had been more romantic and less rigid. I wished the circumstances had been different for both of us. I wished I didn't have an STD to manage, and I was sure Lucas wished I hadn't been so irresponsible with my time here. I felt more confused and less happy than before he'd come. Lucas had brought with him a mirror of the Western world, and I hadn't seen my reflection in it. I felt lesser, broken, and unworthy—embarrassed, overweight, and directionless, trapped in my own negativity and plagued by a handwritten marriage proposal.

As my once-called muse pulled away in the taxi, I finally exhaled. After being here for seven months, it was clear I had regressed even further. Before coming here, the list of improvements I'd wanted to make in myself had been short: *stop playing victim to my past, be more worldly, be more hardworking, be grateful,* and *learn not to depend on a man.* But I hadn't accomplished any of those things. Instead, I had pages of handwritten attributes and character strengths to acquire.

Lucas was right; I had needed to experience life on my own, but it had brought out the pain from Kateryna I had been avoiding. I made a beeline to the nearest pharmacy to feed her. I felt disgusting inside.

8

THE LAYOVER
(FEBRUARY 2015)

Two weeks passed in a blink of an eye, and my departure from Cairo to Kyiv was in three days. Per Lucas's request, I was to work in Kyiv to earn a ticket to San Francisco, where we would start over in his new apartment. Each day, I felt more like an imposter. How could I settle down in San Francisco with Lucas when I was half the woman he'd met years ago? Now that I was properly acquainted with my drawbacks, how could I keep playing pretend? More importantly, how could I begin to quit my drug use?

I was sure that with the aftermath of my Cairo experiences and the pressure to meet Lucas's three-thousand-dollars-a-month rent expectation, I would crack if opioids were still in the mix. My addiction was heavier than ever, and in a big city like San Francisco, I feared I'd end up on the streets or find the wrong drug dealer or, worse, get caught by Lucas and be exposed as a fraud. I had to kick the habit and come to Lucas with at least drugs off my slate.

I couldn't detox in Ukraine. My mission was to find a job and purchase my ticket back. Detoxing meant spending a month or more on the couch, and I had read articles about the dreadful process. It would be a full-time job in itself, especially since I would have to hide it from everyone. I would need to lie about being sick just to cover up the lie that I wasn't a drug addict.

These thoughts overwhelmed me, but I found distraction and peace on dates with Amir. I really liked him. Really, really liked him. He had a way with words, especially when he told me sweet little nothings. I figured any relationship we could have would be one I could partake in while on the Californian West Coast. He, on the other hand, was in love with me.

"Even if I can watch you from a distance, and I will, I will come to San Francisco and love you from afar. Doesn't matter where we are, I will love you. Always," Amir said with teary eyes, as he drove me to the airport.

"Please, Amir, don't say that. We have to move on. I'm glad we met. I just wish it was in a different time and a different place," I told him. I started to cry. "I'm sorry for everything."

"Don't ever be sorry with me. I am so happy to have found a love like you. I thank God for that. And please, don't cry. God counts your tears, and He will make you happy. You will see. This is not our end," Amir said, crying and kissing my hand.

He walked me into the terminal, rolling my bags. I was shaking and crying uncontrollably. I was terrified of finding my way back home again because being lost and carefree had become my normal. I was beyond scared of how I would settle down with Lucas; I was not good enough for him. And my little sidekick, opioids, needed a lot of attention, whether I was going to quit or get back to my healthy dose of half a pill a day as I'd been doing in Reno. I was sad to leave Amir. He was the only one I could trust in the aftermath of Rami. He cared about me, and I could see he truly loved me.

It felt like another movie moment for me: late night at Cairo International with an Arab prince who was ready to take me as I was, while I was on a mission to prove my self-worth to another man who had the highest expectations for a closet pill popper. Unlike when Lucas had taken me to Reno International Airport with no promises of what was to come, here was Amir, telling me to call him for whatever I needed, that he would do everything to keep me safe, comfortable, and happy. *Life is so unfair,* my thoughts screamed in my head. *So unfair.*

"This doesn't feel right," I said, gripping Amir's fingers.

"You have a plan. And inshallah, God will see it through. I want you to be happy, remember that. Do it for me," Amir said, kissing my forehead.

"I don't even know what I want anymore. I don't even know *me* anymore." I continued to sob.

"You are beautiful inside and out. A strong woman! Any man should feel lucky to have and to hold you," Amir replied. "Yella, go. Don't miss your flight."

He walked away, wiping his tears. No man cried in public in Cairo. God, how I would miss those deep, dark, large almond eyes and the smell of his Oud Wood cologne.

I could really have used a friend at that point, but my best friends from Alaska were both heroin addicts, and I had distanced myself from them even before leaving Reno eight months ago. I only received a few Facebook messages from them, mostly asking for money or telling me how much they loved and missed me—a byproduct of heroin euphoria. My Ukrainian roommates were the closest girlfriends I had, but their hidden agendas and shady stories had kept me from forming true connections with them. They hadn't even said their farewells; I'd yelled to their closed doors, "Goodbye, I'll miss you!" and received silence in reply.

The only friends I had at that time were Amir and my younger sister, Masha. So, I called her and sobbed in her ear.

I'd been visiting Ukraine every summer and sometimes in the winters for the last seven years. Coming back this time, in the dead of a bone-chilling winter, felt less climactic than usual. My grandma, mom, and sisters sat around our small kitchen table, taking shots of strong homemade wine. I could almost taste their disappointment in the air. Their chatter was shallow, and I felt like the black sheep.

"So, where are you going now?" my drunk mother asked, snapping into a pickle. She had sat in silence, watching me since I'd come home from the airport, and this was her first word to me.

"I am going to San Francisco to live with Lucas," I told her sheepishly.

"And do what?" she asked nonchalantly.

I hesitated. "Work, build a future, and start a family with Lucas."

"Katya, are you stupid? No, really, you don't see he is wasting your time. All this travel bullshit. You've been chasing him around the world with no direction. He will never settle down. What does he have to prove, anyways?" my mother asked.

"We wanted to do it together, Mom. He's working on his career in travel," I said.

"Exactly. His career. His plans. He just needs you for his own pleasure," she said, taking another shot of wine.

My silence said that I agreed. I almost never took my mother's advice; her track record didn't warrant it. We barely talked as it was, but what she said affirmed the anxiety I was feeling about my whole situation.

"I hated that you went to Egypt," Mom continued. "And all that bullshit that happened there. Where was Lucas then? Huh? You think he cares about you? Ha! You think you will have kids with him? Please don't make me laugh."

Like bricks hitting me in the face, my mother's blatant, hurtful truths woke me up. The fact that she cared made me feel a sliver of her love. That care from her was so rare that I complied.

"You are right, Mother," I told her. "I think he doesn't care about my future. Oh, and please don't be mad, but I need to see a gynecologist. I haven't had a period for five months now."

"What? Why do you think so?" She sat up, concerned.

"I stopped taking birth control, and the periods stopped," I replied, embarrassed.

"Katya, what birth control? How long have you been taking it?"

"On and off for...ten years now," I said, my head down.

My mother and grandmother were furious. They lectured me about how it was better to get an abortion or put a baby up for adoption than take chemicals to alter my body. They warned me that my body could go into early menopause and I would become a 'bezdetnaya' (an insult for a childless woman). They told me that no man would want a sterile woman. They feared I would be sterile and told me their hopes for grandchildren from me were gone. My grandpa suggested I schedule an appointment with the best gynecologist in Kyiv. I started to cry out of fear of never being able to have kids.

"Don't worry—we will fix this. But promise me, for God's sake, never take those pills again," my mother begged. "Lucas wants you to take them, huh?"

"Yeah," I said.

"You are not going to San Francisco. Wake up! I don't care what you say. You are staying here until we get your health back in order," my mother said.

I said nothing and left the room. It had been a rough day spent in two countries. The wine, my anxiety, and the health scares knocked me out for the night. Before I fell asleep, though, I noticed two things: Amir asked if I had arrived safely even though it was 8 a.m. PST in Cairo, and Lucas, who was an early riser, hadn't texted or called to check in.

The following morning, I woke up to a notification-free phone screen. My first thought was that Lucas had broken the first rule on my contract: communication. My thoughts were swirling, and anger overtook me. I called Lucas on Skype.

"Hi, are you going to ask if I've arrived in Ukraine?" I greeted him.

"Come on, Katya, of course you have," Lucas said. "If something was wrong, you'd let me know. Hey, don't start with defensive talk. I was busy all day. My mom is here, and we were picking out carpets for the new place in San Francisco. Had to put out a fire in Reno from an insurance business claim. Lots of shit going on! Let me send you a photo of the rugs; you can help me."

"I don't want to see it. I'm not happy that you don't care. I mean, I expect at least a call or text from you," I said.

"I'm setting up our house together here. I'm working long hours to make the astronomical rent here for us. I care that you are comfortable here. How do you not see that?" he pleaded.

I'd heard this spiel before. He always emphasized that things were 'ours' and that he paid for 'our mortgage' and 'our electricity.' I argued back that, whether I lived in his house or not, he would still be paying for all those things. My contribution was food expenses, cooking, cleaning, and working to save money for *his* travel plans. Moving to San Francisco wasn't my choice; he had planned that without me. Now it was supposed to be my problem that rent was high.

"A call or a text takes three seconds, Lucas," I continued.

"You know what, you are there now. You're fine. Stop, seriously."

"Anyways, I'm going to see a gynecologist today. *You* call *me* later tonight. I don't want to remind you."

After a long day of visiting different doctors in the fertility clinic, getting pelvic ultrasounds, giving blood and urine samples, and recounting my entire birth control history to every specialist, I was diagnosed with secondary amenorrhea. This absence of a period usually pointed to polycystic ovarian syndrome and/or endometriosis. Whatever the problem, it was entirely blamed on taking birth control and not allowing my pituitary gland to regulate my hormones and menstrual cycle naturally.

I didn't know then, but I had chemically turned off my pituitary gland, and it was struggling to work. Receiving hormonal treatment for that gland and my ovaries became the first step to getting my menstrual cycle back. The last specialist I saw referred me to a doctor of holistic medicine to treat my hormonal imbalance with herbs. Most Ukrainian doctors were very much against synthetic hormone therapies and rarely prescribed birth control pills. My doctor said that only around five percent of women in Ukraine used modern contraceptive methods like the pill. I was shocked when I Googled and found that nearly sixty-five percent of American women were on the pill.

Lucas didn't call when expected, so at around 10 p.m., my time, after three glasses of strong wine, I called him again. My mother came into the room, sat on the bed, and listened to my conversation.

We fought. I yelled into the receiver about his inability to make me a priority. I complained about my medical condition and how birth control had harmed me. I asked what he thought would happen when I moved to San Francisco and why he had let me go to Egypt so easily. Lucas said my Egypt trip was my own responsibility. I reminded him that Cairo had been 'our' idea. He then insisted that San Francisco was the path to a brighter future.

"What future? Your future, Lucas? Should I keep doing what is good for only you? Like taking birth control is good for you? Why don't you snip yourself or wear condoms?" I asked, winded from anger.

"I've only wanted what is best for you, too," he said.

"Well, taking birth control pills was not best for me. I did not want to take them, but you needed that assurance. I was fucking scared to go to Cairo, but you didn't try and stop me. Did you think it would be best for me, too? I wanted to go to London and study, but that was not best for you either," I reminded him.

At that point, my mother got on her knees in front of me and mouthed, "Break up with him now," while making a cut-throat gesture and staring deep into my eyes. I began to sob, torn between two people deciding what was best for me. Two wrong people, at that. Why was I allowing them to decide for me? I wasn't sure. I was too desperate for someone's approval to see the unhealthy cycle of dependency I had with my abusers. I had never dared to make my own decisions, not because I didn't trust myself but because I was programmed to be a people pleaser. But between Lucas arguing his points and my mother making prayer hands, I chose my mother.

"We are done, Lucas. I am not going to San Francisco. I am breaking up with you, for real this time," I said through my tears. My mother gave me a huge thumbs up and hugged my leg then left the room.

"Wow, Katya. Okay, don't call me anymore. Good luck with everything," he said and hung up.

The rest of the night, I mourned the loss of Lucas. Being with him was half of my identity, and breaking up with him meant I had to relearn what I wanted. I walked all night in the gently falling snow until 6 a.m., wandering around my neighborhood and swinging in playgrounds. I cried hard, remembering all of our trips abroad: experiencing the slums of Mumbai, living in Spain, dining at Michelin-star restaurants in Bangkok, painting our entrance door red, taking a beautiful boat ride on Inle Lake in Burma, exploring the caves of Vietnam, and tearing up dance floors in dozens of countries. I kept looking up at the sky and asking God for the strength to let go of these memories. I was deeply grateful for all the experiences Lucas and I had shared, but the voice in my head kept saying, *You only miss the moments, not him.*

Saying I was in shock is an understatement. I was in pieces. I despised the hand of cards I was dealt. I hated that I was left to navigate my mind, choices, and current shit-show alone. I wept harder in self-pity. I wished I had a normal life and normal people around me who made the right decisions and set good examples. A normal mother and father who weren't alcoholics or breeders of negativity. A family who made sure their kin were following some sort of expectations, with concrete values and family reunions. A father who got mad at me for making a mistake and gave me a long, hard lesson with a, "Make me proud, kid, and know that I am always here for you." A mother who asked, "Did you eat today?" Instead, I had been left alone and without an idol to follow, clinging to a fantasy of having a family but never really knowing what that actually looked like. I cried even harder, knowing that I was a great person despite all my wrong turns; Kateryna inside me was worthy, but no one ever noticed her.

I will prove them all wrong! I am worthy and capable! Getting up from the bench, I packed all the hurt into my already full backpack of pain and marched forward. This time, I had a plan to make it back to the USA and build a stable future like I wanted.

I needed a lifeline, a friend. I remembered that Amir had said he would be there for me any time. After a two-hour phone conversation, he offered to help me move to NYC. He had family there and said it would be easier for me if I knew someone in the area. It was an offer I couldn't refuse. Amir helped me find an apartment for rent in Manhattan via Craigslist, bought me a one-way ticket to JFK, and sent extra cash for the first week. He said he would visit me in mid-March.

It all happened so fast, and no one did anything to stop me. Not my grandmother, my grandfather, my father, my mother, or my sister. The plan took all but two weeks to map out. On the rebound of my failed relationship with Lucas, I made every decision without a second thought. I was not afraid to fail, as I had nothing to lose. I didn't say much about my plans to my family, still angry at my mother for inserting herself into my relationship.

After a month of taking seven different herbs three times a day, I finally got my first period in eight months. I had never been so happy to see blood! I felt like it was God's way of rewarding me for finally letting go of Lucas. Getting my health back under control gave me hope that coming to Ukraine was somehow part of a grander plan. I didn't say goodbye to my passed-out, drunk mother, and I boarded a 6 a.m. one-way flight to JFK.

Ukraine had been a short four-week layover, wherein I had made many impulsive decisions. I wondered if every girl who was traumatized with early abandonment, rape, and mental abuse did the same thing—packed bags and kept running. Impulsive decisions were my mom's normal, however, and "we live for today" was her coined motto.

When I was fifteen, my mom and her boyfriend, whom I'd never met, stormed in on Halloween night, demanding we pack up and move out immediately. I hadn't seen her in two months and had been taking care of my four-year-old sister, Masha, with no heat for a month. I cooked hot dogs on an open fire outside and drove Masha to her scheduled visitations without a driver's license to protect my mom's custody rights. Her boyfriend forced us to move to Anchorage to avoid paying the next month's rent. He locked us in his second-floor apartment, making us fast for eighteen hours a day and giving us only watermelon for dinner. We escaped by passing a note to his friend at a New Year's Eve gathering. My mom eventually married that friend—Oleg, the pilot—and had my last two sisters with him.

My instinctive move to New York City was as ridiculous as my mother's examples growing up. I hated knowing I was a product of my upbringing, and I was smart enough to reflect on that. However, I wasn't strong enough to love myself and break free from it, although I fantasized about it. My only options were staying in Ukraine with my unloving mother, being with Lucas and his bullet-point expectations, or running away and starting over again. Getting on a plane to an unfamiliar destination seemed like the best option; besides, I'd done it many times before.

I was determined to make my world stable for once. I had myself and Amir to rely on now and hoped that together we would thrive; two good people should get good things in life. I wanted to believe that Amir was a good person. And I prayed that my spontaneous move wouldn't end up like my mother's Halloween escape plan—in regret at trusting the wrong man.

9

THE EMPTY CHASE
(MARCH 2015)

I needed physical distance from my past and the parallel future I could have had with Lucas in San Francisco. I needed a blank canvas to paint a brighter reality in which I could mold myself into the woman I wanted to be, not the woman Lucas had described in bullet points. Moving far from the West Coast seemed like the only way to keep thoughts of Lucas out of my head. I kept his contract close by, reading it whenever I started to miss him, reminding myself of why I had to leave.

My transition to the NYC metropolis was hazy and impulsive, nothing I wasn't used to. With limited resources, I had to go with the flow, saying yes to everything and not caring where life took me next. Perhaps New York held the answer to my never-ending quest for self-worth and a family of my own.

I landed in JFK, thrilled to be back in the Western world. The city buzzed with opportunities, and I vowed not to miss a beat. My body surged with estrogen again, but my mind struggled to process my complex emotions. Was I in love with Amir or just the hero role he played in my life? Did I have severe daddy issues that made me seek lovers to feel whole? Was I rebelling against the rape? I still had vivid dreams of Rami's face and sometimes thought I saw him in crowds. Those emotions ran deeper than my surface wounds, but I didn't know where to begin unpacking them, nor did I have the luxury to focus on my mental health. My mission now was to find employment.

My apartment, beautifully furnished, sat on the corner of 37th and 9th Avenue, just a few blocks from the Lincoln Tunnel. With a rent of almost three thousand dollars a month, Amir could only afford it for a month and a half, through the end of April. The traffic noise was louder than in Cairo but had less honking, so it was manageable. I printed forty resumes at a nearby office supply store and hit the pavement. I felt so free walking the crowded streets without being harassed at every turn. After a couple of days of distributing resumes, I received a call back from Mexicue, a Mexican tourist restaurant with a full whiskey and tequila bar. They were opening a new location in NOMAD on 5th, a block from Madison Square Park. I'd be back to waiting tables and mixing drinks at minimum wage, but it was better than nothing. Plus, it was only a forty-minute walk from my apartment.

Amir and I grew closer. He always seemed to be awake, ready to answer any text or call no matter the time in Cairo. His promises of "I will move to NYC and be with you," and, "My uncle can help me find a good job in finance, we can live a great life!" made him seem too good to be true. It had always been his dream to live in the USA, but his mother couldn't bear for him to live so far away. He fed me hope and motivated me to strive for a brighter future. I mostly loved how he loved me, always asking caring questions like, "What did you eat today?" and, "Did you get home at a decent time and get good sleep?"

While I wasn't working a double shift—which I did four days a week—I explored NYC by foot and public transportation. I visited a childhood friend from Ukraine who'd recently moved to be with her Italian boyfriend. She was busy going to school and awaiting permanent residency. It felt nice having a normal, healthy friend.

There was, however, the issue of my drug needs. Since leaving Egypt, I had managed to cut down significantly. In Ukraine, pharmacies sold low-dose opioids without a prescription, so I brought a small supply to NYC. Without health insurance, I couldn't afford a doctor's visit to play my con game. Fortunately, one of Amir's friends, living near Wall Street, invited me to his home at Amir's request. In his bathroom, I found a bottle of Percocet. I asked if he needed them, explaining I had terrible tooth pains, and he gladly gave them to me. I was set for a month or more if I snorted and rationed them. Drugs always had a way of finding their users.

Meeting Amir at JFK airport felt awkward and was not what I had expected. He didn't look as magical as I remembered. Among my fellow New Yorkers, he seemed out of place and insignificant. The fairytale effect of our secret love story had worn off, as being back in the Western world had reset my perspective on life. I didn't need him to protect me on the streets, he could easily come up to my place without sneaking past a beweb, and we could kiss and hold hands at restaurants. However, feeling his warm embrace was still nice. And the fact that he had followed through on his promise meant a lot to me.

I had more time to observe Amir now that he was out of his natural Egyptian habitat. He became very protective of me whenever onlookers passed by. If someone checked me out, he would squeeze my hand a little tighter, a sweet gesture acknowledging that he noticed the attention I received from men.

As we walked down Times Square hand-in-hand, a homeless man yelled in our direction, "Chocolate Milk! My favorite!"

"You know, you look different blonde," Amir told me. "Blondes were never my type, but don't get me wrong—you are still beautiful!"

"I had to go back to feeling like myself again," I replied, smiling through my codeine-numbed face.

Riding in metros, Amir cradled my face, gently kissing my forehead, lips, and eyes. "You know I love you, right?" he whispered in my ear as we sat on the Brooklyn Bridge, gazing at the city skyline. He woke up earlier than me, made us coffee, and greeted me with the biggest smile. He held me with so much lust, and I melted into his arms. We stayed in bed for hours, making love all afternoon, only leaving the apartment when hunger motivated us. With him, I felt wanted and needed. He never once judged me for my turbulent past or for not being able to provide a life for myself just yet.

We did it all in NYC: fancy restaurants, Central Park, clubs, bars, and even shopping at Macy's. We only bumped heads once, and that was when I danced too close to a man at PHD nightclub. Seeing that, Amir withdrew, sitting alone at the bar. His jealousy spilled over in a calm yet firm reminder of what he'd told me in Cairo: "You are my woman and a reflection of me. Dancing too close makes him want you and makes me look bad." He'd emphasized that this was how a woman respected a man, and with that respect, a man would do anything for her. I got defensive at first, remembering how Rami would dictate my actions, but later apologized for my reaction to a trauma Amir hadn't committed. I promised to be more aware of my behavior. It was the least that I could do for the man who had rescued me.

His two-week visit was coming to an end, and we needed to address the elephant in the room: What was our relationship, and where was it going? I wasn't sure what I wanted from Amir romantically. I hadn't had time to process my feelings about my last years with Lucas and the abuse with Rami, and I knew it wasn't healthy to bring all my baggage into a new relationship. I wanted Amir to help me and to be there for me like he already was, but I couldn't understand what should come next. I eagerly wanted to know his thoughts and for him to help me decide what mine were. I was too numb on Percocet and had too many problems from the past swept under my emotional rug to decide for myself.

"So, you leave tomorrow. What's next for us?" I asked him, as we laid in bed, hungover from bar hopping.

"That's a good question. I mean—I'm in love with you, Katya, I hope you can see that. And I will do my best to come and visit you as much as I can."

I wasn't fully convinced he was in love with me. I felt his lust for me, and I fulfilled that need for him. I knew we had a good connection and good communication, and he accepted my past and present, taking me as I was. But a part of me wondered if I was the right person for him. I was complicated, rootless, spontaneous, and an addict, which he wasn't aware of. He would have to love me as much as I loved Lucas and take the huge risk of moving to another country and starting over. I hoped he was capable of that kind of love because I could see it working if we weren't living on different continents.

I decided not to reply. Hadn't he said, "I will move with you to NYC," or had that been a lie? Why the mixed signals? The air became too thick to breathe, so I rolled an American Spirit cigarette to clear it. My instincts told me I was just being used. But what about the apartment? I couldn't make more than three thousand a month serving tables. Where would I live? Was he abandoning me? We'd been having unprotected sex. What if I was pregnant? I needed an escape from the tsunami of fearful thoughts, so I headed straight to the bathroom for a small line of codeine to bring down my heart rate.

While in the bathroom, I could hear Amir talking on the phone in frantic Arabic. I heard the voices of what sounded like his parents and another female. "Wallah! Wallah!" ("I swear! I swear!") was all I could make out. Something was off. As I came out, he motioned a finger over his mouth to silence me. Their conversion continued for an hour, during which he locked himself in the bathroom. "Mish— heya!" ("Not her!") I knew that conversation was about me.

"What's wrong? Who was that?" I asked him when he finally emerged from the bathroom.

"Katya, let's talk. Come sit." He paced around the room while I sat on the couch, watching him align his belongings and begin to pack in his OCD way.

Before Amir spilled the tea, I did a quick mental inventory of my situation. I didn't want us to break up; I needed him for my stability in NYC. I also needed him so I didn't look foolish in front of Lucas. My goal of showing Lucas my worthiness had always been my top priority; it was like a broken record on replay: *What would Lucas think of you, seeing how you are not succeeding yet again?* I also had very little money to support myself on a minimum-wage job in an expensive city. And I had nowhere to call home but this fully stocked apartment. Whatever he had to say next, I had no choice but to work around it for my own benefit.

"My parents know I'm with you here in NYC," Amir said, with sweat beaded on his forehead.

"Oh, okay, I thought they knew. What's the problem with you being here with me?" I asked.

"We're not married. I cannot be staying with you in the same apartment," he said, sitting at the breakfast table, far away from me, as though he'd just found out I was infected with the White Plague.

"Hmmm...I see. How do you think they found out?" Living alone under the same roof and not being married was not unusual to me, but I knew that almost all Muslims followed this Islamic rule.

"Well, my ex saw the photo you posted on your Instagram. The one with shopping bags and me standing with my back. But by the way, can you delete it?" he said, searching the room for my phone.

"Wait. You have an ex? How recent? How does she know my Instagram? Why would it matter to her?" I asked. Amir had never mentioned he had been in any relationships, past or present. Then again, I had never asked; there had been no clues that he was juggling two relationships. He was always present, always available, and always made every conversation about me and my life.

I watched him intensely as he digested my questions. I'd studied people long enough to know when an answer was forced—when they tried to make a lie sound as casual as telling me what they had for breakfast.

"We've been broken up for a long time! She's just obsessed with me and doesn't get that we're done. She came over to my parents' house, put photos of us in my room, and wanted to get back together. Her friend saw us out in Cairo once and found you on Instagram. She came and showed my parents the photo at Macy's."

My stomach dropped. I could read the lie in his facial expressions. I felt certain that he and this 'ex' were still together. That voice I'd heard on the phone was hers. Everything but "we've been broken up" was true. He'd added details to convince me that the whole statement was true—a classic move.

Katya wanted to unleash all hell, but Kateryna reminded me that that wouldn't be wise for my situation. She had been the catalyst in all my recent decisions and decided to take some responsibility for the outcomes. I remained calm and figured that I should get as much help as I could from Amir until time and distance pushed us apart.

"My parents are judging me! Yes, I'm lying to them. I told them I'm staying with Ziad. But she's crazy to come to my house and get me in trouble. Can you please write to her and tell her you're just my friend and I was with Ziad?" he begged.

"Come here. Come sit next to me," I said. Amir lay in my lap. *Poor boy*, I thought. He'd do anything for premarital sex. He was chained by religion and expectations and just wanted to spend a nice holiday with me. He had paid a lot for these past six days, including my housing, ticket, and new wardrobe. I was grateful for that. I felt for him—for the mess he had to clean up back home and the tight leash his mother would keep him on. Part of me felt sad for being the sin that would eventually break up him and his girlfriend, but it was his fault for not telling me in the first place. I had been transparent with him from day one.

Thanks to the high level of codeine in my bloodstream, I managed this situation calmly and without anger. I felt his strong feelings toward me and recognized all the sacrifices he had made to spend two weeks with me. I wished he had been honest from the beginning; then again, if he had been honest, I might not have accepted his offers and might have been on a different path.

"It will be okay, Amir. It will be just as it should be. I'm happy to have spent this time with you. But now that they know, and it's haram, you probably won't be able to visit me here in New York anymore," I said, petting his buzz-cut head. "And sure, I can write to her if that helps you look good among your friends and society," I added. I knew what it was like in Egypt to be caught in a mess like this—the loss of honor to the family name, the possible shaming by society, and the extra Friday prayers to wash the sin away.

"I will see you again! I know that. I just don't know how, where, and when. I'm sorry," he said. "Katya, I don't want to date you, I want you for something more serious."

I stopped petting his sweaty head. I had waited years to hear those exact words from Lucas. I wanted that status above all else. To be something serious meant I belonged; I was wanted above the rest; I was not a trial; and no one was wasting my time. It meant my man saw me as I was and didn't mind sharing the burdens of my demons. I wanted someone to whom I could say, "I didn't choose my upbringing. I'm fighting that programming every day to be a better person than I was designed to be. Thank you for loving me and giving me a chance," without being judged or belittled. I wanted to say that to Lucas.

I never imagined that just ten short months after leaving Reno, I'd be sitting on a couch in Manhattan with an Egyptian man, navigating his complicated world while he told me he wanted to be serious with me. I had always imagined returning to my life in

Northern Nevada, planning a wedding with Lucas, and riding mountain bikes along the Truckee River with our green-eyed son.

I needed to let go of my past wants and accept my stark reality. So, I chose not to reply. I wrote the message to Amir's 'ex'; in it, I said that I was a friend of Ziad and that we had gone out to dinner that night as a group. I reasoned that a little white lie would make Amir more comfortable, regardless of whether he was actually with this 'ex' or not. Since he was a year younger than me, I thought he still had a lot to figure out about his feelings. I hoped the hint at marriage was not a lie like the rest of his words. I struggled to pinpoint whether I was truly in love with Amir or just in love with the idea of him being the stable partner I'd always wanted.

Amir left the next morning in a cab, looking like a dog with his tail between his legs. He abandoned his machismo, knowing Allah had caught on to his game. He left me all the cash he had, two hundred fifty dollars. I almost didn't take it, already feeling like a prostitute. He said he couldn't help me pay for next month's rent and kissed me on the cheek. Even codeine couldn't soften the harsh reality I was experiencing. As I waved to the yellow cab, I genuinely feared that I would end up on the streets in NYC, wrapped neatly in addiction. Both Lucas and Amir had made their messes with me and run back to their normal lives.

I needed a strong man, or just a stronger human next to me, so I didn't have to carry my load alone. But again, my mother's point had been proven: the world was a bad place, and everyone was out to use me. I found myself drenched in stupidity, silence, and solitude, standing in front of my apartment building watching Amir's yellow taxi blend into traffic. I shouldn't have hated him or Lucas; I should have hated that I was so desperate to have a normal relationship. I was clearly not meant to have that. In three weeks, I'd be turning twenty-six. I wasn't sure what most twenty-six-year-olds were up to, but it definitely wasn't what I was doing: wasting away. I cried the rest of the day on the couch.

I thought I was wise beyond my years, but every man I met treated me like a child. Life had taught me a lot, yet I constantly failed to apply that wisdom. I knew that I was doing wrong by getting into pointless romances, aimlessly roaming the world, and putting drugs into my body, but I kept running from myself.

On April 29, my birthday, I packed my two bags of clothes and my two flags—Ukrainian and Egyptian—and vacated my apartment before noon. I had exactly forty-three dollars in my bank account and subway directions to the next place I'd call home. I'd found a room for rent in Astoria, Queens, a block from the N metro line. My roommates were an older woman in her fifties with major OCD and a Thai girl who was younger than me. I was happy to know I wouldn't be living alone, and I was among women who wouldn't get me into the wrong groups. They kept to themselves and worked solid nine-to-five jobs. But the strict rules on kitchen use and noise level alongside my single bed with pastel yellow sheets kept the apartment from feeling homey. I didn't want to spend my birthday sitting on the yellow bed, looking at my pathetic belongings. Thank God it was a Friday—that meant going out to work the nightclubs.

After Amir left, taking with him all his promises of getting me on my feet, I had to find another job to pay for rent. Being completely on my own now wasn't scary. I could always take care of things on my own, but I believed I shouldn't have to when a man was nearby. I gave him my body, my time, my care; I washed his laundry and cooked his meals, and in return, I believed he should provide a roof over my head. I'm not sure why I clung to those traditions because I hadn't grown up being taken care of by anyone, especially not a man. I figured I'd always wanted to be helped and had never received that help, and that drove me to seek out men who could take care of some of my needs, especially so I could take care of my expensive opioid needs.

My second job wasn't what I had envisioned for myself. The opportunity had come up when I'd least expected it. One day, my colleagues from the Mexican bar took me out to a club called 1 Oak after work. There, I met Sammy, a second-generation Russian Israeli Jew in a baseball hat. He made me a proposition: "Hey, you seem friendly and outgoing. How about I pay you two hundred dollars a night if you find me ten cute girls to come to the clubs I promote? If you find less than ten, it's only one hundred dollars." In my drunken stupor, I accepted without hesitation and started working every night from Thursday to Saturday, walking around the Meat District and Greenwich, inviting groups of girls to LAVO, Marquee New York, 1 Oak, and Avenue. Sammy was like a big brother to me, always protective whenever weirdos approached me. He liked that I had a psychology degree and admired me, as his dream career was to be a social worker. I couldn't complain about making an extra five hundred dollars a week.

That night, I asked Sammy to pick me up for my birthday. He came with another Jewish friend, and we went to our usual spot, 1 Oak. I thought I was going to work, but Sammy surprised me with a bottle for our table. The DJ called me on stage for a birthday shoutout. I had a lot of fun but felt lonely in the crowded room and a bit indebted to Sammy. I hoped he didn't expect me to sleep with him for his kind gesture. I got stupid drunk and later went to some strip clubs and house parties with MDMA in Brooklyn, using Amir's abandonment as my excuse for my reckless decisions.

I woke up around 5 p.m. the next day, overwhelmed with a guilt that made my stomach turn. This was the first time since Kateryna had emerged in Egypt that I felt guilty for my poor decisions. Katya wouldn't have batted an eye; she'd have brushed off the act and told me, "You are young, wild, and free," without feeling ashamed and embarrassed. Maybe Amir's talks about decency had rubbed off on me. Maybe turning twenty-six and being alone in a big city made me second-guess my rebellious and reckless behavior. The woman I was last night, trashy and without boundaries, didn't deserve respect from men. I seemed to have gotten comfortable with feeling shameful.

Why couldn't I just get my act together? Most people had nights like this regularly, but my morally questionable behavior didn't sit right with me. If my parents couldn't punish me, I knew that life would. It's really hard to raise yourself, but I was blessed with a moral compass that worked from time to time. That morning, it pointed to what I had been lacking...faith.

Maybe it was because my brain was completely depleted of serotonin or because I had engaged in all seven deadly sins the previous night, but I got on my knees and prayed. I prayed and cried and cried. I hadn't cried like that in a long time. My mantra during the sin cleansing was, "I'm sorry... I'm sorry... I'm sorry." My heart ached so much that it took my breath away. I knew I couldn't stay in NYC for long, as I would get sucked into a darker world. Given the circumstances, I also felt that Amir's cookie-cutter plan, even if based on Islamic expectations, could be the best path for me to follow. It was a direction with a destination. I stayed kneeling in prayer until I fell asleep on the floor.

The following week, I reached out to Amir.

Amir,

I have been meaning to write to you, but I waited for the right time in your busy schedule.

From one point of view, there is this relationship you, as a Muslim, are trying to establish; answering all other questions and concerns from your life, among many other things. I understand, we have very different cultures.

But you said, "I will not date you; I want something more serious." Did you really mean that?

I hate not knowing where we are heading.

Some nights, I wake up thinking—is all of this worth it? Can't I just throw it away and start anew? New opportunities for my personal future. I am not afraid of new beginnings; it's actually a very strong mental skill I have acquired.

I have been preparing for both answers you might give me. The risks of both are high. But with the marriage answer, the risks are higher due to many unknown factors. I think there would be more unknowns in our marriage than unknowns that being single would bring. By unknowns, I mean all these physical and living needs, all the logistics, all the planning, all the differing viewpoints on rules, religion, culture, and lifestyles.

However, the chances of meeting a soul like yours and connecting like this are rare. We both know this. Thus, all of these unknowns can be discussed, assembled, and set in motion. For now, I am waiting for this flower to bloom. I will just let it be.

Love,

Katya

In a moment of codeine-free clarity, I reread the email when I didn't get an immediate response. It sounded absurd to be in such a fantasy world. Marriage and family. Another sliver of a pill put me right back in a space where I felt normal. Amir's response came later, with promises of rekindling our relationship after his lies to his parents were settled. He promised to make the right decision for both of us, in due time. I loved him, so I gave him space. When one door closes, another one always opens.

My mother reached out with an invitation to stay for the summer in Viana do Castelo, Portugal. She and her husband had purchased a home there, overlooking the Atlantic Ocean. She needed my knowledge of Spanish to help her get settled in with utility companies and for me to help watch my two younger sisters. With no direction in NYC, I took up her offer without hesitation. I had a purpose. I didn't have to work bars and nightclubs anymore, and I could reset my priorities.

On June 12, almost a year after leaving Reno, I packed the same two bags that had been with me to three countries and took them to a fourth: Portugal. I left New York City without even calling my employers. I just disappeared without a trace, doing what I did best: running into the hands of people I desperately wanted to please.

10

PASTEL DE NATAS & WHISKEY (JUNE 2015)

As with all my recent flights, I got a one-way ticket to Porto, Portugal; it was an open-ended journey. I felt almost one hundred percent certain that this stay with my mother would heal my wounds and be a time wherein I would receive the advice, support, and encouragement to get back on my feet. I could once again feel hopeful about myself if I could only pour my pain into the one person who had the power to heal me. But if someone has the power to heal you, they also have the power to destroy you. This fear lingered in my mind, but after enduring so many misfortunes in such a short time, I didn't expect fate to be cruel yet again.

My beautiful mother, 5'2" and skinnier than usual, with brown hair and hazel eyes, didn't say much when I arrived at the train station in Viana do Castelo, a slow-paced retirement city forty minutes north of Porto. I received a small, awkward hug and a, "Daughter, happy to see you." I was happy to see Anka, my two-year-old sister, and Sveta, my six-year-old sister. My sister, Masha, ten years younger than me, also came to support our mother in her transition to another country.

Mom and Masha had more positive memories to chat about than Mom and I did, but I chimed in with appropriate laughter. Masha had been living with our grandmother in Kyiv for a year, away from our mother, while our other two younger sisters from my mom's third and current marriage moved to Portugal. No one mentioned how unjust this was to Masha, who was still a minor. Yet, I saw Masha as the luckier one since our mother hadn't introduced her to any addictive substances, and Masha had our grandmother—a saint compared to our mother—to care for her. Masha was favored more than me, but that didn't bother me; I was happy at least one of my sisters was doing well.

We celebrated our arrival with stops at vista points along the Atlantic and an extravagant seafood sampler dinner with a whole grilled pineapple garnish. "I'm so happy all my girls are together. All four of you!" my mom said without making eye contact with me. My plan to confide in her and get her help looked grim only hours into our reunion. She looked at me as though I was plagued with a disease, keeping her eyes distant.

After seeing the slight jealousy in Masha's eyes when Sveta said, "We have seafood like this all the time!" I felt annoyed and angry that Masha had been left in Ukraine. Masha had never had dinners like this or seen the ocean, but maybe being with our grandmother was better and gave her less trauma to carry. It was like Mom knew I was judging her for her spontaneous move with her equally crazy husband, Oleg, but she was too embarrassed to have me, or anyone, question it. So, I just smiled at her, leaving the snake where I'd found it. The little Kateryna in me was still relentless in seeking her love, even at twenty-six. Even the smallest gesture of genuine care from her would send me to the moon. But her hard breathing and long stares, half a bottle of Vinho Verde in, confirmed that she was very unhappy with my directionless life—one whose creation she didn't understand her contribution to. I could smell an uncomfortable conversation brewing between us. It was just a matter of who snapped first. Almost always, it was her, after a few pulls off the whiskey bottle.

Her three-bedroom apartment with wooden floors and an equally large glass balcony was lovely, to say the least. It was luxurious compared to what I was used to in New York City and Cairo and Reno, or what Masha was used to, living in a five-hundred-square-foot apartment with our grandparents. The kitchen, of course, was stacked with unwashed dishes, and laundry piled sky-high in my mom's room. That was to be expected. The freshly lacquered living room space wasn't fully furnished, but not much was needed. The sunset-facing side of the apartment was all glass and brought enough ocean into the space that anything more would have distracted from the feeling of sailing in the open sea. Masha and I shared a room and had our own queen beds. I envied my mother's linen bed sheets and goose-feather pillows. And again, I felt sorry for Masha and myself for not having our mother support us or provide us a stable home.

After a week passed, I started getting antsy and irritated. There was only so much Vinho Verde I could drink and so many pastel de natas I could eat to mask my withdrawals. I hadn't had a dose of codeine since our seafood dinner, where I'd finished the last of my score from an NYC acquaintance. I needed my drugs to handle babysitting my youngest sisters, the never-ending dishes, and the growing tension between my mother and me. I was barely getting through each morning, but I noticed my mom having sporadic bursts of energy throughout the day. She seemed extra nice and generous at midday, not her usual self. "Do you need some clothes? Here, take the credit card and go buy whatever you want," she offered one day. "But take the girls with you, it's a nice day out."

A drug addict is always aware of who may be the next source, who their kin addicts are. The fact that my mom carried her handbag around the house and even slept with it was a dead giveaway she was hiding something in there. I needed to get a hold of that purse. I suspected she was on pills, but just like I couldn't call her out on this crazy new lifestyle she was trying to attain, I couldn't question her about doing opioids again. Maybe she had never stopped since our Alaska days. I'll never know.

On day nine without opioids, my body started to ache intensely —a pain I had been avoiding for years. It felt unbearable, as though bugs were crawling under my skin; my joints were on fire, and ice-cold sweat poured out of my pores. That was my cue to seek out codeine.

Like a hunter, I snuck into my mom's room at 3 a.m., pausing before each step to ensure the wood didn't creak under my weight. I grabbed the purse off the bed and exited the room even more slowly, my mouth salivating at the thought of what was inside. If I knew one thing about my mother, it was that she would never offer to take me shopping unless she was high. She was chronically miserable, so any happiness from her was most likely chemically induced. I remembered my childhood in Alaska; her generosity and spontaneity had been byproducts of her opioid euphoria.

Jackpot! It felt like déjà vu; I was fifteen again, stealing pills from my mom's purse. My hands shook as I took out the sleeve of eight 1000mg white pills. I didn't even read the name; I instinctively knew they were narcotics. I popped one out from its aluminum foil restraints, feeling a pang of guilt, and I bit off a bitter chunk. Disgusting. Fifteen minutes later, I felt normal again: no anxiety, just a gentle grin on my face and unjustified butterflies in my stomach. I felt happy to do anything, to make plans and fantasize about my bright future. These pills were very strong. I typed their name into my phone and crawled back into bed, ready for a night of restful sleep after ten days on the edge of the razor.

"That's weird, why is my purse in the kitchen?" my mom asked us over breakfast the next morning. I pretended to be consumed by my phone.

"I didn't touch it," Masha said.

I could feel my mother's laser stare on me. Who cared? I didn't anymore. I was high and happy as a kite; unbothered, untouchable.

Getting a box of those pills was simple in Cairo and elsewhere, just not in the USA. In Portugal, I just walked to the pharmacy. I dressed decently and asked for the pills by name in proper English. "My doctor in New York recommended these. I had back surgery a few years ago, and I don't know if it's the flight or the hills around town, but I can't sleep because of the pain," I lied. The next pharmacy heard a similar story, and the next one heard about a violent car accident in the Lincoln Tunnel. I got creative with my stories, and for four to ten euros, I secured enough high-dose codeine pills to last a month.

However, they didn't last a month. The ease of getting the pills and my greed increased my tolerance. I went from a quarter of a pill a day to two whole pills a day in a month's time. With ten pharmacies in town, I visited each one twice a month. I stocked up. Life was sweet.

My mother caught on to my drug use, as addicts easily spot the signs. She knew I had caught on to her by snooping in her purse. I stopped making eye contact with her to hide my pinhole pupils, and my mother did the same. We walked around the house wearing sunglasses, as funny as it looked, hiding our symptoms from each other. However, she had more to hide than I did.

The narcotic warning of "do not mix with alcohol" is valid. Drinking on top of taking pills can stop your heart and kill you, but it also increases the potency of the opioid. Drinking is like tossing a coin and hoping it lands on heads. It is worth the gamble; just one sip of alcohol sets that euphoria on another level.

"Masha! Quiet, but come here," I whispered to my sister in our room one evening almost two months into our stay.

"What? What are you doing?" she asked, as I pulled her to our mother's room.

"Jesus, look what I found." I pointed inside my mom's closet.

Inside, behind the extra blankets, were roughly fifteen empty whiskey bottles.

"Oh my God, I knew it was bad, but I didn't know it was this bad," Masha said, somber-faced.

Masha never sugar-coated any of our mother's shenanigans, but she was better than me at blocking them out. She saw the good side of our mother, one I still can't see to this day. Usually, she would withdraw, not wanting to stir the pot further. "Just leave it, Katya. Mom isn't all that bad," she'd say, protecting her, after I spilled all the rotten memories from my childhood. Her protection infuriated me but also left me questioning why I was so obsessed with airing our mom's dirty laundry in front of the family. It was my cry for help, my attempt to expose the abuser who'd left the scars I desperately hid from everyone. I had to justify my flaws by exposing our mother's.

"Yeah, it's bad. No wonder she is sleeping half the day," I replied.

"What should we do? We can't tell her," Masha said.

"I don't know. If we tell her or ask her anything, she will flip out. We know that! Remember the incident in Makoshyne? Those vodka bottles Grandma found hidden in the walls?" I asked.

"Don't remind me, please," Masha replied. "But I thought she was just doing wine. We all drink here together. I mean, yeah, I'm not eighteen, but it's just wine. So, she goes into her room and drinks more behind our backs. Wow..."

"Yeah, once an alcoholic, always one. I read that they save bottles as a cry for help. I mean, why not throw them away?" I said.

Right then and there, I almost told Masha that I also knew our mother abused pills. However, I didn't think Masha needed to know that. She didn't need the additional hurt of realizing that the hugs and kisses she'd been receiving on this trip were just the opioids talking. Besides, if I revealed my mother's drug abuse, she would retaliate by exposing my drug use to the entire family. I wanted to stay righteous in Masha's eyes and in all my sisters' eyes since they looked up to their older sibling.

I bit my tongue and reasoned—in my codeine state—that Masha had endured enough abuse. After all, Masha had moved in with our grandparents just a year before because our mother got blackout drunk in Ukraine and became convinced Masha was a demon. She chased her with a garden hoe and hacked down her bedroom door, all the while screaming, "I should have never come to the USA and had you from the Devil that is your father."

"I'm really scared, Katya. We can't leave the girls like this. She is passed-out drunk half the day! But I'm just scared to confront her. Don't touch these bottles, please, leave them," Masha said.

I left them for Masha's sake during her stay. She was terrified, like all of us, of the alcoholic giant inside our mother's small frame. I decided I would expose my mother in due time. For now, she was my bread and butter, and a distraction came at the perfect time.

Amir came back into my life like an Atlantic storm. He confessed he couldn't stop thinking about me, dreaming of me, and wanting me. He asked questions he'd never asked before, catching me off guard, but my addictive side handled them effortlessly. He asked if I would ever consider converting to Islam, and if not, if I could follow his cultural rules as a wife and if I'd be okay with raising children the Muslim way. He assured me he wouldn't force me to convert if we ever got married because in Islam a Muslim can marry a non-Muslim woman but not the other way around. That was a relief because I could never convert—not because I didn't like his religion but because I'd never liked the concept of religion in general. I was born Orthodox, raised Catholic in Alaska, and forced to attend Baptist churches with Mom when she had a month of clarity. God, to me, is separate from religion.

Almost every night, we had three-hour phone conversations about life's philosophies and met on middle ground if we had polar-opposite viewpoints. With each deep conversation, I was indoctrinated into his pious life expectations: do well unto others, maintain good standing with our families, pray, don't drink, don't eat pork, be a decent woman as she is a reflection of her man, and save money for a good future. I agreed to his rules but challenged his expectations about raising children. I insisted that if we had kids, I would teach them my culture's etiquette and rules and celebrate our Christian holidays. Even though I was not a big fan of Christmas, I believed a mixed-cultural baby should be enriched in both parents' backgrounds. He agreed without much argument. Our nightly conversations were the perfect escape from my dysfunctional world with my mother.

"Katya, I need to see you. The boys and I were planning a trip to Romania in mid-August, but it looks like they can't go. If I get you a ticket, will you come with me to Bucharest for four days?" Amir asked.

"Of course! Is that even something to question? I miss you so much," I said.

I missed how he cared about my comfort in public, clearing the way for me by gently pushing crowds aside. I missed his soft smile and big almond brown eyes. I missed the way he asked, "How do you feel now? Are you cold, hot? Do you need anything else before I go?" I missed our physical chemistry and how magnetic it was, our different skin tones, and our cultural standards meeting in the middle. His care and chivalry were intoxicating and highly addictive for a woman starving for self-esteem.

"I just have to find a way to tell my mom. She doesn't seem too happy with me right now. I'm not sure she even likes you. I told her about what happened in NYC, so, now, to tell her I'm going to see you again..." I trailed off.

"Hmmmm, she doesn't like me, huh? Never met me, but okay. Maybe I'll meet her soon, and I promise she will love me!" Amir assured me.

I thought that was a big promise to make. My mother had been drunkenly content with our choices when Amir had sponsored my move to NYC, but when she called to selfishly invite me to Portugal, she found out that Amir had left me and learned the details about his ex-girlfriend discovering our stay together. He had let me down, but so had she, more than once. I had excused and forgiven my man, but I had never thought about excusing and forgiving my mother. Instinctively, I knew my mother would be disappointed that I was running back to this Arab man.

On the other hand, did I even deserve a trip? I wasn't working except for helping my mom around the house and entertaining my two-year-old and six-year-old sisters. Instead of taking trips to meet my lover, I should have been focusing on finding stable housing and a job. Feeling like a lowlife, I did the obvious thing; I blamed my mom. Instead of her helping me, motivating me, and caring about my past year of mayhem, she only wanted me around in support of her drinking habit. With me around, she could sleep through most of the day without being burdened by watching two toddlers.

I hoped to find the time to talk to my mother, but through the codeine haze and daily responsibilities of caring for two young children, I couldn't. I wanted to ask, "Hey, what do you think I should do next? I don't have a home or roots anywhere, so what do you think is best for me?" like I had planned on asking before coming here. Instead, again, I was faced with figuring out how to raise myself. Amir, yet again, became my guiding light to some kind of 'normal.'

"Mom, I'm going on a short trip...with Amir. The Egyptian guy," I announced to her over our evening cigarette break.

"Hmmmm...where to?" she asked, blowing out smoke.

"Romania for four days. It will be after Masha's birthday in August, after she leaves back to Ukraine," I said.

"And you'll leave me alone with Anka and Sveta?" she continued, never making eye contact with me. She was already thinking about how she wouldn't be able to drink as much while being a full-time single mom. The girls' father, Oleg, visited every couple of months, his job as a trans-Atlantic cargo pilot keeping him away.

"Yes, but not for long. And Oleg is coming that second weekend in August, remember?" I asked.

"Fine, go," she said with disappointment. Or was it jealousy? I couldn't tell.

The trip to Romania with Amir reignited the love I felt between us. It was a love rooted in unhealthy attachment but still filled with attention and care. The healthy part of me, looking out from behind the codeine curtain, saw that his caring ways attached me to him. Small gestures, like asking me to finish all my food at the restaurant and neatly folding the clothes he ripped off me the night before, were enough for me to call my feelings *love*. His presence reminded me that I could be a woman who deserved companionship. I didn't know what 'worthy of love' really felt like, but the novelty of a Middle Eastern man with his dogma on courtship and high priority on marriage made me feel truly important.

Amir didn't come with contracts or high expectations like Lucas did. His few expectations, like "don't dress so provocatively in public," were much more manageable than Lucas's demand of "don't let your body go and get all fat on me." Amir didn't expect me to make a certain amount of money or run a business, as Lucas did. Amir was simple; he only wanted us to live a pious life, and who could argue with that? I craved and needed healthy structure, even if it was provided by Islam.

Unlike the Western man, Amir didn't demand I split payment for meals, tickets, or gifts. "While you are with me, I take care of all your needs," he would say. I felt like the luckiest woman in Europe! I was grateful not to be spending any money, as all I had were two hundred euros I'd managed to get from my mom when her pills kicked in.

Our time together was amazing. However, on our second night at the Bucharest hotel, after we came back wasted from club hopping, Amir threw a curveball at me. Calling me to the bathroom, he took out a gram of cocaine in the most nonchalant way and lined up two mountain ranges.

"Where did you get this?" I asked.

"It's a long story. I asked a cab driver where to get some. He took me to a drug lord's house; it was a hostage situation, but he said this is the best stuff around. I know you like this, so it's for you and me," he explained.

I hadn't read the Quran yet, but I was pretty sure mind-altering substances from Romanian drug lords were not part of a pious Muslim lifestyle. The two lines of cocaine on the sink instantly took me back to my party days with Alina in Cairo, when I'd lived the frightfully intoxicating double-standard reality. I reasoned that Allah slept at night and accepted Amir's offer.

"I don't like this stuff. I really don't—I mean, I do it, I've done it, but I like—okay, just one," I said, pausing before saying the other 'c' word.

I'm not sure what that substance was, but it wasn't cocaine. It was closer to meth or something else they mixed out there. I immediately regretted taking it, as this drug took the reins on my anxiety away from codeine. The comedown brought intense thoughts of suicide, regret, and restlessness. It was horrible compared to real cocaine. We stayed up in bed, holding each other until 7 a.m. It was a terrible experience. Amir flushed the rest down the toilet, and I applauded him for it.

Back in Portugal, I deep-cleaned the house out of guilt for leaving and disappointing my mother. I then counted how many times I'd flown in the last fifteen months since my departure from Reno. The total was eight times, with multiple layovers in Ukraine between Cairo, NYC, and Portugal. Amir had already planned another trip for me in September to Hurghada on the Egyptian Red Sea, and he would visit Portugal for his weightlifting competition in November, hoping to meet my mother. That would bring the total to ten flights in seventeen months. With this, I happily considered myself a nomad, with lessons to teach others.

Awaiting my next trip to the Red Sea, I stopped sweeping up

cookie crumbs around the elephants in the room that no one addressed: my unstable, sporadic travels and wasted precious years. Why hadn't anyone in my family intervened? Even during my layovers in Ukraine, my father had said nothing about my ever-changing lifestyle. At the kitchen table, no one dared to offer their opinion. I was just a passerby, a husbandless, childless, nomadic gypsy. I ran to Ukraine every chance I got, seeking guidance and a warm meal, but they seemed to think I had it all figured out. It was too late to ask my drugged-up mother; she, like me, was in another world, chasing the elusive white pill.

In my addiction-controlled world, I came up with a brilliant idea: if I couldn't get my life together, maybe I could help others find their path. Life coaching made sense to me; I had experienced a lot, lived in many countries, and lied just enough to make it seem like I was managing my mind. Like many people, I was good at giving advice but never took my own. I had enough trauma to help others over-come theirs, and my background in psychology could be put to use. So, I spent my spare time studying for a life coach certificate. Deep down, I believed coaching another lost soul was a way I could feel useful in this world. Once certified, thanks to extra drug doses, I even built a website. I called it "Wanderlust Therapy" and wrote blogs on topics like "Travel is the New Form of Therapy" and "The Recipe for a Perfect Life." A notable blogger at that time actually reposted one of my articles, but I've long since forgotten what it said.

My mom did her best to support me from inside her crazy world, saying, "You're wasting your time. We should just rob a bank. No, I'm serious. Working and studying is all bullshit. Did you know this whole world is run by thirteen Jewish families?" I just sipped my coffee and kept blogging on my website about a utopian world I knew existed outside of my mentally impaired cage, hoping someone would read my articles and get some use out of them.

Amir was my saving grace and the only person who truly cared about my sanity. I started venting to him about my mom's lack of concern, care, or consciousness. To distract me from her, he would ask about my lifelong goals, where I wanted to travel next, and what kind of jewelry I liked. His questions removed me from my daily toxic environment of seeing my mother passed out on the balcony sunbathing, reeking of metabolized alcohol. My only job was to check her pulse to see if she was okay and to offer water. Amir gave me hope that this was all temporary, and if I could dream it, he and I could achieve it. And with that, weeks flew by until we met again.

Amir and I had an unforgettable trip to Hurghada, Egypt, that September. We stayed in a villa on the turquoise sea with flour-white sand. However, I almost overdosed after taking 400mg of codeine and drinking three gin and tonics on the beach—nearly twice the maximum daily limit. Amir was my hero again, wiping me down with cold water under my armpits and neck back at the hotel room. "Did you take anything else?" he asked, panicked, as my heart rate dropped below fifty. I was limp, my lips turning blue, and I struggled to breathe, but I managed to lie, "No." Despite this, the Egypt trip was filled with positive emotions. I met all his friends and his sister and rode horseback in the desert. I almost stayed in Egypt, but the five-dollar opioids in Portugal pulled me back to my mother's house like a black hole.

"Mom, the world is not fucking flat! Enough. Please. You are crazy!" I finally snapped one evening, screaming at the top of my lungs. I had heard her Flat Earth Society propaganda for five months. This was typical of her character. She jumped from one conspiracy to the next, as someone who hadn't worked for a decade often does. Mostly, I played along just to earn my two-hundred-euro allowance, doing distance experiments in the dark to disprove the curvature of the Earth. But tonight was not a good night, and I'd had enough.

Amir and I had just had a serious fight, one that might not be resolved. He had left the week before after visiting Portugal and competing in the world powerlifting championships. Our fight had been about deep subjects like family values and morals, and I'd gotten very defensive about him picking apart mine. He had been particularly upset that I'd still been with Lucas while we'd been seeing each other in Cairo. He'd implied I might be capable of cheating on him based on my history. I'd argued that he, too, hadn't been honest about his girlfriend at the time. I'd reminded him we were in the same boat. He'd also been angry that my mother hadn't wanted to meet him. She ruined all my relationships whether she was present or not, against it or supportive; she leaked negativity and polluted those around her, especially me.

"Don't ever talk to me like that! You know what? You're ungrateful! You're shameful to look at! Living around here—useless! Just flying around the world and fucking men. Muslim, low-life men!" my mom yelled back.

That was it. It was the conversation we should have had almost six months ago. She'd avoided eye contact, any contact, and sitting too long in the room with me. She'd never asked how my trips with Amir went or what my plans were, whether I was moving out or not. Since Masha had left, she'd been even more distant. I understood why; it was because we both didn't want to ruin our opioid buzz and face reality. I decided to settle this conversation using the best communication tools she had given me: insults and rage.

"I'm fucking shameful to look at? I'm useless? Look at yourself. You lay around all day. You don't even try to teach your kids anything or take them anywhere. Your room is a fucking mess! And you haven't worked a day since 2007!" My whole body was shaking.

"Ha! See, you are ungrateful! Who brought you to the United States and got you that passport? You think I didn't work hard on that farm and got screwed over by Masha's dad? Where are your children? You can't even do that! I don't need to work—I have a husband! You can't even find a boyfriend. Good thing Lucas left you —if he only knew how messed up and ungrateful you are!"

"Shut up about the States! That was like eighteen years ago! I don't owe you anything! You decided to go there! I was a fucking kid! Oh, yes, that's right—I never was your daughter, just your excuse!

And you told me to break up with Lucas! Or were you too drunk to remember that?"

"Maybe you need to take another pill, Katya. To calm down! You're a drug addict!"

"Why don't you give me one? You have them in your purse. Where is it?" I stormed to the living room to find her purse. She followed.

"Don't touch my stuff!" she demanded.

"You take narcotics just like me—don't even hide that. Oh, and," I stormed into her closet, "you're still a lowlife alcoholic! All these fucking bottles. You think we don't know? You think your daughters are happy to know you're a drunk? They fear you! They hate you! I showed Masha these, too! You will never stop."

I sweated with fear of what would happen next. I had confronted her about her drinking many times before, and each time she had defended the bottle over our relationship. Her typical responses included threatening to disown me, grabbing my hair and throwing me down, or calling a family member to have me committed to a psychiatric ward. This time, I had gone too far—I had exposed her pill habit as well.

Sadly, my two youngest sisters saw and heard everything. I went over to the couch and hugged them, to protect them and to shield myself from her.

I sat there with my eyes closed, breathing slowly to lower my blood pressure. All I could hear was slamming drawers and cabinets and loud thuds. My mother cursed repeatedly, "You little fucking bitch," as the commotion in my room continued for a good ten minutes.

"Get the fuck out!" she screamed. She had packed my bags and threw them by the front door. "Get out now!" she demanded.

I froze, my legs refusing to move. "I'm so sorry," I whispered to my sisters and kissed them. Poor Anka and Sveta couldn't escape this, and they still didn't understand what Mom was searching for at the bottom of all those colorful glass bottles. Maybe it was better for me to leave, to prevent any more heated adult arguments from reaching their little ears. I couldn't save everyone; I was still fighting to save myself. Tears ran down my face. "I'm so sorry Mama is like this. I love you both very much. You will be okay," I said to them.

I put my shoes on and grabbed the first coat I saw. My mother pushed me outside the already open front door, threw my luggage at my feet, and slammed the door.

"Where is my passport?" I banged on the door.

"Oh! Now you need your passport! Now you're grateful for it?" she raged back.

"Give me my passport and my purse, or I will call the police! I swear to God I will have these kids taken away from you." I used my last bit of ammo.

Moments later, she threw my purse and passport outside the door, along with the key to rock bottom. I sat on my bags under her apartment building, grateful for one thing—our Wi-Fi reached the curb. Her balcony was just above, and I could smell her burning cigarette. "I feel so sorry for you," I sobbed under my breath. Cringing at my own words, I called a cab. I should have been worried about myself, crying and panicking about my situation, but I just wanted to hug my mother and tell her, "I want to help you. I love you no matter what. We all need you to be happy."

This was my superpower. In the face of adversity and survival, I shined through. I had enough heart for even the worst of people. Yet no one in my life seemed to value that part of me. Lucas kept telling me to "dig deeper" and "stop playing victim." But I was already at the bottom of myself—wasn't I? I hated being this strong and kind when I should have been cold. I never used my superpower for what really mattered: my own well-being. I didn't know how to do that; my happiness depended on everyone else being happy with me.

I was so confused with myself. Where was the fear one should feel when sitting broke and homeless in a foreign country? Yet again, I was unafraid to step into the unknown abyss. I knew I would make it out; this situation was nothing compared to the magnitude of my family's dysfunction. At the core of my being, I knew that even though it was a monster who had made me, who didn't love me, and who left me to navigate a cruel world, I was better than her. Whatever life threw at me, whatever she did to me, I loved life more than she ever could. I thought of the smiling faces of mothers in the Mumbai slums and their love for their children despite unbearable poverty. My mother would never be able to feel that. I was not going to let her negativity destroy the light inside me.

I had exactly eighty-seven euros and half a battery charge on my phone. The cab dropped me off at the train station, and I got the last train to Porto for thirteen euros. Close to midnight, I checked into the ten-euro-per-night hostel my sister and I would stay at during weekend trips to this historic wine city. I lay in the fetal position and cried myself to sleep.

Early the next morning, my rock-bottom instinct was to message Lucas. Not my father, grandma, sister, or Amir—I wanted Lucas. He, out of everyone in my life, had seen this side of my mom. When we'd visited her in Ukraine a few summers ago, she'd dragged me out of the house by my hair in front of Lucas when I'd yelled in her face that she was drunk after a heated vodka-infused conversation. He'd stepped in to stop her, but she'd hissed in his face, and we'd left in absolute shock.

'Hi, my mom kicked me out because I told her she's an alcoholic. I'm stranded in Porto, Portugal. Can you help me?' I typed, trembling.

His response struck me in the heart: 'Hi Katya. I'm sorry to hear that. Your mom is crazy, that is a fact. Can you ask Oleg for help?'

Typical Lucas—helpful but removed; he offered a solution but watched from the sidelines.

'Thanks, I will try,' I typed and went back to bed to continue sobbing. Her husband wouldn't be on my side. By now, my mom had probably already messaged him and everyone else, lying about why she had kicked me out.

I had enough money for two more nights at the hostel. The hostel offered a simple breakfast of bread, jam, and coffee, and that was all I ate for the day. Feeling ashamed for stuffing the stale bread in my pockets and searching the streets for half-finished cigarettes, I had no other choice but to call Amir.

"...I just want someone to love me. I'm not a bad person, I do have morals. I know what it looks like from the outside! How can your own mother just kick you out? But I swear, Amir, I just told her she needs to stop drinking. I'm not a bad daughter. I can't be around her... I can't. She hurts me over and over again. I don't even have money for food. I stole fucking bread today," I poured my heart out from my hostel room.

"Katya, Katya, I get it. I'm sorry for all of this. I will get you out! I'm your man, aren't I? Now, stop crying," my hero sang to me.

"Where can I go, Amir? Where?" I continued sobbing.

"Well, I've been thinking, and hear me out first, but...what if you come and live in Egypt? We will find you a decent job, I'll ask my mom to help and get you an apartment. I want you to meet her. It could be good for you...for us," he said.

Horrible flashbacks of the rape, the pollution, the crowded streets, the harassment, and all the struggles I'd had in Cairo flooded in like a bad infomercial. I let the memories and Amir's suggestion process for a few silent minutes.

"Okay, I just, umm," I breathed out heavily, "I just don't know if I can live there forever, Amir."

"It won't be forever. When I said I wanted something serious with you, I meant it. Come and get to know my family more, and we can plan our next steps. Maybe we'll move to the States, maybe to Europe, we can figure all of that out in time," he assured me.

"Okay. Let's work on getting there together. I'll come," I said, closing my eyes and hanging my head as though in prayer.

I couldn't afford to be selective or hold out for better options in my dire situation; beggars can't be choosers.

Amir sent me money to cover my hostel stay and food for two weeks. Then he purchased my ticket to Cairo. By late December 2015, the taste of the prized Portuguese treats, pastel de nata, made me nauseous. I was ready to leave this imposter country my mother called home. With my trusty one-way ticket to Cairo, I vowed to see that place with fresh eyes, to find the good in the ugly, and to embrace the man, the lifestyle, and the opportunity life had offered me. Maybe the grass would be greener when I was there as part of an Egyptian family rather than just a Western expat.

As I awaited my departure at the Porto airport, I made a deal with God: I would quit my pills for a better life, find stability with my partner, build a nuclear family, and ride into the Reno sunset with my foreign prince when we moved back to the USA. If Egypt and Amir were my calling and this was my second chance to get my life right, I had to follow it with a sober conscience.

11

CAIRO, TAKE TWO
(DECEMBER 2015)

re we sure about this? my paranoia nagged. My blood was almost clear of opioids, and instead of lounging in a luxury apartment overlooking the Atlantic, I was crammed into the back seat of a reckless cab on a Cairo highway. I forced myself to calm down, thinking, *Amir is here, it's okay.* I pleaded with God for a sign that this was the right decision. The universe responded clearly, confirming I was on the right path. I arrived in Cairo on December 27, at my apartment on 27th Dimashq Street, on the seventh floor. Seven is my favorite number—this was my sign!

I stepped into the apartment to find all the French Victorian lights on and not a speck of dust in sight. As usual, the nicer Cairo apartments looked like antique Parisian storefronts. With an almost nine-hundred-square-foot, double-living-room space, I felt so lucky to call this place my new home.

"Oh my God, this is so nice! Please thank your mother. I can't believe this," I said to Amir, feeling utterly grateful to have a roof over my head. Here was a mother I'd never met, renting this apartment for me, while my own mother had never done anything like this for me.

"You deserve this, habibti," Amir said, gently hugging me. "Here are fresh towels and bedsheets. The fridge has some cooked meals and breakfast stuff, too."

I was so overwhelmed by the generosity of the Sabry family that I couldn't control myself and burst into tears. Gratitude, fear of what was to come, and hate for my mother stained Amir's Oud-Wood-scented shoulder. He tucked me into bed, laid next to me until I fell asleep, and sneaked out in the middle of the night.

Third time in Cairo in three years. That was my first thought the following morning. I sure didn't miss waking up to noisy streets and the call to prayer. *Can we worship God without the daily broadcasts?* I was happy I didn't have to roll out a prayer rug. The winters here were the worst: cold, windy, and dusty. It was even dustier and colder than I remembered. Out of habit, as though responding to my own call to prayer, I searched my purse for a pill to drown out the mental chatter only to be slapped in the face with reality. I had none.

You decided to quit, remember? clear-conscious Kateryna chimed in.

"I was kidding! I can't do this right now. I'm not ready to meet you," I said, panicked.

Keep searching the bag! I need a dose! codeine-fiend Katya demanded.

I dumped my purse on the kitchen floor while holding a lit cigarette between my lips. I prayed a sliver of a pill had gotten crushed at the bottom. I was prepared to lick the bag but came up empty-handed.

"No. We are doing this," I told myself. I had bargained with God for the family life and bright future I might have deserved. If I showed weakness, I knew I would lose Amir and be stuck in Cairo again. Or, worse, dead after a gang rape at some party. Starting over in Cairo was already an uphill battle. Popping pills to avoid my pain hadn't worked so far. I was terrified of what clarity would feel like, but I knew I couldn't keep going like this. I would die sooner rather than later.

Quitting cold turkey was the hardest thing I'd ever experienced. Not the aimless traveling, not my mother's abuse and neglect, not the rape, not living out of a car on the streets of LA—nothing had prepared me for what I would go through over the next thirty days. And the cherry on top? I did it in complete solitude and secrecy, in a cold apartment in the middle of Cairo. Looking back, I should have been under medical supervision. I didn't know then about opioid withdrawal syndrome and its life-threatening consequences.

Gaining clarity felt like slowly dying after being hit by a bus at full speed and bleeding to death face down on the porous asphalt. It was sheer torture—every joint in pain as though on fire, the uncontrollable twitching and twisting muscles, and the tsunami of depressive, judgmental thoughts. Cold night sweats and vivid dreams of falling and spinning had me waking up gasping for air. I would vomit uncontrollably at night, sobbing from the pain of even my feet touching the bathroom tile. During my puking episodes, my newfound clarity was not glamorous as I watched cockroaches scurry out from under the rug. I would scream and drop to my knees, holding my vomit in my hands, too scared to put my face in the toilet next to the skittish roaches.

I'd come close to full withdrawal mode, but it'd never been like this. I didn't even have alcohol to numb any of the symptoms. The first week of detox was hell on Earth. Every hour felt like an eternity without opioids in my system. Sounds, smells, and the sensation of touch were all amplified without the curtain of opioid bliss. The sensory overload brought on excruciating headaches. I took a lot of ibuprofen to manage the pain, and sometimes my body produced a placebo effect, tricking itself into thinking they were my special pills. I wanted to reach out for help, but in this hell, I was completely alone.

My ex-therapist would have been shocked to learn that I was a functioning addict, and even more so that she hadn't seen any of the signs. I wished my mother could be a friend since she had gotten me hooked in the first place, but after the confrontational episode in Vienna, I knew we probably wouldn't speak for another year or two.

By day, I became the new English teacher at Urban Toddlers, singing *Twinkle Twinkle Little Star* and dancing to the Madagascar soundtrack. With heart palpitations, hot flashes, and body aches, I struggled to keep my energy up. I told them I was sick. By night, I was Amir's girlfriend, attending gatherings with his friends and smoking shisha till midnight. He also thought I was sick. After midnight, I turned into my own therapist. I took cold showers and talked to myself in the mirror until my body shut down from exhaustion.

Think of your future, think of your kids, think of how much life you should be living. You are not your addiction. This is only temporary. This will pass.

I chanted these thoughts over and over, begging my brain to believe them.

A small victory came when I had a normal bowel movement without laxatives for the first time in ten years. I braced myself out of habit, wrinkling my face and biting down, but the waste came out easily. Stunned by this perk of sobriety, I felt a wave of guilt for hurting my body for so long. This emotional moment marked the beginning of the third week of sobriety, when my physical withdrawal symptoms finally subsided.

Minus a constant runny nose and trouble sleeping, the full-body exorcism became tolerable. But in week three, true anxiety set in. It was not the kind of anxiety I'd felt beneath the opioid blanket—this was restlessness and fear unlike anything I had ever experienced in my adult life. This anxiety was real, raw, and unfiltered.

In the hours before sunrise, I lay on the couch, unable to dream, watching the street below through the dirty living room windows. Then a blinding light went on in my head—I became aware of a horrifying truth so vivid that my soul hurt: I had completely ruined my life. I let out a long, silent, agonized scream. I had ruined my life. In that moment, it felt like I'd woken up back in my fifteen-year-old mind. The last ten years flashed through my head like a trailer to a new Stephen King movie. I hated myself for letting pills control me for a decade. A *decade*.

I replayed my college years and saw opportunities lost and wasted. Why had I left my high school sweetheart for Lucas? I'd never processed that choice, too high on pills to feel. We had been such a good match. And why had I let Lucas fly me around the world aimlessly in pursuit of his happiness and career? What about all the choices I hadn't made, like pursuing a career path I was proud of, because I was too preoccupied chasing my next fix? Who was I if I was not an addict?

I felt like a fraud, meeting myself for the first time. None of the pain I was running from could be healed with truckloads of synthetic opioids. Instead, the pain was amplified, as though I had been keeping it down like an inflated ball underwater. Everything, down to the gritty details of my sad childhood, came bobbing to the surface in that first conscious moment of clarity, awaiting to be processed.

To keep the tears coming, I fantasized about the life I could have had without pills. I replayed the last ten years, year by year, imagining different outcomes. I pictured myself as a typical American college graduate, sharing stories at BBQs about how my high school sweetheart and I had gotten to know each other at thirteen. I imagined hot summer nights in the hot tub, half-drunk beers, and our German Shepherd licking our faces.

I missed the life I could have had, with hair extensions and Sunday-night football games, camping trips, Metallica jam sessions, and the highlighted pages of graduate-level course books. I envisioned my mother visiting, us wearing matching stone jewelry, her smelling like lavender oil and inviting us to stay at her timeshare in Lake Tahoe. In my fantasies, she was sober and clean.

My real-life story repulsed me; it seemed foreign. I didn't want the memories of my bad decisions, my lies to get pills, and snorting said pills off toilet lids stored in my hippocampus. I didn't want the past few years I'd spent in Cairo, the rape, partying, Lucas, my mother—my entire childhood. Could I somehow reset that part of my brain? I didn't want to be me—not one bit. Shame and guilt coursed through my veins.

That morning, what was left of me in the mental boxing ring was a beaten young woman, stripped of her identity and chemical euphoria, in a smoked-out apartment on a rundown street in a third-world country. I prayed this would be my moment of complete transformation. I prayed for God's mercy to not let me down. I held myself, chanting, "It's going to be okay... It's going to be okay. I don't know how—but it's all uphill from here."

I calmed my tears, but anger soon followed. I despised my mother for her part in my pain. She was weak and had dragged me down with her, and I hated myself for allowing it.

Blaming her brought no peace to my new self. I still felt ashamed of who I was. But I had only been fifteen when I'd first gotten addicted to pills, my mind reasoned. That wasn't an excuse. I threw more punches at my ego. Self-loathing peaked as the sun finally rose over the Cairo Zoo. I wanted pills so much that I was sure I would relapse. The addict inside me plotted a visit to the pharmacy next to my work on Zamalek—a fresh one I hadn't yet conned. But a splash of cold water to my face brought me back.

Acceptance, my saving grace, was still out of reach. I wasn't ready to forgive myself. As sick and twisted as self-sabotage felt, I enjoyed feeling like a martyr. I wasn't done punishing myself. I finished my last cigarette from the pack and managed to say, "Thank you for being strong," to my wide-open pupils in the mirror. I looked more beautiful with a swollen face than I ever had with a numb, glossy-eyed opioid expression.

Closet detoxing was my biggest transformation to date, with no one there to witness it but God. It was all for Him, after all. There was no nurse or therapist cheering me on in a lobby full of loved ones. No release papers or referrals to specialists and yoga studios. No professionals reminding me that substance abuse and mental health disorders are chronic. It was just me, my thoughts, and the burning cigarettes.

Still raw from detox and fragile in my own skin, I met Amir's family about a month into my move. We arrived in his father's borrowed BMW, late at night as was the Arab world's routine, and I was reminded of the crutch my pills had been all these years. *God, I hope I don't embarrass myself and turn beet red,* I thought as we rode the elevator to the penthouse of the eleven-story building. Back home, I would have shown up with at least a glass of wine coursing through my veins, but that night I had to put my best, sober foot forward.

"Wow! You are so beautiful! Welcome! Come, come," Nadeen said in broken English, kissing each of my cheeks. Amir only smiled in approval and followed me in.

Mr. Sabry appeared with a wide grin, shaking both of my hands gently and adding a small bow. Amir's sister ran out of her room and swooped me into a tight, Western-style hug, the kind reserved for sisters.

It was clear Amir had painted me in the brightest light on their family's walls. As we ate a spread of lamb leg, chicken four ways, rice, salads, and lentil soup, the conversation circled around my travels, the States, and the New York City restaurants the Sabrys frequented.

Not once did I feel uncomfortable or judged. For a few hours, I even forgot I was an addict in detox, seamlessly blending into their large living area lit by three chandeliers and filled with polished French antiques. I spoke freely and was even allowed to smoke my cigarettes indoors. Apart from slipping away to the bathroom a few times to settle my post-opioid stomach, I didn't want to leave their company.

The evening ended with family photos and grainy home videos —Amir dancing on tabletops as a toddler, and Nadeen posing with her perfectly groomed children, dressed in a velvet-tight dress and a choker far too stylish for the nineties. Only once did a craving hit, when I fought back unexpected tears, realizing that a mother—not my own—was capable of grace, love, and overwhelming hospitality; and she offered it, without expectation, to me.

In the months that followed, I fought cravings three to four times a day, relying on extra nicotine to get me through. I focused on the fact that I needed a new persona; there was only so much self-hate I could tolerate. Before, I'd hidden behind the pain of my trauma; my identity had been defined by my broken childhood. My excuses for making mistakes had stemmed from being an addict. Now, getting used to my new high—clarity—left a big gap in my self-perception. Slowly, I began to accept that my slate was now clean. I had survived the worst of my journey on Earth. This had to be the beginning of something extraordinary. God should be proud—surely, He would reward me for all this hard work.

However, I couldn't accept the chaotic environment I was in. I felt like a wrongly accused inmate, awaiting my trial date and release while trapped in a dirty cell. That cell was Cairo. Apart from the refuge I sometimes sought in the Sabrys' home, I became aware that I was too good for Cairo by living the same night over and over again. There were only so many dinners out I could take, shishas I could smoke, and friendless days I could spend. Not to mention the sexual harassment on the streets and the fact that my Arabic was getting good enough to understand when I was referred to as a "prostitute from Hurghada."

"I'm depressed, Amir. I don't want to live here. I really want to move back to the USA. We can go together and start a new life there. You always talk about opening a cafe and shisha bar. We can do that in the States," I vented to him over tea and shisha one night.

"Maybe that's not a bad idea," he said. "We need to come up

with a business plan and let my parents know. But we aren't married yet; they won't just let me go."

"I want to see the mountains. I want to ride my motorcycle and go on road trips. I want to paint in the park on Saturdays like I used to do back home. I want to run again. I was doing five-and-a-half-minute miles! I need to see trees, grass, and big open spaces. I want to do my art. I want to go on hikes. I want to do all that with you. I want to live with you!" I pleaded, tears forming behind my eyes.

"I see... Katya, life isn't only about trees and mountains. I'm doing all I can to make you happy. Don't you see that? You need to try and adapt to being here. What about getting more friends? We can move you to Zamalek, near your work. There are a lot of trees there, by the way," he said.

"I try to be friends with the girls in your group. We are just too different," I replied, dropping my somber gaze to the floor.

It was true; my contributions to their conversations were too far-fetched. I wanted to talk about the economy and foreign politics, learn Arabic, and discuss the unfair wages for women in Egypt. But most of them didn't work and were rich and taken care of. They didn't have hobbies like I did—art, running, writing, and cooking. Their conversation topics were shallow, revolving around cute clothing styles, the best cafes, and vacation spots. Even though they spoke English fluently, by the end of the night, everyone switched back to Arabic, leaving me sitting there blowing smoke rings from the shisha pipe.

"Okay, you know what? We should go to the North Coast! Or maybe to the Red Sea for some seafood. I need to sell a few more apartments and check my finances, but we can plan an amazing trip. A good reset," he said, lifting my gaze from the floor.

"That sounds nice. I do need a reset," I quietly agreed.

"And after that, we can see about moving you to Zamalek! There are a lot of foreigners living there you could meet. Now, cheer up. I don't like to see you sad and crying. You are too beautiful to be sad," he said, reaching out his manicured hand to touch mine.

. . .

Zamalek was no better. It was just another turd covered in gold foil. It was loud, polluted with standstill traffic, and filled with harassers —albeit with better English—on every corner. Despite being a third-world country, this man-made, one-square-mile, affluent island in the middle of the Nile housed many trees, which made me feel closer to my past life in Reno. Most foreign embassies and many European expats lived here. Rent was hard to come by, but saying you lived in Zamalek carried a certain prestige.

Amir—with the help of his loving mother—moved me and completely furnished my new tower. I lived at 35 Ahmed Heshmat Road, third floor, apartment 'a la shimel' on the left. The corner building faced a relatively quiet street, at the time.

Since we rented the place during the holy month of Ramadan in mid-June, we failed to notice the secondary experimental school for girls and the nuisance it would bring. I didn't know what they were experimenting with, but when school was in session in September, groups of twelve-year-old girls would catcall and hiss at me, forcing me to defend my dignity with my broken Arabic.

Every bus and micro-bus, unloaded these new types of harassers, parked bumper-to-bumper right on the cross street, precisely under my bedroom window. "TAILA, TAILA, TAILA (COME, COME, COME)!" the parking man shouted each morning around 6:40 a.m., helping the big buses back up into the narrow, now unusable, street. The cars parked so tightly you could barely squeeze between them on foot, and the traffic on the one-way Ahmed Heshmat moved an inch a minute.

Earplugs didn't help. My new Ikea bed sheets and memory foam pillow didn't help. Painting the apartment in my chosen colors— burgundy, Tiffany green, and beige—didn't help. We even got an Italian Mastiff puppy, Onyx, to get me out of bed and scare off harassers. But the therapy dog only left me with flea bites and a piss-stained balcony. I quit my job to avoid walking the streets. Every week, I isolated myself more, finding reasons not to leave the apartment. I couldn't face Cairo, not with my depression keeping me in bed. I lay there in complete stillness, focusing only on the reasons why I needed to leave this country: I needed more personal freedom, to go on hikes, to drive my own car, maybe even to go back to school and continue my career.

"Come on, Katya, be happy, please," Amir asked me. He came by every night to either take me out of my tower for dinner or bring takeout. Then we would smoke grape-flavored shisha, copulate, and part ways before midnight. Our intercourse became problematic for me; it was an unprotected daily occurrence and the only thing that brought me pleasure in my mundane existence, creating another unhealthy attachment.

"What would you do if you came here one day and I was gone?" I asked him one night during our pillow talk.

"Nothing," he said, running his fingers through my hair.

"You wouldn't chase me?" I asked.

"No, if you want to leave, then leave. It would just tell me that you don't appreciate anything," he replied.

Suddenly, the apartment warped into a familiar hell. The Arabic infomercials blaring in the background and the weird shadows the swaying banyan trees painted over the walls reminded me of a place I'd felt trapped in before. I teleported back to the apartment in Los Angeles where I'd been forced to live with the handicapped professional pervert—the child abuser who'd made me watch porn and model lingerie for him.

My mind reasoned that it was my depression and opioid clarity playing tricks on me, removing me from my comfortable reality. How could I compare the man I loved to the child abuser from my teenage years? *Stop that!* I told myself.

I snuggled deeper into Amir's chest.

"Do you think you're addicted to sex?" I abruptly changed the subject.

"I enjoy it very much with you. I want you all the time. I don't know. Isn't every man addicted?" he replied.

"I guess I'm worried I'll get pregnant," I replied.

"I would love a child from you. You know, I dream of having a beautiful little girl with you...one day," he said.

"If I got pregnant, would you marry me?" I asked.

"Taban! (Of course!) Without hesitation," he said.

"I, too, want a little girl," I said, kissing him on his full lips.

Maybe he would move for the child, I thought. I wasn't planning on getting pregnant as just a ticket out, but I believed he would leave Cairo if a child's future was at stake. How could anyone not want to leave Cairo? As an American, I could bring him to the States with my citizenship if we were married. Surely, he'd want his family to have a better, freer, and cleaner life than we could in Cairo. I needed to give him enough reasons to move with me. I needed to get out of Cairo, but I didn't want to lose him in the process.

After another month of staring at the ceiling, I forced myself to snap out of my longing for a life back in the USA and accept my reality. The new persona that clarity had left me in search of had voluntarily chosen me. My ruthless, under-the-influence decisions had chosen me. Lucas sending me off to Cairo was an action that had chosen the new me. His contract to marriage had filtered me out of his life and put me in this lonely island apartment. Amir rescuing and supporting me had left me on the only real path ahead: to someday be his bride. I had to set aside my desire to run away again and face the honking cars' music.

On one hand, it wasn't fair to Amir to be constantly unhappy when he was doing all he could to keep me comfortable. On the other hand, I hadn't been in my right mind when I'd made those decisions and ended up here. I hadn't been right in choosing my next wanderlusting adventure, especially in leaving Reno to experience life abroad. I had to stop being a victim of my poor decisions and make the best of the cards I held. But doing so sober was overwhelming.

'Looking for expat friends on Zamalek,' I posted on a Cairo Facebook group. I needed Western friends. To my surprise, I gathered a group of five women. We regularly met up at the island's coffee shops. I became close friends with three of them: an American/Mexican flamboyant chica living here with her American diplomat boyfriend, a talkative and classy Canadian married to a mega-rich Egyptian man, and a shy German girl living with her Christian Egyptian boyfriend. I liked Pascal—the Canadian—the most.

During our meetups, we did our best to keep it positive, but our conversation often drifted negative. We needed to vent and complain about how crazy life in Egypt was for us. It was cleansing and therapeutic, but sometimes, it turned too dark.

"You can't take Egypt out of an Egyptian. And don't have kids with an Arab. I've been in Cairo for seventeen years now. Not by choice but to be with my son. My ex and I got married in Florida, and he took our son back after a year living there. My son is almost eighteen, and I can't wait to leave," said the Florida woman. She was the most bitter.

"I'm sorry to hear that. Amir is not like that! His family is very Westernized. His dad works for the Office of Arab Affairs, a respectable man. I love his mother very much; she is so nice to me! Takes me clothes shopping, brings me home-cooked meals. Plus, they have family on the East and West Coasts of America. I do believe Amir when he says he will one day move with me back to the USA," I countered the negativity.

The Sabry family seemed very Westernized at the time. They spoke English and had close family in the States. His mother didn't wear a veil, his father admitted to drinking wine with European diplomats, his sister could barely write in Arabic, and I never saw her pray. Yet, Islam still wove through their daily lives. His sister couldn't ride in cars with boys, no one drank alcohol at home, no one ate pork, Amir and his father attended Friday prayers, and no one could move out of the house unless married.

"Ha! You caught the MMID syndrome!" The Florida woman laughed in my face. "My Mohammed Is Different," she said, wiping tears from her eyes. "They are all the same, honey. Remember that! No matter what he says to you, what their family does, or how much they travel. Their blood is thicker than tar."

I never invited Florida woman to coffee again. Her words, which brought back memories of Lucas, felt like a glitch in the matrix. I needed to focus on the positive aspects of my unconventional life. I had been accepted into a prestigious and kind Egyptian family. They took care of me more than my own parents ever had. I'd quit pills! I was ten months sober already, and with that, I knew God wouldn't let me down. That was our deal, and He'd shown me the sign of repeating sevens. I was on the right path; the devil was in the details.

12

BRIDE OR DROWN
(OCTOBER 2016)

Amir and I had a good—even great—relationship by Egyptian standards. These were standards I didn't fully agree with but had to accept due to our circumstances. Our biggest problem, aside from not being able to plan any life-changing events until we were married, was living in Cairo. We were stuck in a Muslim society with rules to follow, unable to escape the social expectations that defined Cairo. The Egyptian web had been spun, and we were both trapped in it.

Amid the silent nights and loneliness of living in Zamalek, I realized our relationship was very codependent due to these social rules. I depended on Amir for everything: money, entertainment, food, shelter, friendship, mental support, and, most importantly, my future. He held the keys to it all.

Could I get a high-paying job here? Most likely not, as I wasn't connected within their society. I could teach English and make very little money, but working for a company would require not only fluency in Arabic but also extra protection from Amir to ward off men in power and their harassment. Most women here, even my expat friends, didn't work. Amir took care of me fully, and in Egypt, they would call him 'caring,' 'supportive,' and 'the ultimate provider.' But in the Western world, those are all red flags for total control and manipulation.

I was torn between accepting the codependency, thereby giving him the control, or sticking to my Western expectation of being independent. I convinced myself that I would still choose Amir as my partner even if we had a wholesome Western relationship. I loved him, right? Or was this so-called love merely a byproduct of victimhood and disappointment from Lucas's contract? It was hard to find an answer amidst the guilt of being an ex-addict.

I regularly woke up with a knot in my stomach, as though caught sneaking back into the house at 3 a.m. on a school night. My thoughts immediately jumped to Lucas. He would be so disappointed in my current situation. He would tell me, "Do not depend on a man." His contract had explicitly stated that.

"No, Lucas. You are wrong! A woman should depend on her man," I would say to my dog. He would wag his tail in support. How could I make sense of what was really best for me? Codeine would have known the answer! She always did. But it was Clarity that I'd chosen to make sense of the mayhem.

I kept Lucas's contract by my bedside, re-reading it to reassure myself that Middle Eastern values were more aligned with my Ukrainian ones. I hoped that the more I accepted the Muslim family expectations, the less Lucas's contract would make sense. Slowly, I surrendered to the path of a soon-to-be wife of a Muslim man.

Whenever Amir and his family discussed real estate—with its high prices in Egypt and the lack of a banking system to secure loans—I'd always redirect the conversation to how wonderful mortgages were in America. When he complained about his low commission split for selling high-dollar apartments, I'd remind him that in the States, agents could charge five or six percent. His mother would complain about the high cost of imported goods in Egypt—fruit, designer clothes, electronics—and I'd quickly respond that our outlet malls were fantastic and produce of all kinds was readily available year-round.

Amir could sense that I was on edge. My contributions to the conversations around his family's table started to sound more like complaints than helpful suggestions. He knew all too well that I could leave at any moment, given my history of sporadic traveling. He noticed I'd lost the sparkle in my eyes. I stopped meeting him at the apartment door with lustful kisses and spent more time on the phone with my Canadian friend, Pascal, complaining and comparing the world we lived in with the world we'd left.

What Amir didn't know was that I was pill-free, making it impossible to make any decisions. The addict in me had created this mess; when the mask was removed, I couldn't believe I'd made so many impulsive decisions. I wanted to take back fifteen years of my life and start over.

Lacking self-esteem and any ability to make clear decisions, I put my trust in Amir, hoping he would make the right decisions for us. After all, being the leader in the family is the pious Muslim responsibility.

"What's your biggest fear?" Amir asked one evening. We'd been silently smoking our shisha, and I hadn't smiled at him all night.

Being stuck in Egypt for the rest of my life, I wanted to say.

"Drowning," I replied. *Actually, that's what being stuck in Egypt feels like.*

"Really? Why's that?" he asked.

"It's the only unknown that truly terrifies me. Like, does it hurt when the water fills your lungs? Does fresh water burn more or less than salt water? Is it easier to let go with water in your lungs? Does the person fight till the end? Or do they come to the conclusion that it's pointless and just surrender to God's mercy? It must be terrifying, knowing you are fighting for your life but your time has come to move on to the next," I said.

"I can see that. I guess for me, burning to death would be worse," he replied.

"Maybe. But drowning is an ironic and an almost romantic way to die. We once breathed fluid in the womb. Drowning would be the ultimate way to go out of this world; the same way as you came into the world, breathing water," I continued.

"Wow, you've really thought about this. I love how deep you are," he replied.

"Ha, maybe that is a little too deep," I said. I was shocked to realize that my response had come from Kateryna, the little girl who spent too much time alone, lounging on a tree branch, contemplating how the brain actually worked.

If Katya still ran the show, asking for more pills to silence the know-it-all, way-too-deep Kateryna, I would have had a different response to Amir, one that wouldn't have derailed his small talk. She would have said, *Base jumping! But we should do that someday anyways!*

"What do you want most?" Amir continued. His questions were different than usual, and he wasn't fully lounging in his chair. "Wait, I will answer—living in a forest in a tree house!" He laughed.

"That would be amazing! And I will someday. But—I guess I want a family. A healthy family," I said, almost sheepishly.

"You'll have that one day," he said with a big grin on his face.

Yeah, but not in Egypt, I wanted to say.

Family. Coming from a few broken ones, it's a fairytale concept to me. But it's all I want and hopefully deserve. I marvel at marriages that last decades. "How do they keep choosing one another day after day?" I asked my mother once.

"Cheating," she replied. "Men have to cheat and keep spreading their seed in order to feel fulfilled. You know, having sex with their wife, a prostitute, or jerking off in the bathroom is the same for a man. That's why they can buy sex and still orgasm, because the sacred act of procreation to a man is purely physical sensation, never mental. They need a warm, moist hole to get out their egos and still can go home to their wives because they are taking care of them and making them feel wanted. They are just children at heart, and not one man wants to be lonely and unneeded. They can't survive alone. They need constant reassurance that they belong. A woman can." She gave me this reply as though reading from her burn book on men. A part of me agreed with her; the other part knew that people could be faithful to one another, and that true love does exist.

I wanted to ask Amir what he thought about cheating. But what man would say it's okay? According to Islam, a man can have many wives, but only after the first wife gives her blessing. I didn't feel like getting into another religious discussion with him.

"Katya, I want to take you tomorrow to pick out rings," he said, eyes as bright as the day I'd met him.

"Rings for engagement?" I asked, scooting to the edge of my seat.

"Yes. In Egypt, we exchange rings in front of our family and get their blessing. I would like to do that. Will you marry me?" he asked, blowing shisha smoke out of his nostrils.

Did I love Amir? *Yes, I'm still in Cairo for him—I must love him.* I loved how he'd cared for me over the past two years. He'd supported me physically and mentally, chasing me around the world no matter the circumstances. The only thing I wanted to change about our relationship was for us to leave Egypt and start fresh in the USA. There, I could be happy, too; my current lack of happiness clouded my understanding of whether I wanted this marriage.

But if we were married, I reasoned, I would have a lot more say in setting my expectations. Muslim men are required to maintain their bride at the living standards she was accustomed to at home. Where was my home? What standards had I shown Amir to maintain? A nomadic traveler with mom issues. Homeless and thrown out by her own parents.

"Yes! I will. I do!" I answered, holding his outstretched hand. We were in public and unable to exchange hugs or kisses.

. . .

We got engaged on October 28th, 2016, ten months after my return to Cairo. The Sabry family, mom, dad, and younger sister, were all gathered around a round table in the bustling dinner lounge of the Ritz Carlton.

"Yella!" Amir laughed, all giddy, pulling the ring out of the black box on the table and motioning for my hand. He slid the gold band on and sealed it with a kiss to my forehead, as Arabic house music played in the background. It was nothing like the traditional Islamic engagement, usually hosted in the bride's home with both families present and the Al-Fatiha—the opening verse of the Qur'an—recited to seal the promise. And it was nothing like the engagement I had envisioned, overlooking a valley from the top of a mountain as my sweaty groom-to-be pretended to tie his shoe before pulling out a ring on one knee.

I struggled with his ring as his sister filmed me gritting my teeth, pulling exaggerated faces, and wiggling the band until it finally slid on. Everyone broke into laughter and clapped. "Welcome to the family!" his father yelled.

Nadeen pointed to her husband and said, "Same! Like me," reenacting the struggle I had just gone through with Amir's ring.

"You will be the most beautiful bride!" his sister said, raising her voice above the music.

We all stood from the table to exchange hugs and kisses. Nadeen wiped happy tears from her eyes, kissed my ring, and held me in a long, warm embrace.

We celebrated our engagement, unconventional in both cultures, by cutting a large cake topped with tropical fruit, then gathered for group photos on the terrace overlooking the twinkling lights of downtown Cairo and their reflection in the Nile. That night, I couldn't wait to post the photos and videos of my gold band and curly hair on social media. I wanted everyone to see that I had made it—that I was doing the big-girl thing, getting married to a handsome foreigner at twenty-seven years old.

I was relieved to be engaged, but I also hoped Amir loved me enough for the both of us, because my love depended on us leaving Egypt, just as I had wanted from the beginning. I had a plan to keep myself from drowning: we would marry officially in Kyiv to begin the immigration papers to the USA. The United States recognized Ukrainian marriages under common law, whereas Egyptian marriages were only valid if done as a civil ceremony in court. I didn't want Amir jeopardizing this by settling for a ceremony and a 'writing in the holy book'—a purely religious wedding. It wasn't that I doubted his desire to take me as his bride and eventually immigrate with me to the USA; I simply didn't trust the Egyptian system, where faith and law were so tangled together.

13
UNION AND REUNION
(JANUARY 2017)

'A woman is like the river,' I wrote in my journal on Christmas night in Cairo. *'She flows with force and emotions and turns as she pleases. Like water, she carves her path despite obstacles and unruly terrain. She gives life and carries life. The man; he is the river's banks. He is to be strong and stable so she can lean into him. He is to contain her force and build up higher walls if she is to overflow. He is to support and guide her powerful flow. He is to give her structure and wholeness in life. He gives her purpose and beauty. Together they are in harmony, one incomplete without the other. A woman is not her true self without the need of support; and a man prides himself on being that supporter and bearer of her happiness. When in balance, they are both unstoppable.'*

I hadn't journaled since my travel days with Lucas, when scribbling in notebooks kept me grounded in foreign places. Now I had picked it up again. My true Kateryna self had been making many appearances, mostly in my late-night thoughts and on those pages. I was slowly getting to know Kateryna—the version of me I'd buried in my teens. It felt as if I were letting her catch up to the real world after she'd been asleep for over a decade. She still had a lot of processing and learning to do, and writing out her beliefs helped.

Amir and I arranged to be married in Kyiv at the beginning of 2017. He was the bank to my wild, raging river. I expected him to be strong and stable so I could lean into him. I felt powerful when standing next to him. I felt wanted, accepted, and valued. I truly felt that his love for me would carry us to a fresh start back in the USA, where my water wanted to flow. I figured I'd made my wants clear and that he'd accepted them with a promise of marriage. We even searched for places to move to in Sacramento and explored housing options. Together, I was willing to go through anything, as long as it was not in Cairo.

I didn't want to believe that—with such a serious commitment —he had another agenda. My heart longed to believe I was worthy of a healthy, true love between a man and a woman, especially after being let down by so many people around me. My mother always saw the world as bad, convinced that everyone was out to screw her over—and that was exactly what she got. Your thoughts create your reality, and I chose to focus on the positive to shape a better outcome for myself.

With all that in mind, I still wasn't entirely confident in our marriage, but I brushed off my doubt as cold feet. Looking back, I realize my perspective on romance had always been idealistic. I idealized Lucas, and now, I was doing the same with Amir, painting him in a glowing light. Perhaps it was my longing for a perfect, healthy love that made me overlook his flaws. If I focused on the positive and believed in this love, maybe it would manifest. But a part of me still wondered—was I just repeating old patterns, chasing an ideal that might not exist?

. . .

Amir and I landed in Kyiv and were welcomed at the airport by my father, my step-grandpa, and Masha. I felt a surge of excitement as I watched my father give Amir a big hug and carry his luggage. By that point, my father had accepted him, though it hadn't always been that way. At the beginning of our relationship, he would remind me, "I am not saying they are bad people, I'm just saying they are different, and eventually you will come to see that. But let's hope it all works out!" I took his comments with a grain of salt, as I always did. Now, I was happy to see my father welcome Amir with open arms.

But my father had always been more of an advisor than a parent —forever grateful, I still loved him, forever eager to please me. His hug to Amir was just another reflection of that, a way to show me his support in the choices I made. Watching them together reminded me how far I'd come on my own without my father's guidance—or perhaps, how lost I'd become without it.

Arriving at my grandma's apartment in the dead of winter felt depressing. The gray sky, monochrome block apartments, and sad faces at the bus stops added to the gloom. I thought, *Wow, I've come such a long way from here.* I'd gone from a five-hundred-and-forty-square-foot apartment in which five people lived to the USA, then I'd become a world traveler and a bride-to-be to a high-status Oud-Wood-smelling Egyptian powerlifter. Right then, my mother's toxicity sabotaged my happiness: *If it wasn't for me taking you to the USA, you wouldn't have such a nice life.*

I grew up poor in Lysoviy Masyv, a neighborhood on the northeast outskirts of Kyiv, at the last stop on the red metro line. Despite its high crime, drug, and alcohol abuse rates, I have only fond memories of my childhood. Locals know Lysoviy Masyv for its big outdoor secondhand markets and as the departure point for cheap fare for buses heading farther east. We learned to avoid needles on the ground but were encouraged to collect empty glass bottles from drunks passed out in ditches and the surrounding forest. We recycled these bottles for five kopiok each; if we collected enough, we could buy bread and butter for the week.

My mother and grandmother had my aunt and me gather cigarette butts in a jar to salvage the tobacco so they could roll their own cigarettes. My dessert was often the ends of the bread loaf dampened with water and sprinkled with sugar, and, if we were lucky, drizzled with honey we got from the neighbors. Despite the poverty and harsh conditions, I felt happy and free, with a hundred-acre woods as my playground just a minute's walk from our nine-story block apartment.

Amir was on his best behavior around my family, being polite and social. I felt so proud to show him off as my groom. During our brief visit to Ukraine in the summer of 2016, he had already become accustomed to our Ukrainian middle-class way of life. However, the Middle Eastern flair didn't quite fit in with the Soviet blocks in Lysoviy Masyv. I asked him not to wear so much cologne and to leave his Prada shoes behind, as people here were merely surviving. I warned him that he might get jumped. Amir's nature was to show off his status and designer tags, as it was customary in the Arab world to gain respect. In Ukraine, only the corrupt rich oligarchs did that. I asked him to blend in as much as possible. Arabs faced some discrimination in Ukraine, as they were often seen as dirty businessmen.

I called Victoria, our Ukrainian lawyer with whom I'd been working via Viber. "Do you have the papers ready?"

"Good day, Kateryna. Yes, we should be ready to go. I'll text you Zak's address. You're planning for tomorrow, correct?" she answered.

"Yes, tomorrow! Very excited." I smiled, looking at my husband-to-be as he ate the eggs I'd made for his breakfast.

To celebrate, we went clubbing in the wealthy area of downtown Kyiv that night. The best-rated clubs are hangouts for wealthy and super-wealthy men, watering holes for the hairy Turks, Middle Easterners, and Israelis. Amir was the son of an important Egyptian diplomat, and he fit right into the crowd. This was the perfect place for him to show off his Prada shoes. We dressed in our most luxurious outfits and took an expensive cab to a club on the bank of the Dnipro River. The music was deep, but the crowd was shallow. I left Amir at the bar for a few minutes to go to the ladies' room, and when I came back, an elite prostitute was fishing for him.

"Excuse me, I was here first," said the Barbie-doll brunette, edging me away from Amir at the bar as I wedged myself between him and the seat she had just taken.

I broke out in hysterical laughter. The woman crinkled her nose at me in disgust, her head cocked slightly to the left.

"He is my husband. I am not here working," I said loudly enough for the rest of the onlookers to hear.

The girl stood up and left quickly with her sidekick.

"What was all that?" Amir asked, looking innocent. "What just happened, Katya?"

"Come on, Amir, you didn't know they're sex workers? She was hitting on you. What was she saying?" I asked. When I'd walked back from the bathroom, I'd seen the prostitute talking into his ear and Amir laughing and throwing his head back. He'd turned and looked at her dead in the eyes as he'd sipped his drink, seemingly about to respond before I'd interrupted.

He started laughing. "Come here," he said, pulling me into his chest. "You don't have to worry. I am your man, you know that, right?"

"Yes, but you were talking to her. I saw you. Never mind," I said, forcing a confident smile. For the first time, I felt jealous. My heart raced; I didn't like feeling threatened.

I hadn't expected anything or anyone to ruin our outing, but Amir's need for attention already had. He was handsome and craved attention, especially as a foreigner amongst Eastern-European beauties whose ideal image of a man was him: bearded, dark-skinned, exotic, and wearing a Rolex—and Amir was well aware of this. I knew my soon-to-be husband well; he put on a persona as if he was experienced with many women, but I knew I was his third, maybe fourth woman ever. He was just a boy still and didn't know what to do when he got attention from a beautiful woman. I brushed off that encounter.

Waking up on my wedding day in my childhood home felt surreal. Never had I thought I would be back in my home country on such an important day. I always dreamt of eloping, and with Lucas. I could hear my father's and grandma's voices in the kitchen already. I sat up slowly, looking out the window to see a crisp yellow winter morning. I turned to Amir, sleeping beside me, and thought, *This better be the best thing for us both.*

Instead of feeling joy, my mind raced with the challenges ahead: immigration, the Egyptian wedding, the business Amir still needed to complete to afford the move, and my lack of resources to help financially. Our cultural and socioeconomic differences suddenly seemed glaring; his family owned mansions by the Red Sea and had servants while my family was in a five-hundred-and-forty-square-foot apartment in Kyiv's ghetto. No one in my family could afford name-brand shoes, let alone Prada. Despite my doubts, I smiled at him, knowing he loved me for who I was, not for my past or upbringing.

"Good morning *wife*," my father said once I left our bedroom. He was sitting in his coat on the couch.

"Good morning," I said, sitting on the stool next to the small dining table.

"Here it is," he said, pulling out a plastic liter bottle of what looked like Pinot Noir. "Homemade wine!"

Grandma was rinsing out the glasses. "I'm coming, too!" she said with mischievous laughter.

Dad poured me a tall glass of moonshine wine. Without saying a word or waiting for a toast, I drank it down in four big gulps.

"Wait," Dad said. "Grandma, come here and have a drink with your granddaughter, soon-to-be wife."

Grandma, still dressed in her robe, sat next to him and held up her glass. "Katya, don't worry, all will be well. He is a wonderful man, and you deserve that. All the other little things will work out. People change their lives all the time. Just laugh and think about having kids with him. Once you are a mother, things will settle down. Ha, and maybe I get to visit you guys so I can share stories with our neighbors." She spilled out her toast with a big smile then chugged her glass.

Amir had been very polite around my family. He stood up when my grandma entered the room and made a slight bow when greeting my father. He asked if my grandma needed groceries when he ran errands and always brought something back for her, my grandpa, or my sisters. He insisted on paying for everything, always asking how much things cost and leaving money on the counter. He knew exactly how to act as a guest in someone's home: bringing gifts, cleaning up after himself, and engaging fully in conversations. Unlike Lucas, who had brought tampons when coming to stay at my Cairo apartment, Amir brought artifacts from Egypt and exotic Middle Eastern pastries into a Ukrainian home.

"Yes, he is wonderful," I said, already feeling the twenty-percent alcohol content of the wine hitting my head. How did they know I was hesitating? If I were still taking pills, I would have passed up the drink and been content with my codeine high. I probably wouldn't have been hesitating, either, as my doubts would have been silenced under the opioid spell. It'd been thirteen months since my last dose, and I was proud of myself for getting that far.

At that moment, Amir walked in, gave a small wave, and said a broken, "Dobroe ytro!" before heading to the bathroom.

"Good morning! Husband! Look at you, so sweet!" my grandma said in Russian, smiling at him and grabbing my arm.

"Drink?" grandma asked in her broken English as Amir came out of the restroom, motioning to him to come over to the couch.

Amir came to the couch and shook my father's hand with both hands. My father smiled at him, patted him on the back, and poured him half a glass of homemade wine, a simple gesture of acceptance. He was proud to offer something from his own hands to his soon-to-be first son-in-law. I could see the anticipation in his eyes as he awaited Amir's reaction to the taste.

I was glad my father was here, supportive and contributing in any way he could to make Amir feel celebrated. Even if he didn't truly want to, he still tried. I never asked for my father's honest opinion on my marriage, knowing I wouldn't take his advice if it was negative. If my mother were here, she would have been making it clear that she did not accept Amir, stone-cold and leaking wrath. She was too honest in her opinion, especially after a drink of moonshine wine.

I sensed that Amir was as nervous as I was that morning. We tried to hide our nerves with alcohol for breakfast. I stared into Amir's eyes across the table, and he stared back. Something in his eyes kept me moving forward. Eventually, I smiled, and he did, too. In my buzzed state, I felt sure that all these leaps of faith had brought us to this very moment, and the big finale was soon to come.

The last time I'd sat at this table, I had been dealing with my breakup with Lucas, and Amir had been assuring me it would be okay. Now, I was moving forward to my next chapter, with my then-friend becoming my husband.

"Let's get dressed. We have to be there in two hours." I stood up, grabbing Amir's hand.

I despised winter celebrations. Apart from New Year's Eve, celebrating anything in the dead of winter felt uncomfortable. Everything was cold and indoors, with muddy, snowy boots from flu-infected guests. I hated stepping outside for a cigarette break and dealing with coats piled on a couch, lost gloves, and sweaty hats. Dangerous road conditions and drunk drivers only added to the misery. Of course, I never expressed this and just 'accepted and adapted.'

January 24, 2017, marked a cold celebration I had to accept and adapt to. Years of moving around with my mother, traveling out of a backpack, and lacking the self-esteem to stand up for what I wanted had ingrained in me this 'accept and adapt' mentality. On my court wedding day, I wore a salmon-colored office dress because I couldn't find a white one. I settled. I wanted a big curly blowout, but the blizzard outside closed the nearest hair salon, so I settled for small roses plucked from my cream-and-white bouquet pinned into my bun. I put on dark red lipstick, which I never wore.

Looking in the mirror, I noticed that I looked like my mother had on the day she'd married her American husband. She hadn't worn a traditional white dress, either; she'd worn a hideous, light purple Barbie dress. She'd also worn small white and purple roses in her hair and dark red lipstick. I absolutely hated our resemblance and felt struck with fear that my marriage would end up like hers—leaving me a divorcee with a baby in my arms.

Was this a coincidence, or was I following some generational curse, haunted by the need to break it? Somehow, even by not being here, my mother was ruining my wedding day. Despite the physical resemblance to my mother, I was not manipulative, a drunk, or a drug addict anymore; thus, I figured, there was no chance for me to be following in her footsteps. "Please, let this be the right decision for myself and my future," I asked of God, just to be safe.

Eleven of my family members gathered at the Zaks marriage court branch to support my decision. Amir and I arrived feeling pretty buzzed. We walked in and greeted everyone in the carpeted room in which a large Ukrainian flag was draped in the background.

My Ukrainian isn't very good. I understand about sixty percent of the spoken words, but since I grew up in the USSR, we were taught Russian more than Ukrainian. I worried about not understanding what the lady would ask us during the swearing-in and that I wouldn't know when to answer. The homemade wine in my veins helped me relax a bit.

Standing next to Amir at the podium, the petite brunette officer asked me first, "Do you, Kateryna Dunko, take Amir Adbel Khir—I'm sorry I can't pronounce all of this—Mr. Sabry, to be your lawfully wedded husband and vow to be there for him through sickness and health?"

"Da," I said in Russian with a smirk.

"Please sign here," she replied, pointing to a line on a pink-boarded marriage certificate decorated with a large Ukrainian Coat of Arms at the top. The Ukrainian Coat of Arms looks like a trident with the word "воля," (freedom) encrypted into the image. I have that trident tattooed on the back of my neck.

"Do you, Mr. Sabry, take Kateryna Ivanova Dunko to be your lawfully wedded wife and vow to be there for her through sickness and health?" She turned to him with a sweet smile.

I translated into his ear.

"Tak," he replied in Ukrainian. I watched him from the corner of my eye as he signed on the line.

Amir stood confidently, bowed slightly with his eyes, and gently squeezed my hand in excitement. These were all telltale signs of authenticity; he was fully on board with the marriage. Even if I butchered the translation, he was committed to this marriage. But was I on board?

"Love, protect, and respect each other! Today you are handed your first family document—a marriage certificate. I pass it on to the head of the family. Take care of it, and may your life never be lonely but be a real holiday where joy and mutual understanding reign," the officer proclaimed to us and my family.

As Amir received the processed piece of tree bark, my heart raced as I did my best to translate those powerful words into his ear. "May your life never be lonely..." *I am already lonely back in Cairo*, I thought.

We sealed our civil Ukrainian marriage with a kiss, and my family cheered as though Ronaldo had just scored a winning goal.

I didn't feel as happy as our spectators did. There were obvious bad things about this decision that I just couldn't shake: I was still living in Egypt, and now, as my husband, Amir controlled my every move and how much money I had and what I spent it on. Amir had said, "A bride will be a reflection of me and my family." Did that mean I had to be a certain way?

My family, clapping at our new married status, was nothing like the elite Egyptian family to whom I now belonged. I felt almost angry at them for giving me away for Amir's taking. I felt especially angry at my father for not having asked Amir about his plans for me and for not having told Amir, 'My Katya can only be your bride if you can provide a life for her outside of Egypt.' That was what any Muslim father would have done.

My family took turns gifting us with flowers, and we all posed for group photos. My smile was wide, but that salmon-colored dress, I felt, ruined every picture. The whole ceremony lasted just fifteen minutes. Afterward, we rented a large dimly lit dining room at a nice Georgian restaurant in downtown Kyiv. Amir and I fed each other cake, drank shots of vodka with Grandma, and endured a cold, joyous indoor celebration filled with awkward silences. By 10 p.m., I was sick of translating and called it quits. We had been drunk since 9 a.m. My new husband and I passed out in our clothes for the night.

The magic and excitement of our wedding day were forgotten during our three-day, self-inflicted hangover. We drank homemade wine at breakfast, yearning to solidify our new status as husband and wife. I had dreamt and wholeheartedly believed our marriage would make me feel different, honored, and more secure. Instead, I felt more anxious than before.

Amir left four days after the wedding to get back to work. I felt relieved to get a break from translating and eager to start on his immigration process. He didn't resist my need to stay in Kyiv and even left money for legal fees. I stayed to have our marriage certificate translated into English and to await the much-needed apostille by the US Embassy in Kyiv, ensuring our marriage was recognized both in Ukraine and the United States. This would secure my position in getting Amir and I out of Egypt.

―――――

My life has been full of twists and turns, but nothing could prepare me for what happened next. February 12, 2017, haunts my nightmares, waking me in cold sweats and tears even today. I replay and rewrite the outcome in my mind. That day feels like a punishment, though I'm not sure why.

It was the day I handed Lucas my report card on how I had become a stronger woman, during a joyous winter reunion unlike any other—a closure two years in the making.

I assumed he saw my wedding photos on Facebook. He reached out to me, asking if I wanted to meet up sometime soon, and I was shocked to learn he had moved to Kyiv just a few months earlier. We weren't friends on Facebook at the time because Amir had asked me to unfriend him for his own peace of mind. I couldn't type a faster response to him:

'Hi Lucas, yes, let's meet up for coffee!'

I was ecstatic about seeing him; I needed to see him.

I met Lucas outside the touristy Golden Gates in downtown Kyiv in the mid-afternoon, in the small square defined by benches and manicured bushes. It was the heart of winter; a freshly fallen, shallow layer of snow blanketed the shoveled piles of frozen ice, creating a delicate white cover over the ground. I walked with purpose, kicking the airy snow into small whirlwinds behind me. I was on a mission to see the man I hadn't known I'd been missing until I'd seen his message that morning.

When I spotted him in the busy tourist pedestrian walkway, he was sipping English Breakfast tea from a to-go cup outside the corner coffee shop. I could pick him out from any crowd by the shape of his head, even when he wore a thick mustard-yellow beanie. He looked perfect. Taller than I remembered but still with the same magnetic pull as the day I'd met him. We hugged in silence, and in that moment, I forgot everything that had happened between us. I looked in his eyes as though for the first time. We stood there comfortably smiling at each other.

He thanked me for meeting him and asked if we could go for a walk. We mostly talked about what he was doing in Kyiv and why he'd decided to move there. His interest in Kyiv puzzled me, as did how he managed to live abroad while still running his remodeling business at home. He wouldn't move to London for my education, but he moved to Kyiv and made it the central hub for his travel plans. He seemed different from the last time I'd seen him in Cairo, more mature at thirty-nine. I was blonde again, doe-eyed, and looking beautiful wrapped in fur. He had never seen my face without the effects of opioids—pin-needle pupils and a drooping expression.

"Why did you break up with me?" Lucas broke the permafrost ice, gazing into my right eye. We'd been wandering the empty frozen parks in Kyiv for an hour and had stopped at a cafe.

"My mom begged me to. And, honestly, that contract was just too much. It turned me off. There's no way, no way you could find a woman like that," I explained, my voice rising in distress.

"No, Katya. No one made you. Don't say your mom made you. Take responsibility for your actions; you did it. Forget about the contract, that was stupid of me! Get rid of it!" he cried.

Shame filled his eyes as he repeated that c-word back to me, looking past me as if searching for an explanation on the horizon. I gave him the excuse that perhaps neither of us had been in our right states of mind during our last trip to Egypt. I hadn't been in the right state of mind for sure, and he must have still been confused about why I'd broken up with him and perhaps wondering whether it was Rami that had influenced my decision.

"Yes, okay, my mom didn't make me, but she supported me. My family all felt like you were wasting my time, and they worried you'd never settle. We were just always traveling, and I wanted to build a future with you." I felt relief unlike ever before in finally telling him how I felt. "I kept that contract, honestly. I read it over and over. It was just too much."

He started to tear up. "Fuck, this is hard." My muse rubbed his eyebrows. "I don't know what to do right now. Should I fight for you? But it's too late, isn't it—it's too late?" he asked in a quivering voice, looking into my right eye again.

My knees shook under the table. I held my breath, holding back tears. I touched his hand and bowed my head in sadness. Unlike during our first date, when I'd touched his hand to ask for sugar, this time I touched him to convey my deepest regrets.

How could I tell him that I knew he spoke to the soul when he looked only into my right eye? How could I tell him that I knew he just wanted to be loved, appreciated, and live out his dreams, just like I did? How could I tell him that I knew he was searching for what childhood had deprived him of in foreign lands, just like I was? How could I tell him that I knew he wished we could go back, just like I wanted to?

I couldn't. That precious metal on my right ring finger held me hostage. It duct-taped my mouth shut. My Ukrainian vows kept me from throwing myself into what I've always believed were my soul-mate's arms. This was another movie moment Lucas and I shared, and I just barely held it together.

I wanted to scream at him, to ask why it had taken him two years to reach out. All this time, I'd been secretly waiting. Never mind his contract to me; had he not read mine and seen that I only wanted communication, love, and respect? How had this not been simple enough? I didn't need him to make a certain amount of money, have a perfect house, or perform manly duties. I just wanted him to be himself and sail with me in the same boat down the river of life. I wanted him to see that maybe I'd failed at my motley experiment of living abroad, but I wasn't able to find the emergency eject button. I needed him to notice me spiraling out of control.

What a shame to have lost everything we built. We'd overcome so many hardships as a couple, watching over each other in the daily unknowns while travelling and never questioning whether we would wake up holding each other or not. I'd boarded a plane to the middle of the hostile Arab world to prove to him that I could thrive without a plan.

My love for him at that time was stronger than my body and mind could handle. It was not meant to be contained within my traumatized human existence—it was a connection my soul needed to experience on Earth.

Swallowing hard, I became furious at how unfair this whole situation was. I didn't want to hear him regretting our breakup; I wanted to know he was confident in being without me, that he had moved on. But to fight for me? Now? That had been an option years ago! It had always been the only option I'd wanted him to choose. Why hadn't he offered to help get me out of Portugal? I'd sent him that pleading text. Why hadn't he stopped me at the Reno airport? We probably wouldn't have been sitting here now. Why hadn't he fought for me during those nights in Zamalek when I'd been crying and rereading his marriage contract, blaming myself, thinking I could never be good enough?

I'd wanted him to fight for me back then, not now that I'd found stability and someone who wanted me for who I was, flaws and all. Amir proved I was worthy of being kept, promised to, and fought for, without contracts. Lucas wanted me to be enough, but Amir showed me that I was enough with a ring and a vow.

You should tell him you were an addict, I suggested to myself. I figured it might justify my shortcomings in our relationship. *Bad idea,* I thought. I didn't want him to think any less of me than he already did.

"It's too late now, Lucas," I forced the words from my lips. I tried to blink my tears away.

But God only knew I wanted to say, *I love you so much that I'm willing to merely exist knowing my feelings for you will never be replaced. I will always love you so deeply that I'll be forever holding this energy in me, lost and not knowing what to do with it. Throughout all these years, I've just been waiting and hoping you could guide me, show me how you needed to be loved. I don't yet know how to navigate the yearning in my soul or how to express the love inside me through my human condition.*

Stop, I told myself. *He's just regretting and in shock that you're married. But you gave so much of yourself to him, and he didn't even meet you halfway,* my mind reasoned. Amir was a more practical choice, and Lucas was never going to happen. It was time to let go and move on. Amir was now my choice.

"Let's get going," I said, noting the time. We left our tea unfinished and still steaming hot. His eyes were red from holding back tears, and I wiped mine gently so as not to ruin my eyeliner.

We continued to walk through the snowy, closed amusement park on the left bank of the Dnipro River, a metaphorical reminder that there had been good times, but the season had passed. It felt good to be by his side again, exploring and experiencing new things, even for a brief moment. His familiar gait was imprinted in my subconscious mind after months spent following him through jungles, mountains, and third-world cities. In those short few hours, he was my little bit of 'home,' a familiar warm past.

We walked along the riverbanks back toward the nearest metro station. My feet felt frozen in the thin boots I wore, so we stopped at McDonald's to warm up.

"Do you want a coffee?" he asked.

I smiled. "Just like our first date, but this time, let's actually get the coffee as promised."

He stood in line to order, adding a pastry because he couldn't go a day without chocolate. Everything felt so familiar and calm. Then his tone shifted. "Do me a favor and don't disrespect him."

I already am, I thought, *by spending the day with you.*

"Lucas, I'm sorry for all I said to make you feel that. I was not in my right mind. I'm learning to not be defensive and will do my best with him, too. We were just not communicating well, and I was naïve and didn't know better," I pleaded, still seeking his approval. With Amir, I would have probably debated, wanting to understand what he'd meant and why it was important to him.

"Just don't, please; it really sucks when he's trying so hard, and I'm sure yelling 'Fuck you' on an airplane won't go over well with an Arab," he said, reminding me of the time I'd completely disrespected him in public.

I was jonesing for a fix of codeine so badly on that flight from Jakarta that I feared I would shit in my seat. After we returned to Reno, I moved to Cairo. *Lucas must have been stewing over this to justify his ability to let me go to Cairo*, I thought, *it all makes sense.*

Tell him your real dark secrets, Kateryna urged me. *He needs to know the truth.*

I can't portray myself as a victim, I mentally replied. *Lucas hates that.*

"Okay, yes. I won't," I answered, embarrassed that he'd remembered *that* flight back home. "And for your next love, appreciate her efforts and give her the time she deserves. Don't be so selfish with your own future," I put my two cents in, desperate to save him from himself.

I'm not the only one that needs saving, Lucas, I thought. *You needed me for your own selfish reasons.*

"I should have given you more attention, I know," Lucas responded, taking his last dose of chocolate cake.

A lot more, I thought, *you failed to see you were living with a real addict.*

"We live and learn," I said, hoping to end the conversation, as I was overwhelmed by my thoughts, my pain, and our memories.

"I really needed this closure. Thank you," he said. "Just promise me one thing: Don't have children with him, please."

I couldn't take on another request from my fallen hero. *Does that mean you will have a baby with me? I highly doubt that.*

"Lucas, please, I don't know what will happen. You know I want children. My family is pressuring me, too," I said quietly.

"Just do it when you know one hundred percent that he is the one for you. Divorce sucks, as you know, and the kids always suffer," he said, looking again into my right eye.

"I don't want to be like my mother, yes," I said, nauseous. I was terrified that history would repeat itself and I'd be too powerless to stop it.

At that moment, I felt more than ever that I may have made a mistake in getting married. It wasn't Lucas's tears, the love we still felt for each other, or the beauty of our meeting in my home country that triggered this feeling. No, it was the present moment in that McDonald's, the freedom in my fellow Ukrainians' social behavior, the fact that no one was surveilling our conversation or judging that I had a wedding band and Lucas did not. It was the clean waterfront park we had just walked through, the crisp fresh air, and the kissing couple in the corner.

I dreaded the world I was about to return to, the madness of Cairo—the pollution, the social etiquette, and the sky-high expectations.

Fuck. I started to panic. *Freedom* is tattooed on the back of my neck. Freedom, as I and Ukraine would say, is my religion. I was betraying freedom.

I wish you were my riverbank, Lucas, I thought.

"Okay, are you done? Let's go, I should be getting home soon," I told my muse.

We headed back to the metro, and I kept finding excuses to stay with him a little longer. "I'll ride with you to your station and catch the red line from Zoloti Vorota," I said. We boarded the crowded train and pressed together in a corner, his scent intoxicating me.

How had I ended up in this position? How could I tell my soulmate that I had to go home? Life was so unfair.

"You'll thrive," I said under my breath into Lucas's chest. Oh, how I wished he would have said this to me.

At the core of my despair, I felt frustrated because I wanted him to make the same efforts I had. I'd wasted time in Egypt, getting myself into a mess, feeling like he was slowly getting rid of me while my closet addiction ran the show. He'd left all his previous girlfriends with no problem, with an in-person talk and a full explanation, just like he'd left his then-girlfriend for me "after Burning Man on a good note." But with me, our break-up had felt like a drawn-out experiment.

And that ring on my finger, that promise, was what I was now loyal to. I couldn't break it, fearing Lucas would judge my character for being so disloyal, and that he'd bring it up in a heated argument down the road. I was in checkmate. But I wanted him to win the game. After all, that was how we'd played chess at our Forest Drive house—I'd let him win every time.

We spilled out of the subway car into a sea of black, musky coats worn by my fellow Ukrainians. I held onto his slightly bent elbow as we meandered through the underground subway halls to find my platform.

"I wish you all the best. I hope to see you again, maybe," he said, giving me a hug and holding me longer than expected.

I was frozen, limp, and trembling.

He looked me in the eyes and kissed my cheek ever so gently. I closed my eyes and felt weak.

"Okay, go," he said, holding onto my shoulders, tears in his eyes.

"Okay. I am," I managed to say. I took in his body heat and matched my heartbeat to his, lingering in the space between yesterday and tomorrow.

I walked away and descended the longest escalator in Europe. Looking back, I saw him standing at the top, eyes red and blank. We locked eyes until I was out of sight. I realized I wasn't ready for married life. I longed to go back four years—to see Lucas curled up in our tan sheets at sunrise in our 1940s house, to hold his hand through the endless Mumbai slums, to freeze in Catania, Sicily, and to ride our ValenBisi bikes to Spanish class in Valencia. I wished these memories belonged to the man I'd married, not the man left watching me leave.

When I returned to my grandma's house, I didn't tell anyone about my karmic encounter. I went straight to the bedroom, still in my fur coat, and laid down on my sister's bed in the pitch black. Tears streamed down my face as I thought, *You have possessed my heart, Lucas, no matter the past, present, or future.*

Time and space are observable constructs of our physical body. The soul is eternal and continuous across the quantum field. I set my love for Lucas into that quantum field, allowing it to live on in endless possibilities beyond time and space. Our destinies have already been written. I felt so lucky to have known this love and so fortunate to have experienced it in the physical world. I understood why Rene Magritte, the surrealist painter whose works hung on every wall in our small Reno home, floated green apples in mid-air— in the quantum world, that apple can and does exist. My love for Lucas can and does exist, simultaneously.

14
PURPOSE (APRIL 2017)

I couldn't shake my last meeting with Lucas; the snow we kicked up in the river park refused to settle. My reality felt like a glitch in the quantum matrix. The future I had once envisioned—building a life with Lucas in Reno—had now morphed into creating a life with another man from Egypt. Resisting this reality only fed my victimhood mentality. *Why me?* I thought. I wanted to confront every link in this anchor chain dragging me down. If my mother hadn't kicked me out in Portugal, I wouldn't have needed Amir's help. If I hadn't been desperate to prove myself to Lucas, I wouldn't have crossed the Atlantic to Cairo. If I had never gone to Cairo, I wouldn't be planning this wedding far from the trees and the beautiful bluff I'd once imagined. But no matter how I sliced it, those had all been *my* decisions.

As I wrestled with these thoughts, my sobriety added another layer to the battle. Sixteen months opioid-free, I realized that clinging to the past was only dragging me back into a dark place. The only way forward was to embrace acceptance—of the present, the past, and whatever the future held. I had to accept my fate and the choices that had brought me here. Only then could I plan my

Egyptian wedding, see the goodness in my husband, and let go of Cairo's chaos to feel like I belonged.

You should be happy! my mind insisted as I fluffed the pillows on our large L-shaped couch, wrapped in a cream silk robe. But sobriety is hard. Now, happiness and contentment come from the natural balance in my brain, not the artificial dopamine rush opioids once gave me. My stability—a husband, a home, and the future we were building in the US—felt real but no longer exaggerated like it used to. Maybe I would have felt the same with Lucas if I had been sober around him. Maybe sailing through the Bosphorus Strait in Istanbul, sipping tea from a tulip-shaped glass, wouldn't have felt so magical if I hadn't been three Percocets deep. My happiness with Lucas was likely just a product of my opioid-fueled haze, keeping me blind to the cracks in our relationship.

With that realization, I knew I had to stop digging through the past and start finding value in my new identity as a wife. Chasing answers about why I hadn't found my treasure with Lucas was exhausting. My truth now was acceptance—I was married to Amir, and our Egyptian wedding was just two months away. It was time to embrace the life I was building and let the snow from my walk with Lucas melt away.

———

On April Fools' Day, 2017, I suddenly felt unwell. I blamed my low-grade fever and body aches on the stress of wedding preparations and our recent trip to visit Nadeen's side of the family in Alexandria, Egypt. Amir and I had just attended his friend's wedding at a golf course resort in El Gouna on the Red Sea.

Unable to sleep with Amir passed out in a drunken stupor, I called room service at 3:30 a.m. "Hello, I'd like a bowl of soup, a cheeseburger, and a chocolate cake, please, to room 306. Shukran." I had gotten sick earlier at the wedding after just one vodka soda while Amir indulged, enjoying the rare chance to drink alcohol at an

Egyptian wedding. I hoped the food would settle my stomach, but as I ate, I noticed a strange pain in my breasts—something I hadn't felt before.

That morning, still hungover and puzzled by how I'd managed to eat a second breakfast, Amir drove us back to Cairo through the empty stretches of the Sahara. Without warning, I burst into tears, which quickly shifted into uncontrollable laughter, leaving Amir shocked and confused.

"What the hell is wrong with you, Katya? Please, stop, you're scaring me," Amir said, rubbing his brow in annoyance.

I was not in control of my emotional outbursts. Poor Amir had to sit through my crying and laughing, as I flipped between sad and happy songs the entire five-hour drive home.

"Amir, can you stop at a pharmacy before we get home? I have a weird feeling. Can you get a few tests?" I asked as we got stuck in the sea of traffic at the toll booth entrance back into Cairo, framed by sphinx heads and Horus wings on the clay walls.

"A test for what? To see if you're crazy? Because I can tell you right now, you are," he said, laughing.

"No. A pregnancy test," I answered.

"Really? No way. I mean, there is a way. But...no way. Not now, Katya. Our wedding is in four weeks," he said.

"I just feel different. We should check," I said, now more scared by the horrified expression on his face.

We hadn't planned on having children anytime soon, though we talked about it occasionally. Amir always said, "Not until I get on my feet more," and I agreed. But I couldn't shake the fear from my last infertility scare, when my periods had stopped completely and I'd been told that after ten years on birth control, I might not be able to conceive. I needed to know everything was still working properly.

So, before leaving Ukraine in late February, I visited my gynecologist to check my ability to conceive, as I didn't trust seeing a doctor in Egypt. She advised treatment for my PCOS and endometriosis with four localized, hormone-free immunomodulator shots of Etanercept near my right ovary. "You don't ovulate on your right side," she explained. "These shots should reduce the inflammation and give you a chance to ovulate there." She also warned me that conceiving would still be difficult due to my chronic cystic ovaries.

"It's probably nothing," I said, recalling my doctor's disclaimer. The rest of the drive was silent.

I couldn't wait until morning, so I collected my last pee of the day in a cup and squeezed three drops into the test window. Amir, already wearing his thick glasses and his Ralph Lauren pajamas with the shirt tucked in like an old man, knelt on his rug, bowing in prayer before bed.

Two faint lines appeared. My heart raced in disbelief. I grabbed another test and added three more drops. A minute later, the same astonishing result.

It only takes three drops of urine to have your whole world come closing in on you. It felt as if the Big Bang ignited from that test strip, creating a new universe right there in my hands. Looking at those lines, I felt both powerless and divine, incredibly small and happy, overly shocked and inexplicably scared. I had longed to be a mother and have a family of my own for as long as I could remember. Shaking and on the verge of vomiting from disbelief, I stumbled out of the bathroom.

"Well?" Amir asked, sitting up in bed and adjusting his glasses on his nose as I crawled on the wall out of the bathroom looking like a ghost. "No, Katya. No. Really? Say something. Really? You are, aren't you?" he said, smiling in horror. His twisted face was both shocked and ecstatic.

"Yes, Amir, I'm pregnant," I managed to say, still holding on to the wall.

He ran up and hugged me, picking me up and twirling my limp body.

"I'm going to be a mom!" I yelled out in disbelief and sheer panic.

"Oh my God…I need a shisha," Amir said, setting me down and heading into the living room.

We stayed up until 4 a.m., smoking, pacing the room, and planning for the reality shift that was about to hit us. The 'Get out of Egypt now' thoughts blasted in my mind at full volume. We had last talked about this plan in Kyiv, on our wedding day, surrounded by my family. My uncle, a businessman, had even offered Amir job opportunities in Ukraine if he needed extra income while they discussed ways to save money for our move to the USA.

"I can't raise a kid here, Amir. We need to focus on moving as soon as possible," I told him.

"I understand. We will move. In time—I mean, I have to save money and maybe get another job," he answered.

"Okay, well, what about even living in Ukraine for a bit? My uncle had that business proposition for you on the wheat export side. We can be there. I can find work there, like teaching English. We can slowly save to move to the USA," I suggested.

Amir grabbed his notepad and pen, meticulously jotting down bullet points and calculating estimated expenses with his usual obsessive precision.

"We would need at least forty thousand dollars to get us over there. To be comfortable. That's a lot of money," he said, reloading his shisha with fresh sticky tobacco. That was a lot of money to have lying around, even for his wealthy family.

"Not that much. People go there without anything and make it. I'm not afraid to work—I'll clean houses, babysit, work in the kitchen—anything! I don't care," I said.

"My woman will not be cleaning houses, Katya! Are you crazy?" he exclaimed.

"Oh, Amir, if it's for the greater good, I will do anything. Do you think we will be able to save forty thousand dollars in ten months?" I asked.

"I will need to sell twenty-five to thirty apartments to get that commission," he read from his notepaper.

"That is a lot of houses," I said, my voice heavy with defeat. Even if I worked here, making two hundred dollars a month as a teacher wouldn't make a dent in what we needed to save up. My Arabic was still basic, and without being able to read and write it fluently, landing a higher-paying job was close to impossible.

"We also have the wedding I need to pay for. And to get your family over to Egypt for the wedding. The honeymoon. Look, I have enough for all that, but then it's all gone," he said.

"Let's not do a wedding, then. It's too much money. I don't have to have it, really," I said.

"No, Katya, we need to for my family. My mother wants to see her son's wedding, and it's the way we have to do it in Egypt. The marriage is final if done in front of family and friends. In the public eye," he argued.

In Egypt, marriage must be in the public eye; it's a teaching of Prophet Mohammed. If a marriage isn't publicly announced, it goes against the core principles of Islam.

"We can't tell our parents about my pregnancy yet," I told him.

"I think we should. It would be the right thing," he said, unaware of how shaky his voice sounded.

"No, first I need to see a doctor and confirm the pregnancy. I want to know how many weeks the baby is. I remember that no one announces their pregnancy until about week twelve because there is still the possibility of miscarriage," I informed him. "Let's do it after the wedding."

The sunrise pierced through the closed blinds as I lay in bed, cradling my nonexistent baby bump. *This is my purpose*, I thought. *This is why everything I wanted didn't want me. I'm meant to be a mother for this child.* Silent tears of joy streamed down my face as I imagined the life growing inside me. "We won't stay in Egypt, my little one. I promise you won't be in this pollution. Mommy and Daddy will make sure of that," I whispered to my abdomen.

I'd never expected everything to hit me at once: marriage, a wedding, and pregnancy. Each day grew more chaotic, my demands more impulsive than my old codeine habit. Sobriety was already hard enough without an escape, and quitting smoking—my last hold on sanity—pushed me into full-blown hormonal rage.

The first ultrasound confirmed I was about five weeks pregnant. As the shock wore off, anxiety crept in, leaving me restless and on edge. My patience, especially with Amir, grew thin. "I don't care if you're busy; I need to see the doctor today!" I snapped. "Why are you going to the cafe again? We're supposed to be saving money. Just have a shisha at home!" My hormones surged, amplifying my frustration with my husband of only three months.

A new wave of fear hit me—the daunting reality of having a baby in Egypt. The upcoming wedding barely crossed my mind; my focus was entirely on our unborn child. With the wedding just a week away, morning sickness kicked in, adding to the difficulty of hiding my pregnancy.

I was disappointed with my Egyptian wedding. My sky-high expectations clashed with the mediocre efforts of our overpriced wedding planner, who was the Egyptian version of a Karen. I had envisioned vines covering the entire ceiling of the golf country club, The Bear, at Palm Hills in 6th of October City. Instead, I got random fake branches spaced three feet apart, making the venue look more like it was being torn down than set up. Her setup crew arrived late, and when we got there at 4 p.m. for photos, only half of the decorations were done. Everyone was scrambling. The weather didn't help —abnormal heatwaves and a distant sandstorm on April 21, 2017 added to the chaos. My hormonal frustration boiled over, and I vented to Amir, "I told you I didn't want the wedding! It's already a disaster! It looks like shit!"

I had attended dozens of Egyptian weddings, all elaborate and whimsical, but mine looked poorly assembled. We had a twenty-thousand-dollar budget, which I'd thought was substantial for a middle to upper-class Egyptian wedding. Later, I learned that a decent upper-class wedding averages around one hundred fifty thousand dollars. My dress was simple—a mix between a slip and trumpet silhouette with a crystal butterfly wing design on the back, a cathedral-length veil, and no cleavage because I had none to show. After trying on various styles, my petite frame and barely one-hundred-ten-pound body looked best in a simple, classic dress.

Everything that could go wrong did. My acrylic French nails looked like I had dipped my fingers in clay—uneven and bulky. The restaurant staff stole half the seafood Amir's father had brought for the guests, leaving everyone hungry. The worst part was that we didn't get a zaffa—a marching band with bendir drums, pipes, horns, and sometimes a belly dancer to lead the bride and groom into the party. The zaffa is the heart of an Egyptian wedding. "I didn't know you needed one," the wedding planner yelled at Amir. Instead of a grand entrance, I rode in a golf cart with my father. Nothing about it felt Egyptian. It felt like a waste of half our budget to move to the USA.

I was, however, very grateful to have eleven of my family members there, everyone except my mother, my two younger sisters, and my aunt and her crew. Amir made my dream of having my side of the family present come true, paying for their flights, hotels in Hurghada for a few nights, and accommodations near the pyramids. It was my dad's first time abroad and his first time on an airplane. My seventy-year-old great aunt even came, along with a distant cousin from Russia.

My wedding had a few unique touches: perfectly distilled

Ukrainian vodka, Patron from the States, Romeo and Juliet Cuban cigars, and authentic black caviar from Russia.

To my surprise, my friends, Becca and Alex, not only brought the tequila and cigars but actually made it to the wedding. I hadn't expected any of my Reno friends to come when I'd sent out my casual invites. Becca was a close college friend who smoked Prime-Times with me after class and took me out clubbing on my twenty-first birthday. Alex, on the other hand, I'd met while working at the busiest restaurant in Reno. We'd both been servers, and I'd loved her instantly for her dry humor and stoic facial expressions.

"Here, Kat, let's go get a shot! Relax a bit," Alex chirped.

"I don't want to drink in front of Amir's family. They are religious; don't want to give them the wrong impression," I lied.

After his long speech, my father, twelve years sober, also offered me a drink. My bubbly, sixty-eight-year-old platinum-blonde grandmother, who had been dancing in a circle of Egyptian men, led me behind a palm tree with two shots in hand. I politely refused both, blaming the hot weather and again my morals.

"Something's wrong. You're not telling me everything," my father said, stepping up to me on the dance floor. "I can see it in your eyes."

I just smiled, put my finger to my lips, and whispered, "Shhh." He nodded, winked, and kissed my forehead. My secret was out—my father had sensed my pregnancy just from my eyes.

Amir and I left the reception a little after midnight while most of the guests were still partying. His friends were drunk, but I felt exhausted, hungry, and overheated. For eight hours, I had been running to the bathroom every fifteen minutes, paranoid that all the jumping on stage had caused bleeding. Each time, it was only sweat trickling down my legs. My mind remained fixated on the nine-week-old fetus growing inside me.

Despite the cultural chaos, guests showered us with thank-yous, many claiming it was the best wedding they had ever attended. I was shocked by the glowing reviews. All I wanted was to forget the night —Muslim women in veils sitting near rows of Ukrainian vodka bottles, awkward family interactions, and the endless translating I had to do on stage. I pictured Allah, sitting in confusion, calling the whole scene a "soup sandwich of sin and piety." I wondered how many Egyptian brides were two months pregnant on their wedding day. Probably none.

I could have skipped the wedding reception, but I wasn't ready to give up the two-week honeymoon to fit our moving budget. I needed that escape. After putting up with the chaos of Egypt for over a year, I longed to see nature, breathe clean air, eat great food, and go snowboarding. Amir and I went to Rome, the Vatican, then took a train to Milan and up to Zermatt, Switzerland, for snowboarding, with stops in beautiful Swiss towns along the way. Those two weeks were heaven! Switzerland had its challenges, though—the smell of fondue everywhere made me sick. After throwing up in a couple of restaurants, I refused to go inside them anymore.

On April 29, my twenty-eighth birthday, I threw a box of raspberries at Amir in our honeymoon suite because he didn't want to go snowboarding. It made sense, given it would be his second time ever on a snowboard, but my hormonal brain and all-day sickness didn't care. We argued, yet he still followed me to the top of Zermatt Ski Resort. I puked in the tram on the way up, but nothing was going to stop me from snowboarding on Swiss snow—not even a doctor's warning to avoid dangerous sports.

My husband was patient, but I grew more demanding by the day. Each time I looked at him, I felt dread—not because he was a bad husband but because he was Egyptian. My instincts as a mother intensified with every passing day. "We NEED to move to the USA! I moved here for you! We have to raise our child somewhere better!" I would scream at him. Then I'd make up for it with steamy sex and back rubs. I was a mess of hormones and spite, impossible to be around.

Each day brought with it a cocktail of confusion, fear, shame, and frustration as my baby grew. I wanted the world because I had given up mine—for my mother, for Lucas, for Amir—and now whatever was left was meant for my unborn child. I hadn't yet realized that I had a lot of healing left to do before I could be the mother I wanted to be. I told myself that if God made me a mother, I must be ready in His eyes—but I didn't feel ready at all.

What could I possibly offer my child? What lessons could I teach? I felt like I would be pouring from an empty cup. Pregnancy reminded me of the time I'd signed up for the Portland Marathon with only four months to train from the couch. I finished, but the pressure had been immense—and I'd been carrying far less mental weight back then.

As motherhood drew closer, I realized I wasn't happy with who I had become. The hormonal fog finally lifted, and I saw it clearly. I had no hobbies, though I'd once had many, and I had no career to show for the years I'd dedicated to studying. My sense of self was slipping away. Was I still a motocross racer, a hiker, a runner, a cook, a painter, an entrepreneur, a world traveler, a wannabe writer, a pianist, a psychologist—or was I something else entirely? I had spent years chasing men across the world, letting my skills go to waste, and now I was pregnant with shaky plans to restart life, yet again. I knew I had to become a more well-rounded person, someone who could lead by example for my child.

It was shortly after Amir and I had returned from our honeymoon and settled back into routine when my mother's voice pierced through the phone: "You're fucking stupid! Your baby will have no soul! It will be born with the Devil at its side. And those Egyptians you call family will cut off its genitals!"

My guess was that Masha, my sister, had told her about my pregnancy.

"You're a fucking BITCH! Stay away from me! Don't ever call again, do you hear me? I hate you!" I spat back, rage flowing through every word.

"What's going on? Katya, why are you crying?" Amir stirred from his deep sleep to find me sobbing at the edge of the bed. It was 4 a.m., and I was thirteen weeks pregnant.

"She called...said the worst things. I hate her! I wish I was never born!" I collapsed into his arms, sobbing. "It's 3 a.m. in Portugal. She's probably drunk, just needed someone to vent to," I muttered. Years of struggling to make sense of her cruelty had trained me to excuse her, even when it tore me apart. Wiping my nose, I let the excuse hang between us, as if it could dull the pain.

"She will never come near our child," Amir said, pulling me close. "Do you hear me, Katya? I will never let anyone hurt you or our baby. Stop crying, habibti—God counts your tears." His words wrapped around me like a shield as he gently stroked my head, tucked into his chest.

Just a week before this call, we had shared the news with my Egyptian family. It was met with love, support, tears, and prayers, as all of mine and Amir's milestones. My mother-in-law kissed my hands and face, repeating, "Alhamdulillah!" (Praise to God). I cried in response, as it felt foreign to be kissed and praised by another mother.

Nadeen was the mother I had always wished for. She embodied everything a mother should be—kind, nurturing, and attentive. I was grateful our child would get to call her 'Grandma.' Feminine and full of grace and style, she carried herself with strength despite having suffered a stroke a few years back. She had lost her ability to speak and had to relearn how to walk, talk, and function. I was told she once spoke fluent English, but the incident had taken that from her. Still, the purity in her eyes and her gentle smile communicated more than words ever could.

Upon hearing the news of her grandchild, she immediately ensured we had home-cooked meals delivered daily. She even hired an extra maid to take care of the laundry and dusting, insisting I "enjoy my pregnancy and be pampered." Amir's sister stood by her side, and after the announcement dinner, she and I became best friends. She often took me shopping and out with her friends. In the aftermath of my own mother's venom, their love felt almost unreal—proof that another version of motherhood, one rooted in care instead of cruelty, existed.

Everything was falling into place. The Sabry family fully supported our plan to move to the USA. They helped us save money by making larger home purchases, like furniture and bulk groceries for the month. They discussed potential cities with us and even sent links to properties for sale and rent on both the East and West Coasts. Most importantly, they kept Amir motivated with reminders like, "Take care of your wife and child. Allah is watching and blessing your efforts."

With Allah, Amir, and the Sabry family by my side, I felt content. I made peace with my life not unfolding the way I had always envisioned. Motherhood and my Egyptian prince—this had been God's plan all along. My efforts hadn't gone unnoticed; God had been listening. I didn't need my toxic mother disrupting my peace, so I blocked her number.

With my mother out of my life, I turned my focus to the positive people around me, determined to build a better, peaceful future for my child. The warmth and consistency of Amir's family gave me hope that the life of the child growing inside me could be different than the life of pure evil my mother had described. They greeted me with kisses and hugs, and dinners with them were full of laughter and excitement for the great future ahead. There was happiness around me; my life felt full of potential.

But despite this, my mother's words had already taken root in my mind, creeping into my happiness like a toxic vine. I had blocked her number, cutting off every line of contact, yet somehow her cruelty still found a way to echo in me. The insults spread like an invasive weed, threatening to choke the peace I struggled to cultivate. What if she was right about my unborn child? How could she wish my baby would spawn from the Devil?

My mother had never taught me how to be happy. Growing up, I prayed to God to bring happiness to her, yet she was always miserable about everything. I grew up to believe that happiness came from the world around you, from others, something beyond your control. I hadn't yet realized that happiness is a choice, something you create within yourself.

I didn't want my child to inherit my mother's constant disappointment with life through me. I promised myself I'd teach her how to find joy from within, to see the world as a good place. But how could I teach that while raising her in the hostile Egyptian world, a world I was not happy in?

Finding out we were having a girl only intensified my sense of responsibility. I felt an urgent need to protect her from my bad wiring and to give her the best first impressions of the world. As soon as Amir and I left the ultrasound appointment, holding the photo with the tiny arrow pointing between her little legs, I knew I had to protect her even more. I wanted her to grow up free, able to enjoy life without the limitations I had faced, and in a world that aligned more closely with my beliefs.

Amir chose the name Sofie, meaning *wisdom*, and I couldn't have imagined a more perfect name. As I thought more about Sofie's future, I couldn't help but reflect on the women around me in Egypt. Egyptian women seemed restricted and sheltered, stuck in lives they didn't question because they hadn't experienced anything else. Their roles were predetermined, programmed into them from birth. But isn't the point of life to find your own path, to be unique?

The thought of raising a girl in such a restrictive bubble began to terrify me. I realized that my life experiences, curiosity, and everything I had learned were the greatest gifts I could pass on to Sofie. Egypt and its rigid expectations would crush the free will I wanted her to have—after all, it had already taken some of mine.

I hadn't survived all I had just to let my daughter grow up confined to the role of someone's wife, her future dictated by Egypt's wealthy elite. I wanted her to live fully, to make mistakes, and to learn from them—not be bound by rules imposed on her. Religious labels didn't matter to me, but the way women were limited under Islam didn't sit right. I refused to let my daughter be trapped by those expectations. She deserved the freedom to choose her own path, and I was determined to give her that. As twisted as it sounds, my mother was right about one thing: my daughter wouldn't have a soul if she grew up in Egypt—not by my standards. I'm sure my mother meant it in a darker, crueler way, but her words forced me to think deeply.

At the same time, my dear husband also started to change—in all the wrong ways. I couldn't pinpoint exactly when it started, but it came slowly—first with him staying out late, then with him spending money on nights out instead of saving for our future. The air between us thickened, and my 'Get Out of Egypt' propaganda was on full blast.

"And how do you expect to protect her from the harassers on the streets if we stay here, Amir?" I shouted one night as he got dressed to go out with his friends yet again. I was desperate to get him to regain the urgency to leave Egypt that we'd once shared.

"She won't be on the streets!" he snapped back. "She'll live in luxury, always with my driver or me, and go to the best schools."

"That's *if* we stay here, which we're not!" I replied, my frustration boiling over.

"Yes, Katya, we're not. But give me time! I'm working my ass off; I can't do everything at once!" he said.

"In the States, you won't need to worry about luxury. Luxury is going outside without the fear of being harassed," I pressed, urging him to see what truly mattered.

"Oh yeah? And in the States, I'll have to worry about boys touching her at school. Western ways aren't always the best, Katya. She won't be like you; I'd never let her travel alone unless she's married," he retorted, his voice sharp.

"What? So now I'm wrong for traveling? I turned out fine!" I shot back, feeling the sting of his words.

"I'm done with this conversation. Stop worrying and focus on your pregnancy. Be grateful for everything I'm doing for us now," he said, slamming the door behind him.

Now, almost six months pregnant, I felt the weight of everything shifting inside me. As my daughter grew and my organs adjusted, my priorities shifted, too. Motherhood was transforming me, forcing me to confront the magnitude of my choices. *Can I be a good mother after coming from a bad one myself?* I spent hours journaling the pain of my childhood, aching to process and purge the toxins, preparing myself for my daughter's arrival.

The more my priorities shifted toward protecting our daughter, the more Amir seemed to drift away. His late nights, his dismissive comments, and the way he accused me of being "ungrateful for everything I'm already doing for us" stung more with each passing day. Something had changed, and it wasn't just him—it was us. My defenses were on high alert, and the more he pushed, the harder I fought back.

"What's her name?" I asked Amir, as he was heading out for the evening to a 'cafe.'

"Whose name?" he asked, with his back turned to me.

"Your girlfriend's," I answered through clenched teeth.

"You're sick, Katya. This is exactly why I leave every night! You are fucked up in the head! I don't care that you're pregnant; you're also mental on top of that," he shouted, turning around and thrusting his finger at me like the barrel of a loaded gun. He had never spoken to me like that before. *Here it is, Katya, his bad side.*

I had no evidence that he was seeing someone else—just a hunch, as I watched him change in tandem with my swelling belly. He bought expensive clothes, went to the gym more, and shaved twice a day, and his mind was always elsewhere. These were the same behaviors he'd shown when courting me—clear red flags that his attention was on another woman.

When I complained to his mother about him never being home, she and his sister confronted him, asking him to be more considerate. He snapped back, "I'm my own man; I can do whatever I want! Why don't you take care of her?" That ended their pleas. He was the only son, the man among women, and acted superior. I, once having felt like the biggest influence in his life, now sat silently among those women on their couch. I almost said, 'You can't speak to me like that,' but his mother gently squeezed my hand, sensing the fire building in me.

Our house became as cold and lonely as the months I'd spent alone in Zamalek. Amir and I fought daily over his lack of preparation for leaving Egypt, yet I still believed the hero in him could rise. He continued to come home to sleep in our bed, and I convinced myself he was just overwhelmed by the inevitable approaching fatherhood. But when he started staying overnight at his parents' house to avoid me and coming home drunk at sunrise, I knew I was losing my grip on the man I'd once seen as our protector and provider.

I couldn't make excuses for him anymore. My anger boiled over, and I realized I didn't need to raise a man while preparing for motherhood. I had no reason to back out of my responsibilities, and I certainly didn't want to carry him. All his talk about Islam and fatherly roles during our courtship in Portugal vanished as he reverted to a teenager halfway through my pregnancy.

I informed Nadeen that I would spend the rest of my term in Ukraine for three reasons: I wanted Sofie to have Ukrainian citizenship, I wanted to be near my family during the first month of caring for a newborn, and I couldn't stand being around my husband. When she pleaded, "Please, don't leave now. If you do, you will lose your husband; he needs you!" I responded with, "I have a baby coming; I don't need to raise a grown man. If he wants to be there for us, he can—but you are his mother, not me." She knew I was right.

At twenty weeks pregnant, I escaped to my grandma's house in Kyiv, but the fights with Amir followed me by phone. Our screaming matches were so intense, my grandma would leave her own apartment. When she returned, she'd lecture me, saying, "No one should scream like that. It's not good for you or the baby." My sister tried to keep me calm, sometimes taking my phone away.

But I couldn't stop. I knew he was cheating. I felt it in every cell of my body. He just wasn't man enough to admit it. Around twenty-two weeks, I went into preterm labor and was hospitalized for a week. They gave me intravenous tocolytics to stop my uterine contractions. I was so stressed out that my body was rejecting my baby. The father of my unborn daughter was already hurting her and us, and I was in no physical shape to fight that fight.

As I lay watching the medicine drip into the chamber, the conversation I'd had with Lucas in McDonald's less than a year ago flooded my mind: "Divorce sucks, and it's the children who suffer the most." Back then, my intuition had warned me this marriage wouldn't end well.

Proving everyone—especially myself—wrong by believing my choices were for the best became my top priority. I convinced myself

Amir would calm down and leave his mistress once he saw his first-born daughter. I didn't want to seem foolish for choosing him as my husband and the father of our child. I also, more than anything, wanted our daughter to have a fair shot at a nuclear family. It was my responsibility to give her the best life possible. Maybe Amir was failing as a husband, but I prayed he wouldn't as a father.

Lucas would have stepped up, I thought—but only after I met every item on his wife standards list. None of that mattered now. Who'd left, why they'd left, who'd fought, who hadn't, my wrongs, their wrongs—it was all irrelevant. My world was going to change in five months. Those who weren't worthy would stay in the past with Katya. Those who were, I hoped, would stay with Katya the Mommy.

"I will show you all the beauty this world has to offer, Sofie. I promise. Stay in there until you are ready. I need you to survive." I talked to my bump at the hospital. My sweet little girl listened, and we were back on track to her safe development after two fearful weeks of an almost spontaneous abortion.

As my due date neared, I calmed my nerves for Sofie's sake and gave Amir space. I convinced myself that maybe this was how young fathers-to-be transitioned into their new role. Growing up, I'd recognized my mother had never really considered what fatherhood required, and my father had been only twenty—seven years younger than Amir. I tried to be more receptive to our situation, so I stopped asking about Amir's whereabouts and only responded when he initiated. Surprisingly, this approach worked, and he did the right thing by coming to Kyiv nearly two weeks before Sofie's birth, along with his Egyptian family.

A realization hit me like an instinct—my daughter needed a strong father, someone who could provide for her and be a dependable role model. My own father had failed, leaving my mother to raise me alone, but at least he had been there for the first and most crucial years of my life. If I hadn't been pregnant, I would've left

Amir already. Yet I knew it was better for Sofie to have Amir around than not at all. Despite his flighty, adulterous ways, he was still the most important man in my daughter's life, and I had to honor that. But I feared Sofie's path might be far worse than mine, with Amir already so emotionally and physically absent. His grand ideals about Islam and fatherhood meant nothing without real action. *He has to step up*, I told myself. After all, he came from the perfect nuclear family, and his faith called him to be a provider and protector. He knew right from wrong. I left it to him—and to Allah—to find that epiphany.

Early in my pregnancy, Amir and I had dreamed together about our beautiful, exotic daughter. "She'll have my eyes and your brains," he'd say, pride lighting up his face. "I'm going to get her one of those ride-on cars—a black Mercedes—it'll be so cute!" He had been eager to spoil her, and my heart had melted imagining them napping together on the couch. But those dreams could no longer manifest in my reality. Once again, it seemed I had chosen a path where I was alone facing an uphill battle, sacrificing my own wellbeing in the process.

———

It was late on December 11, 2017, four days past my due date. The entire Sabry family had been in Kyiv since early December. They paced around the dinner table, sending anxious WhatsApp messages like, 'Do you think she's coming tonight?' December 8 had been Nadeen's birthday, and when that date had come and gone, they'd grown restless, disappointed that their first grandchild hadn't arrived on Grandma's special day.

I didn't want to spend another dinner with people I knew I couldn't fully depend on to help Sofie and me realize our nuclear family dream. I decided to check myself into the Kyiv Municipal Birth House #2, not because it was time but because I needed a mental escape.

"Grandpa, I think she's coming," I said, wobbling into his room.

Half asleep, he jumped up immediately. "Let's go, sunshine!" he chirped, heading to the front door, where he slipped on his shoes and grabbed his keys and my overnight bags.

"Did your water even break?" the intake nurse asked while inspecting my cervix at the birth house.

"No, but trust me, I'll have this baby in less than twenty-four hours. Please admit me," I begged.

"Fine, we'll get you a room. Not too many babies this time of year," she replied.

I gave a thumbs up through the glass window to my grandpa and Amir standing in the lobby, signaling that I would call them with updates. Ukrainian birthing houses are strict and sterile environments, allowing only staff and expecting mothers to enter the intake or overnight rooms. I felt relieved to have my own sanctuary to focus on getting my baby safely into this world, away from my half-hearted supporters: Amir, his family, and my mother.

Since his arrival, Amir had stayed with me in the small apartment my great aunt had arranged for us to welcome Sofie. It was in the same building complex as my grandmother's apartment, and Masha stayed with us to keep me company. Though Amir had been physically present for nearly two weeks, he mentally was still in Cairo. Every morning, he sat in the bathroom for an hour, chatting online with someone. I whispered to the closed door, "Please, just don't fall in love." Then he headed to the gym, after which he'd take a long cab ride to the nearest shisha place. I paced the five-hundred-square-foot apartment, waiting for his return every night, just like I had in Cairo.

He methodically reassured me after Sofie's due date passed, saying, "Trust Allah, she'll come when it's her time." However, his urgency to leave radiated from him. He filled the nagging anticipation between us with plans for a new tattoo on his chest. I prioritized his wants over an argument and found the best tattoo artist in Kyiv. I spent three consecutive afternoons, past my fortieth week of pregnancy, sitting in the parlor, translating for him. In the evenings, I relaxed into just having his attention by listening to his Arabic pop and pouring him shots of strong homemade raspberry liqueur.

Then there was my mother. She had reincarnated into the body of a somewhat caring individual, but she couldn't fool me. Two months before, a three-way call on speaker with my mother and grandma had bridged us back together. My mother had sounded completely oblivious to our not-so-distant past—kicking me out in Portugal, not attending my wedding, and telling me over the phone that my child would be born without a soul. My grandma had pleaded with me, "Katya, she's sick in the head. She's a drunk. I know she loves you; she just doesn't know how. She probably doesn't remember telling you anything. Please, let's call her and say hi." Because I love my grandma, I'd given my mother another chance to be part of my fragile world.

I neither expected nor wanted her to be there for her grand-daughter's birth, but she showed up in November, driving across Europe with my youngest sister, Anka. At first, I thought it was pretty special of her. In reality, she hadn't come for Sofie—she'd come because she had a long-distance boyfriend she'd been chatting with online. She'd used my pregnancy as an excuse to leave Portugal and her husband. My grandma told me this after my delivery, to avoid upsetting me beforehand. Like Amir, my mom was a cheater and a liar.

My mother acted like nothing had happened between us and even bonded with Amir over a bottle of vodka. Soon, I learned she had a hidden agenda; she was after his money. My grandma over-heard her grooming him to buy an apartment in Kyiv, promising to manage it when we were away. Her real plan was to leave her husband and get someone else to finance a place for her and my sisters. My mother was a swindler, and vodka did all her talking.

Everything and everyone around me was toxic. I only began to see this knowing that an undamaged yet easily programmable child would soon be arriving into this dysfunctional world. As though looking through Sofie's innocent eyes, I knew she wouldn't want this life for us. I didn't want this life for us.

At the birth house, away from everyone else's toxicity, I put on nature sounds and watched the snow gently fall outside the window of my small delivery room. I bounced on a tan exercise ball for two hours, rubbing my three-foot-out baby bump. "Come, my love, it's safe now. Please come and meet Mommy." Without success, I laid down for the night, but immediately upon shutting my eyes, I heard a loud *POP* and felt warm liquid drenching my bottom.

The second hardest thing, after cold-turkey detox, I've experienced in my life was childbirth. I was in labor for eighteen grueling hours. My doctor spent this time screaming at me that there was no way I could still feel pain after a dose of morphine. I probably should have mentioned to him that my pain threshold was lowered due to opioid abuse. I felt everything tenfold. I tried the natural way, but even though my uterus was only two centimeters dilated, I was screaming bloody murder, wailing and howling like the animals I'd been listening to the whole night on my nature soundtrack. Most women didn't feel much at this stage, my doctor reminded me. I responded with pleas to be killed.

Amir was there for the last six hours of active labor. He held my hand during contractions, and I felt sure he would stop talking to his mistress after seeing me in so much pain.

"HOW COULD YOU DO THIS TO ME?" I screamed at him, mostly referring to his girlfriend. He just squeezed my hand harder and dropped his head to avoid seeing the agony on my face. The nurses, however, were impressed by my accentless English.

I was ready to die for Sofie before I even met her. I wanted her more than I had ever wanted anything in my life. I can still hear the frantic beeping of the heart-rate monitor strapped around my stomach, speeding up as she fought for her life while I felt mine slipping away. The pain was overwhelming, but focusing on it felt selfish. I pushed it aside, determined to be stronger than I had ever been as I experienced something no man will ever truly understand.

Our baby girl, Sofie, was delivered by emergency cesarean. I battled the forces of Mother Nature, as my uterus contracted every forty-five seconds while the doctors put two long needles into my spine. In those paralyzed moments on the operating table, I couldn't help but judge myself for not being strong enough to bring her into the world naturally, even though the doctor insisted her head was too big to pass through the birth canal. Still, a part of me felt like I had failed even as I knew I had fought with everything I had.

"Is she breathing?" I yelled from behind the see-through curtain over my stomach, as I watched her limp, blueish-gray body being pulled out of my uterus. Amir was in the nearby room, in line with Ukrainian sterile birthing procedures.

"Yes, she's fine. Look at all this hair! Are you ready to be a mother?" the doctor asked.

"Yes! Yes, I am!" I yelled through my tears.

The nurse wrapped my daughter's seven-pound body in a sheet and brought her close. I kissed her quivering lips, her cries tugging at my heart in a way I'd never felt before. Every instinct screamed for me to hold her, to comfort her, to be the one she needed—but instead, they took her to Amir in the other room while they stitched me up. A growling expression crossed my face as the nurse handed Sofie to her biological father. Through the glass window on the door, I glimpsed him pacing, cradling *my* bundle of joy. Bitterness consumed me as he experienced her first moments before I could.

That honor didn't belong to him; he was already hurting us, an imposter of a father. I knew he couldn't comfort her the way I could, the way only a mother can. He hadn't just endured what I had—the transcendent shift from womanhood to motherhood. That bond, that glue, was mine. It was through our shared pain, Sofie's and mine, that he was given a new label: father. Yet, despite Allah's mercy in Sofie's safe arrival, Amir showed no appreciation. His tearless, blank expression said it all as he helped the nurses wheel me into my recovery room. "You did great, Mama," were the only words I caught as his footsteps faded away from my periphery.

But even with that ache, I still found joy—the birth of my life's purpose. Sofie had arrived on 12/12, the greatest winter celebration I would ever know. I was in a world of my own now, on the other side of my divine responsibility. I had done my part in what marriage and nature intended for me to do: grow the family. But who belonged in it would only be known in time.

I impatiently waited for the anesthesia to wear off in the recovery room, desperate to move my arms, aching to hold my baby. The moment I could finally lift them, the nurse placed her in my arms, and everything changed. As I held my daughter for the first time, my entire perception of the world shifted. It was as if nothing that came before mattered.

Not only was a child born that day—a mother was, too. I was overwhelmed with pride, joy, and awe at this new soul I had brought into the world; everything and everyone else faded into the background. I had created my own family. My body was now forever imprinted with her cells, and in that moment, I knew she wanted me more than anyone else. I felt it as her tiny body stilled against my chest, her kicks quieting. She needed me. She didn't care about the past—only the future. Sofie latched onto my breast as if she had always known how, and instinctively, I knew how to help her. I felt powerful, fearless, and fiercely protective. As we reconnected, body to body, I cried—tears of love and of sorrow—pitying myself for bringing her into a world marked by instability, the scars of my unhealed childhood, and my fractured relationships with her father and my mother.

"Welcome to this big world, my little one. It's just you and me. But don't you worry, I will protect you," I whispered to her precious little face. Sofie was breathtaking: bow-shaped lips, deep brown eyes that mirrored her father's, a full head of dark hair, thick lashes framing those eyes, and the most flawless olive skin. She was my beautiful, fierce little miracle.

I wondered if my mother had felt this way when she'd given birth to me. Had she felt the same overwhelming, unexplainable instinct to protect? Had she loved me even a fraction as deeply as I already loved my daughter, only three hours into her life? And if she had—if she'd truly felt this—how could she have hurt me? No, she couldn't have felt what I was feeling now, I remembered: she hadn't wanted me to be born.

It was just Sofie and me, alone against the bitter Ukrainian winter outside. We spent a total of five more days recovering at the birth house.

On the evening of December 14, Amir came to visit for an hour, just after I was cleared to walk following major abdominal surgery. I wobbled to meet him at the door, making sure my hair was neatly up —hoping to look somewhat attractive. But he didn't even embrace me; his eyes scanned the room until they landed on Sofie. He spoke softly to her while I took photos of them together. Occasionally, he'd signal for a tissue when she spit up, and I carefully pulled myself up, using a makeshift rope from a ripped towel, trying not to rip my six-inch belly incision. Not once did he take a photo of Sofie and me together. When I cradled her to my breast, he shifted his gaze to the window, avoiding my exposed nipple.

"She looks just like me when I was a baby," he said, looking down at his firstborn.

"Yes, your genes are stronger than mine," I replied, smiling because she was so beautiful, like her father.

"Send those photos to me," he added, bending down to kiss Sofie on the head.

I licked my lips for a kiss, but he had already turned toward the door. Tears burned at the back of my throat. *Please, love me again,* I cried silently. *Why am I not good enough?*

Just two days later, Amir's restlessness finally eased, and he returned to Egypt. Disappointment doesn't even begin to cover how I felt. My heart ached as I read his text: 'I'm sorry—I don't have time to come and see you again; I've already changed my flight 2 times. I'll lose my ticket if I don't take this flight.' I had given Amir the ultimate gift—a daughter, a family of his own—yet all he seemed to care about were his material possessions. His last texts weren't about us or the family I had thought we were building together. There was no, *I can't wait to have everyone back together,* or even, *I'm just a phone call away.* Instead, he told me to *be a strong and good mother for Sofie,* as if instructing me to handle it all alone. His deflection, an excuse to distance himself, placed the burden of raising our child squarely on me so he could be free. Then he asked where I'd put his DKNY shirts, his shiny Samsung, and his cologne—things his mistress would surely appreciate more than his own child.

Allah did not grant Amir the epiphany I had desperately prayed for. Instead, I was abandoned on my own battlefield, left to fight for my morals—and, eventually, my sanity.

15
KATYA: THE LEGEND

"I want a divorce!" Amir screamed through the loudspeaker on my phone, stirring Sofie in her sleep. I'd been calling him for an hour, seeing that he was online at 4 a.m. and wondering why he hadn't been answering my messages all day. I could hear distant club music through the phone when he finally answered my call. It was December 22, and sweet little Sofie was just ten days old.

"How could you say this? You don't mean it. Amir, I need your support now! Don't you see that? Please, don't stress me out, I'm breastfeeding," I cried on the phone, hoping not to wake our newborn daughter.

I needed his support as a father and as my husband. But more than anything, I needed him present to sign the important documents for Sofie's future. I still had to transfer my US citizenship to her, just as we had planned. She needed a passport to travel—back to the USA, where we had been planning to live since before our marriage. Even leaving Ukraine with Sofie required his approval. Under Ukrainian law, with his name already on her birth certificate, I had no choice but to follow the legal process. As a Ukrainian citizen in Ukraine, I had to abide by my home country's rules.

"Billions of women have given birth before you, and billions more will after you! You have a child. Isn't that what you wanted? So, take care of it. Stop fucking calling me while I'm out!" he screamed back, drunk.

I should be snapping and yelling "divorce," not him. Hold it together for Sofie's documents, Katya, I told myself, hanging up the phone.

I wanted to escape again, to throw myself out the window and leave behind the hopelessness that consumed me. Explaining to Amir why he needed to be a better man felt as impossible as describing the color blue to a blind man.

'DON'T EVER HANG UP ON ME! ON ANY MAN. YOU ARE DISRE-SPECTFUL,' his WhatsApp message read. My whole body convulsed with the fear of being a single mom, pain, and pure exhaustion.

I was exhausted from the responsibility I felt as a mother—a force that wouldn't let me settle for anything less than a better life for our daughter. I refused to be the mother my daughter cried over, wondering why I hadn't been strong enough to protect her. I wanted to be more than the mother my younger self had glimpsed through a cracked door, crying in a pile of laundry, mourning the past. I wanted my daughter to be free from the helplessness I'd once felt.

While my mother had screamed, "They hurt me—REVENGE!" I wanted to shout back, "I survived! I am not my pain." The path to freedom lay before me, steep and daunting but on which I could finally escape the negativity of the toxic people who had shaped my life. Yet, standing at the base of that mountain, I hesitated. I had grown so accustomed to carrying pain, believing there was no other way to live. Could I find the strength to climb alone? Had I rolled far enough from my mother's tree to become something different?

I figured that being a better mother for my daughter required me to first step over my pride as the betrayed wife and accept that I had made a mistake marrying Amir, as he had proven time and time again that he was not a fit father. But I feared depending on myself as the sole provider of my happiness. My self-worth was measured in the love I received from others, not the love I could give myself. Those shackles were tight around my wrists.

. . .

I knew what I had to do—leave—but I was simply too drained to make the first move, not just from sleepless nights and the physical toll of motherhood but from the constant battle to pull Amir into the present, to make him see the importance of the life we had created, to teach him how to be a responsible man and parent. But he focused more on controlling me than embracing fatherhood.

One thought consumed me: *The cortisol from my stress is in my breast milk, and Sofie is drinking it.* I already felt like a failure for choosing a man like Amir to be her father. And now, I was passing my stress on to her. The weight of mom guilt crushed me. I had sworn to protect her, yet here I was, feeding her my own anxiety and pain.

I saw with crystal clarity how naive I had been to think that bringing a baby into my life would straighten up anyone. Instead, it only exposed how messed up and unfair my 'village' truly was. How could I turn it all around for the utopia I knew could exist? All I wanted was for someone to bring me a glass of water, some kind of relief. But no one came. Sofie and I spent two months in that small room, crying together. I lost all my baby weight, and by the third month, stress alone had given me a six-pack.

I needed help, even though I hated asking for it, especially from my mother. But I had no choice. She was too busy licking her wounds after her internet boyfriend drained her savings and left. I wanted to scream at her, to make her see what truly mattered—her daughter and granddaughter—but she was lost in her own mess. Since picking us up from the hospital, she hadn't visited once, even though she lived just an elevator ride away.

I felt like I was living in a delusion, fighting to stay sane while everything else crumbled. My mother had no excuse for being so heartless, so removed; she came from a loving nuclear family. Her weakness sickened me. She failed to see that I had expanded her legacy—the ovum within me she had carried twenty-eight years ago was now brought to life in her grandchild. I struggled to find the support to nurture this part of her lineage while she lost every chance to bring joy into her later years with her grandchildren. My weakness was believing I could depend on others to rise up; hers was that she simply couldn't see past the next twenty-four hours.

I had no choice but to ask her to watch Sofie while I went to the US embassy to submit the documents for her Consular Report of Birth Abroad and begin the citizenship transfer process. I left Sofie in her care for a mere three hours. When I came back, I heard Sofie crying from outside my grandma's apartment door. Fumbling with the keys, I opened the door to find my mother passed out drunk on the couch and Sofie choking on her tears on the bedroom mattress. I cradled Sofie, filled with anger. I almost kicked my mother's passed-out body but walked out instead, vowing to keep her away from Sofie. And I've kept that promise to this day.

The next time I saw my husband in person was in early February, during our final, necessary visit to the US embassy. He was required to appear in order to sign Sofie's citizenship paperwork—a crucial step for her to obtain a US birth certificate, passport, and travel documents. Without his signature, I couldn't legally secure any of it or leave Ukraine. I had no choice but to keep my composure, to hold it together for Sofie's future. With no support from my mother and no margin for error, I had to stay calm and sane, no matter how hard it was seeing my adulterous husband.

When Amir arrived, he came bearing what I immediately recognized as guilt gifts: a flashy gold knockoff Cartier bracelet for our belated one-year anniversary.

"Oh, Katya, you have to see this. I had an accident at the gym," he said, presenting his gift to me fifteen minutes after walking through the door. His tone was a pitch higher than normal.

He proceeded to take off his shirt and show me his back, where there were eight distinct fingernail scratches. I retracted my worrisome hand and felt a punch in my heart.

"Who scratched you? Did you get into a fight?" I asked in a shaky voice. I could feel the acidic anger boiling up my esophagus.

No, Katya, while you were nursing your baby, your husband was fucking that girl in a hotel room, begging her to scratch him when he finished inside her. Don't you remember? That's how he always liked it, my gut taunted, shattering my delusion of a heated Egyptian gym fight. I couldn't stop picturing sharp red acrylics clawing down his chiseled, sweaty back, reflecting the neon lights of downtown Cairo. *He can't do that to me, to us—not now!*

"No. The squat bar fell on my back. It had hooks on the outside, and it slid, scratching me," he lied straight to my face, as though telling me what he'd just had for breakfast.

Wow, he's a perfect liar. How have I never noticed? "Amir," I said, choking down my tears, "there's no way—no *way*—two hooks could leave eight scratch marks on your back." I wanted to vomit from jealousy.

"Wallahi, Katya, I swear on this cup of water, it was the squat bar," he continued to lie, using a typical Islamic line of swearing on the holy gifts of Allah.

"Amir, swear on your child's life that this was a gym accident," I pushed him, my jaw trembling.

"We never swear on our child's life. I swear on my mother's life, Katya, this is from the gym," he said, looking me dead in the eyes.

The acid reached my face and flushed it crimson—I was livid. Not only because he'd blatantly lied but because he honestly thought that I'd be a fool and believe him. I wanted to give in to my anger and slap him across the face, but I stopped myself. I chose to be the fool in his eyes. I needed him to sign those embassy documents for Sofie's future.

I realized, also, that I still loved him. The jealousy bell rang loudly, reminding me I still longed for him to be mine and mine alone. At the same time, by choosing not to react to his lies, I knew I had just lowered my self-worth even further in his eyes. Yet, every time I looked into his daughter's eyes—like two droplets of water, identical and indescribable—I loved him. I didn't know what to do.

Maybe if you play nice, keep to yourself, be a good mother, and don't nag your husband, he will choose you again. You have to earn that love, Katya! my inner dialogue kept filling the awkward silence between us. I didn't want to believe that he could tear the rug from under me after we'd spent nearly three years weaving it. *We need more time together, as a family.*

Our papers were signed, and once again, Amir left us in Ukraine—back to his mistress and bachelor lifestyle. I was left in a swamp of hopelessness but equipped with a passport and approval letter from Amir for Sofie and I to travel 'only to Egypt.' If I didn't have Sofie, this would have been my chance to finally run. But that was not my reality anymore; I had to keep fighting for Sofie's father.

I knew his mistress's name but had no proof, apart from the gym accident scratch marks and their interactions on social media. I pieced it together, like most women in their FBI internet mode, from the few likes and comments I found on Facebook. They were in the same real estate group, often carrying on coded conversations in the comments. I had a lot of time on my hands while pregnant, and my intuition sharpened with every interaction I uncovered.

As soon as I saw her profile photo—curvy, attractive, and self-assured—and especially the content Amir engaged with in that group, my female intuition lit up. The dead giveaway came in my last month of pregnancy, when she accidentally liked one of my Insta-gram posts from four years earlier at two in the morning, then quickly removed it. She was also the only non-Muslim woman at his work—a foreigner who didn't need to be kept a virgin before marriage—and flaunted connections with Egypt's biggest pop star. Amir loved status and attention more than the Holy Quran.

Yet, I struggled to make sense of the fact that Amir still answered my calls and flew four hours to visit us. He must still want me, right? My reasoning told me that if a man wanted to leave, he would have done so already. So, I blamed the receptionist from his work, seeing her as the manipulator—not the sweet, heroic Amir I thought I knew. *He's just caught up in the wrong crowd*, I mothered him in my mind. I refused to let his mistress's home-wrecking power overshadow mine. I was the woman who had made him a man in many ways. I was counting on his upbringing, and on his sweet mother who loved me and Sofie, to prevail. I just needed more time; he would soon wake up and bond with Sofie, and we would be us again.

We kept fighting our separate battles. Amir's battle was to keep us at a distance while shifting the blame of our rocky marriage to me: "You're crazy to think I'm cheating. You're sick in the head! You need to heal!" Meanwhile, my battle was to keep my daughter's father around and chase my nuclear family dream. Judging by his constant shopping sprees, he had more than enough money to start our immigration process. He resisted, time and again. I fought back—harder each time—refusing to face the imminent reality of my future as a single mother.

The back-and-forth dragged on for six exhausting months—an international battle between Egypt and Ukraine. Flights between Kyiv and Cairo were only four hours apart, and Sofie and I went to Egypt when she was five months old. Each time I boarded the plane, I strode with confidence, ready to seduce and reclaim the second-place world championship powerlifter I called my husband. I didn't look like the woman he'd met two years before; I was skinnier, and Egyptians loved their women full and curvy. I ate as much as I could, but cortisol and tears devoured any extra calories I forced down.

My sweet mother-in-law even bought me lingerie, instructing me to wear it under a mini dress when he came home from work. I tried, but he refused my advances. "Katya, really, now? I have a dinner meeting." We spent two months in Cairo under one roof, but with Amir being constantly cold and distant and rarely home, my Slavik pride pushed me to fly back to Ukraine with my tail between my legs, searching for refuge, again, among my barely involved family.

It felt like I was parading Sofie between Egypt and Ukraine, desperate for someone to notice our needs, for some sense of stability. I kept hoping that forcing Amir to miss us would make him do the right thing, but I was wrong.

Now back in Kyiv, Sofie was seven months old. The Ukrainian summer was beautiful, and I found brief peace walking with her through the city, meeting other moms my age. But Amir kept pulling further away, barely checking in on his daughter. How could the man who'd once chased me across the world suddenly want to keep us apart? My jealousy of his mistress began to consume me, but I still clung to the fact that he could not give up his responsibilities as our rock and safe place. He was Muslim; his purpose was to have a family and take pride in being a supporter. There was no way Amir could abandon his newborn daughter and me, the woman he had once pursued so fiercely.

As a last resort, I reached out to my mother for advice, but her free time was already claimed by vodka bottles. I asked my father to visit his granddaughter, and he did—for three hours, but only because I promised him a hand-me-down iPhone.

I reached out to my Egyptian in-laws for help when Amir denied Sofie and me a flight back to Cairo after our summer in Kyiv. "You're not healed yet in the head! I can't be around you!" he told me. As a last effort, I told the Sabrys everything—about Amir's other girlfriend, the scratches on his back, the random messages I'd found, and his baseless demands for a divorce. In Islam, adultery isn't just a sin—it's a crime punishable by law.

I'll never know exactly what his family discussed after I laid out all my evidence against his claims of "I'm not cheating," but by

September 2018, we were finally allowed back to Cairo, and I felt more confident than ever that, with the women in his family standing with me, we could pull him out of the weeds and back on track as a father. Sofie was nine months old by then, already crawling and eating solids, while my body had long since given in—I'd stopped producing milk with any fat, struggled to eat enough, and now weighed ten pounds less than before my pregnancy. The international battle had taken its toll.

Have you ever had that nightmare where you are trying to run away but keep stumbling on ground made of pudding, and no one hears your screams? That's how I felt in my waking hours. My moral compass told me to have dignity and fight for my daughter's right for a family while my instincts told me to run away from the cesspool of lies, control, and manipulation.

I believed, for a short week after being back in Cairo, I could count on support from his family, but my plan unraveled. His family had turned into my enemies, and my husband launched the dirtiest of games, targeting my mental state and relentlessly pushing me toward the brink of losing my mind. His mental games started subtly, with small things like erasing his steroid doses from the dry-erase calendar.

As I walked into the kitchen, I asked, "Amir, tell me the truth: are you back doing steroids again?"

"What steroids, Katya?" he replied, lounging calmly on the living room couch.

"The ones right here on the calen–" I started, pointing to the now-empty boxes on the board. "What! They were just here this morning! You erased them." I was stunned.

"No, babe, there was nothing there. You know, I'm worried about you, habibti. Your head is getting the best of you," he replied.

Before I realized he was gaslighting me, he was already two steps ahead, setting mental traps. I found a pair of black shoes under the rack and swore I'd never bought them, but he insisted he had been with me when I had, even searching for a receipt to prove it. "You've lost your mind," he said, and I found myself clinging to him for reassurance. This became a daily pattern. He twisted my reality, convincing me I was unstable and insisting I'd said things I couldn't remember—like asking him to stop for groceries. Instead of questioning why it took six hours to buy groceries, I worried about not remembering I'd asked him to go. My thoughts spiraled: *Maybe I'm too anxious. Maybe I'm stirring the pot for no reason.*

His next move was to turn me against my family: "Your mother even told me you don't know how to respect men," and, "They're on my side; they don't love you," he'd repeat whenever I defended my sanity. He reminded me I had no friends in Egypt, blaming me for not "liking it enough to get involved," sneering, "You can't even make friends." He tore me down, piece by piece, until he had full control.

When I found long brown hairs on the bathroom rug, in my bed, and on the couches, Amir calmly dismissed it: "That's the maid's hair. You're again letting your imagination get the best of you!" I knew his mistress had been in our home, which, in Egypt, could send him to prison for up to six months. The more proof I found, the harder he pushed back, and I started to distrust my own reality. *Maybe all that opioid use really did fuck up my head,* I'd reason through my tears.

It didn't take long for the Sabry family to believe him. To them, their golden child could do no wrong. They couldn't accept that their 'perfect parenting' had produced a liar and an abuser.

In a last attempt to be heard, I reached out to his sister. I reminded her of New York, back when even his own family was fighting with him about his time there. I asked if he had been with another woman then. "Oh, yeah—he was engaged. They were picking out tile for their new build," she said, almost casually.

Her words knocked the air out of me. Engaged. Building a house with someone else while I was with him. I cried, "I didn't know, I swear!" But in that moment I understood—the Sabrys had seen me as the homewrecker all along.

I searched my phone and pulled up the photo Amir once sent me of a diamond ring when I was still in New York. "I was looking at rings today," he'd teased, dangling hope like bait. I forwarded that picture to his sister, proof of the lies he spun for both of us. She never replied. The next day she called with a final message: "I can't talk to you anymore about Amir or discuss your marriage problems."

Maybe I imagined it, but I'm pretty sure his sister even suggested I see a psychiatrist. So, I did. I told the psychiatrist, "He says I'm imagining things, but I know I'm not. Then my heart races, and I can't sleep at night."

At my first and only visit, the psychiatrist prescribed Lithium and Diazepam—a mood stabilizer and a mild tranquilizer. I didn't take the medication because I knew I'd been misdiagnosed. But, foolishly, I told the Egyptians about my doctor's recommendations. *Bad idea, Katya,* I told myself one night. *Now you've convinced them you're crazy and an unfit mother. You've just let Amir win.*

I felt the silent scream building inside me as I realized they saw me as a crazy woman who couldn't keep her husband. To them, the problem had to be me. How could their son, brother, and friend—a man raised in Egyptian A-class society, from a 'decent family'—be an adulterous husband abandoning his newborn daughter? I didn't know then, but in Islam, a man can divorce his wife if she is proven to be mentally ill.

Sahar, the maid, was the only person who stood by me. I had met her years before while she'd worked for the Sabry family, going as far back as being a wet nurse to Amir. Always smiling, always positive, she exuded warmth, and I'd tip her each time for her hard work. Every Wednesday, she came to clean the dust from untouched surfaces, offering me a glimmer of hope and a brief escape from the suffocating cage I was trapped in, both physically and mentally.

"Amir is not right," Sahar repeated under her breath as she mopped the already spotless stone floors. "He sees what his dad does. But what about Sofie? Haram!" She shook her head and held her heart.

His father had been accused of having another family by the sister more than once. But what could these women do without witnesses? Nothing.

"Kate, I'm sorry to ask, but do you sleep with your husband?" she asked, handing me my tea.

"Sahar, no, he won't even let me touch his hand. He sleeps here. He has another woman. I know this," I said, pointing to the guest bedroom.

"Haram," she sighed, taking a deep breath.

She was just as trapped and hopeless as I was. There was the right thing, and then there was the Muslim man thing. She didn't need to tell me that men often get away with their dirty deeds, hands wiped clean. I already knew—I just never expected it would happen to me.

I sat there, embarrassed, staring at the steam rising from my tea, struggling to find the Arabic words to explain what he had said to me. But my vocabulary wasn't good enough, so I kept my feelings inside.

Some days, I found the courage to stand up to Amir. But when I did, I was "not a good woman," I had "no dignity," I was "raised by a bad family," I "needed to act like a woman," I was "not appreciative," I had "no principles," and I was "not a decent wife who stood by her husband." I think I heard the word 'decent' two or three times a day. Why had I ever shared my hardships, my family pitfalls, and my traumas with him? He was now using all my words, turning my weakness into weapons against me.

'Decent' means conforming to accepted moral standards. But I wasn't conforming. The meaning of 'decent' shifts the moment you step into another culture. Having lived in both the Western and Eastern worlds, I've realized I don't seem to fit in anywhere. In one part of the world, my behaviors are celebrated; in another, they're condemned. Could I be the problem?

Amir wanted to leave this marriage without the shame of being seen as an adulterer, painting me as the insane villain. That just solidified the thought: I wasn't 'decent' enough.

Every day became a fight for survival. I felt scared, with nowhere to turn and no one to trust. My depression whispered relentlessly, *You can't seem to belong anywhere. You are the problem.* I had lost all sense of self—who I was, where I belonged, and what 'decent' even meant.

Sofie was ready to start walking; just shy of ten months, she was stumbling around on the marble tile. I wanted to enjoy her milestones and share them with her father, but he was never home. Motherhood, without any support, was slowly killing me. My weight dropped significantly. Forcing myself to eat a banana, only to throw it up, was the best I could manage for self-care. I couldn't even recognize my fragile, one-hundred-pound body in the mirror. "This is what Sofie calls Mom," my reflection said to me, and I felt disgusted.

I would fall asleep with thoughts of suicide, planning it in the most real sense. I wanted my Katya legacy to be put to rest; I was done resisting that I was a complete failure. My hopes of Amir, my mother, and his family changing in response to Sofie's birth had vanished as if carried away in a breeze through the already broken window.

16

MOTHERHOOD 2.0

By Egyptian standards, it's the norm for a wife and mother to be 'kept' at home. On the surface, it sounds like a dream—being cared for without the burden of work or bills. But the culture demands that a woman surrender her independence, most social outlets, and career aspirations, and places them in the hands of a man deemed worthy of that trust. Over time, this setup shrinks her identity to fit within the walls of the home. My man, however, wasn't worthy of that trust.

I felt this deeply during my month of complete isolation in Cairo. My only social interactions were a few Friday afternoons at the in-laws' so they could "enjoy Sofie" and brief visits from Amir during his lunch breaks. I was lonely without alternative sources of joy or self-realization. Most new moms in Cairo have their mothers stay with them to help raise the child. The 'it takes a village' concept is taken seriously—except, of course, with me.

My one true friend, Pascal from Canada, had moved away after discovering her husband's infidelity, and the other expats had relo-cated to Europe or returned home. Without anyone to ease my lone-liness, I relied on the TV, which played constantly in the background.

One week, Amir packed his belongings and moved back in with

his parents. I felt it coming as he'd been sleeping in the guest bedroom a few nights a week and would be gone early in the morning. I stopped asking him his whereabouts to avoid hearing more lies. "I prayed a special prayer, Istikhara, and Allah told me to divorce you," he said before he started packing. How could I argue against Allah? I tried to stop him during his first round of packing, clinging to his legs, but he kicked me off like I was a piece of toilet paper stuck to his shoe.

When he returned to gather the rest of his enormous shoe collection, his mother came along to support him. She requested her usual green tea with mint and sat silently, watching him pack. "Why, Nadeen? Why?" I cried in Arabic, pacing the marble floor with Sofie in my arms. Her cold, dead silence terrified me, and I realized how foolish I had been to trust her. Had she only helped me return to Cairo to keep Sofie closer? Would they take Sofie away next?

The Sabry family's once-loving and accepting gaze had grown cold and distant. They didn't want us together. I had become the lie Amir fed them: "She's not a good woman! I do not have a mistress! She's crazy!" My subconscious screamed, *This is a trap for Sofie.* I felt paralyzed, scared to make any move, unsure whether it would be right or wrong. I had no choice but to comply, withdraw emotionally, and remain in isolation.

Amir visited Sofie and his 'kept' wife a couple of times a week. I secretly recorded our conversations, desperate to piece together some sense of reality after he had pushed me so far from it. His constant belittling had left me a shell of a woman, barely able to meet our baby's needs. I wasn't sane enough to see that he was grooming me to comply with my role as 'Ommi Sofie,' (Sofie's mother). To him, my 'mental state' justified my treatment: isolation and divorce. But I still don't understand how much further he wanted to break me—or why. Whatever his motives, one thing was clear: he was determined to protect his image as a decent Muslim man.

. . .

On October 28, 2018, his exotic cologne once again filled the lonely apartment as he spent fifteen minutes pretending to play family. He gently bounced Sofie on his lap, making her laugh with silly faces, while I stood in the bathroom, gluing on my fake lashes. I clung to him like victims cling to their abusers—hoping for change, desperate for love, and blaming myself if it meant keeping him close. I told myself I could bring Papa back for Sofie, no matter what it took. After only twenty-one months of marriage, the father-daughter moment I had dreamed of my whole life had become the fleeting scene of a diaper commercial on Arab TV: forced and rehearsed.

"You have not been appreciative. I took you from your worst situation and made it better, yet all you do is focus on the bad in me. And you're extremely controlling and jealous!" Amir began his predictable degrading.

"Stop putting me down," I replied in a calm yet quivering voice. "Just tell me why you are leaving us like this."

"I'm not putting you down, this is your truth! Wake up!" he said as he pointed a finger toward me.

"You need to wake up, Amir," I replied.

"No, I'm awake! And I'm a person who got a child from you. You'll forever be my problem."

"She will one day know what happened and that you decided to cheat and leave. And that you left her. Is that what you want?" I asked.

"I will let her know, too! I will let her know that things just didn't work out between me and you. I'm much better than you! I'm not going to tell her that you're a bad person. Like you're accusing me now! I'm not leaving her, I'm leaving you because you are disgusting!" His voice echoed off the white marble floors.

In the quiet nights, as I replayed recordings of our conversations, I grew numb to his abuse tactics—gaslighting, deflection, and weaponizing my emotions against me. The fault wasn't ever in the truth, it was in my reaction to his lies.

"You already broke me, Amir," I said, giving the narcissist what he wanted to hear.

"You were already broken! I took you in and tried to fix you, but you were not appreciative," Amir replied.

"How was I not appreciative?" I poked the snake again, more annoyed than anything. *Just confess you found another woman, and let's settle this already,* I thought.

"I got you from being a slut. I choose you amongst sluts. Okay? Because back then in that hotel room, I saw the good in you."

"It doesn't hurt me at all, what you're saying," I replied, bursting into a bitter laugh. In that moment, I saw everything from an outsider's perspective—this dire situation with Amir, my daughter, his cruel words, me being trapped here, and just how immature and ridiculous all of it was.

There is no future here, an inner voice spoke to me. The boat carrying our impossible love story on the Nile had no more room; it drifted now toward its inevitable end.

We need to leave, but how? I thought, struggling to suppress my despair-driven laughter while the same Dettol cleaner commercial I'd seen thousands of times played on the TV.

"I know! Keep laughing! You are mentally ill. As I said the other day, when you heal in your head, soon you'll realize that you've lost everything. You'll regret that we've lost one another," he said.

Isn't he packing his things and leaving us? Or are you imagining that, too?

"Amir, you promised me and your parents that we wouldn't live here—in Egypt! That we wouldn't have children here. You knew what I wanted from day one of meeting me. You couldn't live up to your promises, so you got another girl to lick your wounds," I reminded him.

Sofie cooed, giggling and crawling toward him now, thinking we were paying her attention. Amir smothered her with kisses and tickles. Tears of anger and repulsion stung my eyes as I watched. Even the reality she was experiencing was a lie. This environment, this place, was toxic for her, too.

This cannot go on any further. Sofie deserves more, the inner voice continued.

"No, no, no. I promised you because you only cared about what you wanted. You didn't think about me. You're selfish, always thinking about yourself," he said.

"You did nothing but lie and protect your own image," I argued.

"I can't believe I have to deal with you for the rest of my life!" he shouted, rising to his feet, his face twisted with anger. "And you know what else? I am never moving to the US. You stay by your man, regardless of where you are. Regardless of whether we're married or not! You are staying here, in Egypt, with Sofie. You got that?"

His words hit me like an atomic bomb, obliterating every last shred of hope I had left. I almost shit my pants. My face was pale like a ghost.

He had finally come clean and confirmed my deepest fear: he had been mirroring my dreams to draw me in and use me, and now he was done with me and discarding me. How could I possibly stay in this miserable life? Raise my daughter in a suffocating bubble? Watch her get harassed on the streets like I was? Give her a poor education with little hope for a career? Breathe this polluted air? Fight endlessly for women's equality? Never see the mountains again? Pretend to get along with people who despised me? Absolutely not. Not after everything I'd been through for us, and certainly not after all I'd lived through. I hadn't lived my life to settle for mediocrity in Cairo, Egypt.

You can try to destroy me, Amir, I thought, *but I will never let anyone harm my daughter.*

"You're a fucking liar. You've destroyed my life. All the leaps of faith I took for you—I trusted you with my future. I trusted you to be the father of our child! I left the man I truly loved to be with you! Fuck you, Amir. Fuck you!" I projected all the hate I had through my clenched jaw. Flames burned from my eyes.

"I don't fucking care, Katya. I am leaving you. We talk only regarding Sofie now," he said calmly and left the apartment, slamming the door behind him.

Frozen in shock, I reached for my phone and Googled what it meant to be a divorced woman in Egypt. Under Islamic Sharia law, a divorced mother can keep physical custody of her child until they turn fifteen, but only if the mother stays single. Remarrying means losing physical custody, as the father retains legal guardianship and full authority over major decisions. As a non-Muslim, I'd also have to convert to Islam or prove I could raise my child according to Islamic standards to have any chance at custody. One wrong move, and they could take her from me.

Sofie's giggling once again filled the room.

"I refuse to let this become our reality," I said out loud. I would be trapped by divorce here—forever only the mother of Amir's child, under his watch, bound by his religious expectations, and shamed by his family and society.

Desperate to share my fears and needing someone to confide in for my sanity, I thought of Rana, a woman I had met through Pascal in Zamalek two years ago. An Egyptian woman in her late forties with light skin and natural blonde curls, Rana could easily pass for a German. I searched for her on social media and was relieved to discover she also lived in City View.

I messaged her, asking for advice on my situation, and invited myself over later that day. She welcomed me with openness and honesty. Rana didn't sugarcoat the challenges, making it clear that life here without a husband would be hell. She shared stories of the constant scrutiny and judgment she endured as an Egyptian ex-wife. Divorced twice, she now lived alone in the neighboring apartment complex with split custody of her two boys.

"You get used to it. I still have my outings and friends around," she said.

But I didn't want to settle in Egypt—I never had. I refused to let her reality be mine, too.

That same night, I collapsed on the cold kitchen floor, my silent weeping breaking into quiet, agonized screams. *God, I want out of this country! What do I do now? Amir has turned everyone against me. Where do I go? I don't have a home to return to.*

Then, a shift—I felt something deeper than the fear of starting over: *Life is so much more than this.* It held beauty, even if I'd only glimpsed it. Sofie deserved that beauty. My mother's ill intentions were lessons in resilience, and every storm I'd weathered had prepared me for this moment: to stand strong and fight.

"It's time to do what I do best," I whispered, standing up from the kitchen floor and locking eyes with my malnourished, mentally drained reflection in the mirror. "Run, Katya."

I'd been running my whole life—escaping myself, others, pain, and my past. I'd crossed continents and chased mirages in the desert, but this time, the stakes were higher. If I got caught, the Sabry family would never let me out of their sight. I would be trapped in Egypt until Sofie became an adult. I planned to tear her away from her father and his family, and I feared she might grow to hate me for it. I wrestled with the damage this could cause Sofie—a wound that could last a lifetime.

What's worse, growing up without a father or with a suicidal, depressed mother? Both are devastating. I knew the road ahead would be long and grueling if I managed to escape with my daughter. I understood the harm this could bring her. But what if I didn't fail? What if I rose above it all and soared?

Facing the gut-wrenching realization that the only way to a better life was to escape undetected, I gathered the pieces of dignity scattered on the kitchen floor and reached for my phone. I messaged my good college friend, Becca, in Reno: 'I'm running away. I'm kidnapping Sofie. Can we come and stay with you?' Then I Googled, 'Parental Kidnapping in Egypt.'

Parental kidnapping isn't considered a crime in Egypt until

there's a custody order in place—and even then, only if it's violated. I had no idea if Amir had already obtained one, and I couldn't ask him without raising suspicion. Egypt recognizes dual citizenship, but it refuses to honor child custody orders from any other country. Egypt offers no protection for children abducted from their homes abroad and brought back there. I read the warnings on the British and German embassy websites, each one echoing the same bleak truth: since Egypt didn't sign the 1980 Hague Convention on the Civil Aspects of International Child Abduction—the very treaty designed to return children kidnapped by a parent back to their country of residence—there is no hope for the lost children taken to Egypt. But in a twisted way, that worked in my favor, too. If Egypt wouldn't help bring back children taken from other countries, they couldn't fight to get my daughter back if I took her to the US. But we couldn't get caught.

I'm not a criminal, I reasoned. I just wanted to remove the toxic people from our lives—those who had taken us for granted, weighed us down, and selfishly tried to contain our lives within a bubble for their own satisfaction. *I'm not breaking up a family*—there had never been a real family to begin with.

I spent three weeks processing the magnitude of our escape. The risk of staying outweighed the risk of fleeing, but both options were riddled with unknowns. Would the weight of my sorrows drive me back to painkillers once I was stateside? What if I couldn't provide for Sofie and me, and we ended up homeless? What if Amir realized I was gone before I crossed the border and called the police?

Fear threatened to paralyze me, but I refused to let it take over. I allowed myself only brief moments to feel, staying focused to keep my emotions from clouding my judgment. I wrote down a simple plan: 'Becca buys two plane tickets. I keep my emotions in check around the Sabrys. I don't act suspicious. I get to the airport. I don't get caught.' I needed cash, too—*Sell the little gold you have, Katya.*

When Amir left, he took the gold coins from our wedding and the mother-and-daughter gold necklaces his family had gifted to Sofie and me. All I had left was his knockoff Cartier bracelet, but it would have to be enough for pocket money. As a non-Egyptian citizen without a bank account, I managed to scrape together $1,820 by selling all the gold I owned and my small savings. Without a bank account, I had to rely on the black market and spent two afternoons strolling Sofie through the dirty streets of Zamalek in search of dollar exchange places.

As if fear wasn't enough, paranoia joined the mental ping-pong game. I began to suspect that everyone was in on keeping me and Sofie here. Amir's eyes seemed to follow us everywhere, even when he wasn't physically present. Every time I took the car out, he would call, casually asking where I was going. On longer walks around the City View Compound, I studied the neighbors' routines and the street guards, memorizing their daily and nightly schedules. I noted eyes that lingered too long and realized Amir had the security guards keeping tabs on us. One of his supervisors from work lived just down the street. *How am I supposed to get out of these gates undetected? How do I order a van? How do I get to the airport? Uber is too risky.*

Some days, my overthinking spiraled out of control, but I found a way to channel my anxiety. I poured my racing thoughts into preparing a parting gift, a motivator to keep pushing forward: *When I finish this, I should be gone.* I put paint to canvas and escaped; painting had always been my favorite hobby, one I'd lost touch with while living under the rock that is Cairo—cut off from my needs and wants.

Okay, I'll hide my luggage in the bushes by the curb at night when the guards take their break. Then go down with Sofie in the morning and load into a car without them seeing me. I'll tip him five hundred LE and ask him to drive around to the other gate. The plan could work, but it was risky.

· · ·

Three weeks went by, and my painting was nearly finished. Becca waited patiently for my signal, ready to take us in. She didn't hesitate to offer her room for our stay, and I was deeply grateful to have someone awaiting our safe arrival. We had shared memories of house parties and study sessions on the campus quad, but it wasn't until she'd attended my Egyptian wedding that we'd reconnected more deeply. Since then, we had kept in touch, and she sympathized with my situation, shocked by the dark turn my fairytale wedding had taken.

'That's in 12 days. Are you sure Thursday the 29th?' she replied when I messaged her to pull the trigger.

'They think I've accepted my destiny as a single mother here,' I wrote back. 'We have a schedule. Amir usually comes on Wednesdays around 5 PM after the maid leaves. Fridays we're at the parents' house. No one will check on me Thursday. I've just got to get to the airport.'

'Okay, I found the flight. Booking now,' she replied.

'Delete all our communication. Send me the confirmation on the 29th in the morning. Just send a thumbs-up that you got them.' I deleted our conversation history right after sending this last message.

There's no turning back, I told myself as my hands trembled. I still needed a van and maybe some travel documents I was not aware of. Then it hit me—Rana, divorced and experienced in traveling with her kids, would know more about the process. *You have to tell her, Katya.*

Gripped by fear and hesitation, I finally confided in Rana. Letting her in on my secret was a gamble, but I needed to unload the guilt and fear that threatened to unravel me. I told her about the tickets and begged her to keep it a secret. With tears in her eyes, she urged me to run—for Sofie's future—and promised to help however she could.

Together, we mapped out the final details of my Thursday departure. She promised to arrange the airport van through a reliable company she knew and advised us to create a 'permission slip to travel with child' of sorts—just in case—and printed several copies for me at her work. Rana explained that while this permission was not yet mandated by law in Egypt, border patrol could still ask if the child had authorization to travel abroad. In the document, we listed her male friend's name and number to play the role of Amir Sabry in case the border patrol decided to call. It was risky, but I had no choice but to trust her.

Back at my apartment, I spent two days practicing Amir's impossible signature, tracing it from our Ukrainian marriage certificate against the balcony's glass door until I had perfected it. With the document finished and copies in hand, I thought I had it all figured out.

Three days before my scheduled flight, I woke up in a cold sweat, realizing we needed a roundtrip ticket to support the story that Sofie and I were traveling for a winter holiday. I messaged Becca, who confirmed she had only purchased a one-way ticket but promised to buy a return flight the day before my 7:10 a.m. departure and cancel it within the airline's twenty-four-hour refund policy to save money. Relieved but still wary, I asked her to resend the confirmation once done and promptly deleted our conversation for safety. Paranoia consumed me.

My last Wednesday in Cairo arrived faster than I could grasp. As the sun rose over the Giza Pyramids, I sat in bed paralyzed by fear, waiting for Sofie's cries to signal the start of my day. My heart pounded as the moment to set my plan into motion drew closer.

Dozens of things had to align perfectly for me to escape with my daughter: The maid had to show up, Amir had to pay his weekly visit that night, and no unexpected invitations to the Sabry house could happen, nor could any extended family decide to visit Sofie. The airport van had to arrive on time, I couldn't be seen sneaking out of the house, and we had to cross the border without Amir's father being alerted. Security workers at the airport knew Mr. Sabry. Blonde and pushing a baby stroller, I would stand out like a sore thumb among the Arabs. Not to mention the unknown security measures Amir might have put in place. Had he got a custody order? He could have obtained one without my knowledge. If he had, I would be flagged, charged with kidnapping, and thrown into prison.

"Sahar, it's very clean here. Shukran. Please, no need to come next Wednesday," I said to the maid.

"Hadr, ya Katya. Hadr, habibi," she complied and kissed my cheeks goodbye.

"Sahar," I said from the threshold of the open door. She was smiling and blowing kisses my way from the elevator. "You are a great woman; a great mother. I will miss you," I said with a half-smile and broken Arabic.

"See you in two weeks! Please, eat something. Do it for Sofie! Take care of yourself," she said.

After saying my coded goodbyes to Sahar, I waited for Amir to arrive. Right on cue, I heard the keys turn in the door. I greeted him with a smile—a smile that showed I was happy he had played his part in our escape, just as I had planned. I wore a nice dress and heavy makeup and had dressed Sofie in her best, adding little pink bows to her hair. I refused to let him remember me as the depressed, greasy-haired bag of bones he had grown used to visiting. This was, hopefully, the final time he would see us for a very long time, and I wanted us to go out in style.

"Why are you dressed up?" he asked.

"I was taking photos with Sofie. I realized I don't have any of us together. Do you want some tea?" I asked, now shaking.

"No, I'm fine. Thanks," he replied coldly, as usual.

I made myself tea and watched Amir's fake interaction with his daughter. His sweet words and kisses seemed genuine, but the truth was, he had already broken her heart. He had given up on her before she'd even had the chance to tell him how she felt. I could imagine her saying, "Please stay, Daddy. Mommy loves you. I love you." He'd failed at the one thing she needed him to be—her protector. She needed him to be her hero, the man she would one day look for in a husband. All he'd had to do was pretend, if not for the sake of our happiness, then at the very least for his daughter's. He could have lived a double life, showing up every day to watch her grow. But even that had been too much for him to do. The first man to break Sofie's heart was, sadly, her father.

It wasn't unusual for me to cry while watching them play pretend. He knew I struggled to accept that he had given up on us. But this time, I cried knowing I was about to hurt him—and worse, I had no choice but to hurt my daughter in the process. I didn't want to be the villain, but he'd given me no other choice.

My tea was still hot when he got up to leave.

"Can I hug you?" I asked, stopping him at the door.

"Why?" he asked.

"Cause...I don't get many hugs these days," I said, with a teary-eyed half-smile.

Amir let me approach him and wrap my arms around his chest. He didn't reciprocate, just stood frozen.

As a bargaining gesture with God, I was compelled to love my enemy at that moment. I felt an indescribable mix of emotions: fear of getting caught, fear of what was to come next, pity for myself, pity that we were hurting Sofie, hatred for all his lies, hatred for all my wrong choices. By hugging him, I wanted to show my humility and clear my conscience. Unlike my mother, I was acknowledging that we, man and wife, had failed our daughter, and she would now grow up without the nuclear family every child deserves. Unlike my mother, I was owning up to my part of the blame.

My actions would do all the fighting when he found us missing in a couple of days. A simple hug would make my pain clear to him and perhaps—I so hoped—keep him from coming and taking her back to Egypt.

In that moment, as I leaned on his chest, I was also repenting for the hurt I had put on Amir. Yes, he had broken me, but through Sofie, he had given me the strength to turn our lives around. He had given me purpose for my resiliency. And one day, when he grew up, he would stay up at night, realizing how much he had destroyed. For now, I had to gesture silent forgiveness so I could still look into our daughter's eyes, as they were just like his.

In that last moment of being 'kept,' I prayed to God to help Sofie and me escape safely. The man I had once chosen to love, moved for, and tried so hard to build a family with, turned away and walked out the door for the last time—completely unaware of what was coming next.

I watched him through the door's peephole as he waited for the elevator. My former hero, now turned antagonist, glanced back at the door, as if sensing something. Of course, he did—his role in my life was over. He had given me Sofie, the purpose to stand on my own.

"Goodbye, Amir. I hope you find your happiness, too," I said out loud.

Without wasting a moment, I grabbed my old, trusted luggage from the closet—the same luggage that had carried my memories around the world—and packed frantically for my flight across the Atlantic. It was finally time for us to go *home*.

17
THE NOBLE ART OF LETTING GO (NOVEMBER 2018)

With my plane departing in exactly twelve hours, I frantically packed, hands trembling as I struggled to keep my nerves in check. Every creak and shuffle from the hallway sent me darting to the peephole, heart pounding. *I'm fucking kidnapping my own daughter*, my brain kept reminding me. Under Egyptian law, Amir is the only one who has legal guardianship of Sofie; I just have physical custody, married or divorced. Under Egyptian law, a mother attempting to take her child out of the country without the father's knowledge or consent may face 'serious legal consequences.' That knowledge wrapped around my throat like a noose.

I hadn't figured out what I'd do once I got to the States; you eat an elephant one bite at a time. My only plan was to find a job and get a credit card, but those details felt small compared to the task ahead. My heart raced as my instincts took over, driven by the need to protect Sofie and myself from the danger Cairo had become. Running away was the only thing that made sense.

I focused on taking one step at a time: *Shoes, Katya, pack the shoes.* I crammed them on top of the coats and the few warm clothes I had for Sofie. I had forgotten how to pack—something I'd done a thousand times, traveling to twenty-three countries. But that night, I couldn't match two socks to save my life. My bags were too heavy. I must have opened them forty times, each time forcing myself to let go of something beautiful—my Ukrainian designer dresses, my most comfortable stilettos with their matching purses, my favorite vintage jean jacket. Just material things, I reminded myself, things that didn't define *home*. Home wasn't a place—it was me and Sofie, our freedom, and the uncertain future ahead. Home didn't have a color or a street name; it didn't even have a bed. Home was tomorrow, seeing Becca at the airport. Home was the feeling of breaking free, of no longer being trapped under Egyptian Sharia Law, of no longer believing my life was over. Two light bags with warm clothes and my brains were all I needed. *Keep it together, Katya. Focus.*

Next, I gathered all the necessary documents—my passports, Sofie's passports (US and Egyptian), Sofie's birth certificate, and the forged document Rana had advised me to prepare in case I got questioned at border crossings. It read: "I allow for my wife, Kateryna Dunko, and our child, Sofie Sabry, to leave for Reno, Nevada, on November 29th, 2018. She is visiting her friend there for the winter holidays." *I hope I don't need to use it.* Lastly, I retrieved the $1,820 in cash I had stowed between Sofie's nursery books.

I'm fucking kidnapping my own daughter. The noose tightened around my neck, making it harder to breathe.

'Rana, it's time,' I messaged her on WhatsApp after putting Sofie to sleep.

'Okay, I'm coming,' she replied within seconds.

My weeks of surveillance had paid off, and with Rana now aware of my plan, I would be taking the bags to her house. I'd learned that the six security guards took their nightly tea break together from 2 to 2:30 a.m. in the underground parking garage. By 2:30, two of them would return to their posts near my building, #44. That gave me a thirty-minute window to sneak out the luggage.

Rana arrived on foot about ten minutes later to sit with Sofie. I'd told her to take the elevator from a lower floor so the call button wouldn't ring loudly near my neighbors, and I could use it to take my bags down. We didn't exchange a word as she entered, moving cautiously to avoid disturbing anyone in the building through the paper-thin walls.

Before the elevator doors fully closed, I slipped in with my two suitcases and rode it down. I loaded the bags into my car, which I had parked closer to the entrance that morning. Driving with my lights off, I made the three-minute trip to her house, where she'd left the door open. I wheeled the luggage inside silently.

Nine minutes later, panting, I returned. Rana hugged me briefly and whispered, "I'll see you in a couple of hours," before slipping out and disappearing down the stairs, just as the two security guards emerged from their tea break.

Sleep didn't come, of course. I sat in the darkness, watching Sofie's tiny belly rise and fall. This moment could mark the beginning of a great journey for us—or the end of my freedom as I knew it. If Amir's family decided I was an unfit mother for attempting to kidnap her, I might never see her again. Maybe they would forgive me, but the thought that they could take her away simply because I wasn't Muslim hit me like a train.

What if he already put a travel ban on us? I thought. That thought hadn't crossed my mind until that moment. Sweat slicked my palms as I rocked back and forth on the bed, the motion barely soothing my nerves. I whispered over and over, "God, please help us," clinging to those words like a lifeline.

I watched my 4 a.m. alarm go off in my hand. Already fully dressed with my shoes on, I picked up Sofie from her crib and slid her head under my hoodie so she could nurse. With one hand, I pulled the stroller to the front door and hooked our carry-on diaper bag onto the handle. I stilled my heart, as if steadying myself to shoot a rifle at a distant target. The air around me, the musky Cairo November morning, hung in a quiet haze, as I braced for the chaos that would soon begin.

'Confirmation: Egypt Air Flight MS 895 CAI-JFK...' The email subject flashed on my iPhone screen. Becca's message had arrived, right on schedule. I opened it quickly, my eyes scanning for the crucial phrase: 'roundtrip flight.'

It was time. I unveiled my parting gift—more a gesture of defiance now—the painting I'd been working on, and propped it on the dining table. For a moment, I stood back, taking in my surrealism-inspired creation, a piece that captured the beauty and unpredictability of the human experience.

The acrylic painting depicted a theater scene with a stage framed by pulled-back red velvet curtains and a silhouetted audience. The stage displayed the title, 'Cairo 2018.' At its center were two massive hands—one dark-skinned and veiny, the other pale and fragile. Both hands, their fingers stained with blood, tore apart a massive heart. Between the two ripped halves sat a sad little girl with long hair, swinging silently. The audience screamed insults, the same venomous words I'd endured for the past year: *She doesn't deserve a family! A wife shouldn't be like this bitch! Fuck this child, wish you never had one with her!* My painting was so symbolic, so beautiful.

I hoped the Sabry family might appreciate it, but I knew better. They couldn't grasp the complexity of the injustice of our situation—let alone the depth of a meaningful painting. Maybe Nadeen could understand my hardships, but she was a woman in Egypt, oppressed and obligated to listen to the men. I pushed in the chairs around the dining table, framing the artwork, and left the apartment tidy.

My brain switched to game mode: *You're just going on a trip to see your friend.* I worried my face, terrified and pale, would betray my crime. I took one last look in the mirror, as we do in Ukraine for good luck, and barely recognized the ninety-seven-pound, 5'4" woman standing there. I pitied the bony figure in the tan velvet sweatsuit, wondering who could possibly love me now. I had sacrificed so much for the chance at a family—my athletic stature, my curvy glutes, my health, my sanity, my freedom—all eaten up by cortisol and Cairo. What a shame.

In anger at my situation, I exited the apartment with the stroller, locked the door behind me, and slid my key underneath. My heart didn't flutter one bit.

"Sabah el-kheir (Good morning)," I greeted the security guard at the entrance with a small smile.

"Enty rayha fin (You go where)?" he asked, doing the Egyptian hand gesture of twitching his wrist in circles. It was out of the ordinary for him to ask this.

"Walk, ashen (because) baby, no sleep," I replied in broken Arabic, fumbling with the stroller as I maneuvered it down the three steps.

I kept my walking pace steady while in his line of sight. I was often seen taking Sofie for walks—though never this early in the morning. As I turned the corner of my building, I picked up my pace and took the back garden path toward Rana's house.

Rana was already waiting at the curb of her apartment building, my luggage beside her. She rushed to me, pulling me into a tight hug. "It's time, oh my God. Good luck, honey! May God bless the road ahead of you and Sofie! I will miss you so much," she whispered with tears in her eyes.

"Don't cry now, Rana, all will be well. It has to. Remember, if I text you, your man friend will be getting a call to play the Amir Sabry role. But I hope it won't get that far," I replied. "If you don't hear from me, I'll let you know once I'm in Reno."

"Yes, yes, we are all on standby," she said, holding my face.

The white, unmarked airport shuttle arrived within minutes—surprisingly punctual for Egypt. Rana handed the driver a one-hundred-Egyptian-pound note and exchanged a few quick words in Arabic. I slipped into the back with Sofie, hiding behind the tinted windows, while they loaded my bags and stroller into the van.

Following the plan, we exited through Rana's gate, where the guards didn't know me well enough to alert Amir. As we approached, I ducked down to conceal Sofie. No one glanced into the back seat. *I'm almost free.* Now, I just had to board the plane without raising suspicion.

Cairo International Airport is chaotic for any tourist, and knowing Amir's father was friendly with half the security staff spiked my anxiety. I'd been there many times before, always greeted by one of his connections after my travels. The last thing I needed was for one of them to recognize me.

"...And the return flight is when?" the EgyptAir check-in agent asked.

I froze. I hadn't checked the date on the return flight Becca had booked this morning, meant to be refunded as soon as I crossed the border. Quickly unlocking my phone, I glanced at the email.

"December eighth. We'll be back December eighth," I said, my voice steady despite the panic rising inside me.

"Okay. Ma'am, who packed your bags?" he asked, now standing up and looking at Sofie in the stroller.

"I did," I said, looking at the bags. "Well, my husband was there watching me," I added, stuttering.

It seemed like he was questioning me to buy time until the authorities came. *Fuck, they already know,* I thought.

"We need to check them," he ordered.

Another man dug through my things, his hands moving quickly through the results of my shit packing job—random panties stuffed in corners, coats poorly folded. He hesitated, uncomfortable as the panties spilled out from the sides.

The bags were checked, and my boarding passes were issued. I unclenched my jaw and felt my leg muscles twitch, as I walked toward the customs line. My body was running purely on adrenaline now; I hadn't slept in over twenty-four hours and was struggling to keep my composure intact.

At Egyptian Customs and Immigration, I was relieved to see a female officer. *Thank God,* I thought. *Maybe she understands the injustice of fathers having sole legal guardianship and won't question why I'm traveling.* I handed her mine and Sofie's United States passports, and she proceeded to scan them in a robotic manner. I was still so shaken up from the luggage search that I didn't feel fully present. The female officer was busy having a conversation with a man in the nearby booth, and she didn't even turn and check the contents of my stroller. Sofie sat quietly, patiently awaiting her fate. The passport scanner beeped loudly as it read my passport's barcode, and the officer stamped a random page without hesitation. The same beep sounded from the scan of Sofie's passport. The officer's expression remained unchanged, confirming that my daughter was in the clear —no travel ban.

"Shukran (thank you)," I said in my most respectful, enunciated Egyptian accent. Another small victory. *One step closer to home.*

The flight to JFK departed from a separate wing of the airport. Because this was a direct flight to the United States, every passenger had to go through security screening at two different tables. I was the only White woman with a brown baby amongst a handful of expats, but the passengers were mostly Egyptian men and couples. I paced the seating lounge, dreading the questions they might ask and even more terrified of how I would respond. I'm terrible at lying; my face gives everything away.

They filed us into two lines. Some passengers were held up for a few minutes while others passed through easily. I took my place near the back of a line, hoping the agents would be too worn out to pry into 'the nature of my trip.'

As if on cue, my little Sofie came to the rescue. She was due for her morning nap and started squirming and crying in the stroller. I stepped out of line, moving closer to the jetway, and bounced her in my arms, tucking her under my oversized hoodie to nurse. The men seated at the interrogation tables looked uncomfortable and waved me through without asking any questions.

"Ma'am, excuse me! Ma'am... Wait, please!" a heavily accented Egyptian security gate officer yelled at me from behind at the jetway.

This can't be how it ends. Not like this, I thought. *Not after all I've been through.*

Slowly, I turned around to face our fate and stood frozen as the lanky Arab man approached me.

"Yes?" I replied, clenching the stroller for dear life.

"Is this your watch?" he asked, holding up an Apple watch.

"What? Oh, no, that is not mine. No," I answered, dumbfounded.

Sofie and I were the last to board the aircraft. "Boarding is now complete," announced a voice over the airplane intercom.

Did we actually make it? I'd boarded hundreds of planes, but this boarding was the only one that counted. *Almost there.*

Sofie and I sat in the middle section, in the first row behind the First-Class curtain divider. The man next to us needed a breathing tank; every few hours, the alarm on his tank would go off, and the crew would rush to assist. With all the attention on us, my paranoia grew with each passing hour of the eleven-and-a-half-hour flight. Time seemed to stretch endlessly.

I stared at the flight tracker on the wall, willing the plane to move faster. I kept my emotions in check—no crying, no fidgeting, no letting my guard slip. I felt like a ticking time bomb, ready to explode. Sofie rested in my arms, quiet but wide awake.

Every time a flight attendant yanked open the curtain divider, I flinched. Through the gap, I saw a muscular Egyptian man in First Class staring directly at me. My heart pounded as cold sweat soaked my back. *Does he know?* My paranoia spiraled—he had to be a cop. At any moment, someone would take Sofie away.

Smile; act normal, Katya.

My mind raced. *Has Amir realized I'm gone?* I pictured him stepping into the apartment, spotting the key on the marble tile. I could hear his accented, "Katya, hello?" echoing as he walked room to room, his Ferragamo shoes squeaking against the floor.

He probably wouldn't think I could leave the country with a child. My favorite shoes were still on the rack by the door. I could hear the echo of his angry voice as he sat on the same couch he used to abuse me from, trying my phone and WhatsApp over and over. I imagined him calling his father, interrupting meetings at the Office of Arab Affairs. I could see the sweat on his bald head, his rage building as he stormed to his car. I could picture him speeding off and honking furiously on his way to his mother's apartment.

Get up and move around, I told myself. I paced the aisle with Sofie.

Our plane finally landed at John F. Kennedy International Airport. Since I had a child with me, the attendants allowed me to exit the airplane first, alongside the man with the oxygen tank. To my relief, no police officers waited at the end of the jetway as we stepped onto the terminal carpet.

I walked slowly toward the US Customs and Immigration hall, exhausted and dreading the passport scan. I rummaged through my bag, ensuring Sofie's Consular Report of Birth Abroad was neatly tucked inside the clear folder. This would be her first time entering the country of her citizenship.

As I funneled into the border crossing chaos, the scene was all too familiar. A female officer zig-zagged through the line with a German Shepherd, who sniffed everyone's bags. There's something about border crossings that always makes me feel like a suspect. And that day, I *was* a suspect. Right on cue, Sofie began fussing again, snapping me out of my thoughts. I needed to focus on the task at hand—lawfully entering the United States with my child who was a US citizen, but without her father's permission or knowledge.

Two, four, six, seven, and I am eight, I counted the people in front of me. While standing in line for more than forty-five minutes, I studied the officers as they scanned and questioned passengers. My odds were 50/50—either I'd get the bald, White, Marine-looking officer or the tall, younger Black one. "Please, God, let me get the Black guy," I whispered under my breath. But by the count, I was headed for the Marine. He looked too stern, too serious about his job. If he interviewed me, I was sure I'd blow my cover.

"Next!" the Black officer barked.

"Next, please!" the Marine echoed barely a second later.

Taking a deep breath, I stepped forward toward the Black officer, smiling as I handed him mine and Sofie's passports.

"What's the purpose of your trip?" he asked in a routine tone, his eyes scanning the eagle emblem on our books. Before I could answer, his gaze shifted to me, and he said, "Oh, you haven't been here in three years?" He looked at me dead in the eyes.

"Yes, I was working abroad, teaching English," I chirped, forcing a smile.

"And the child? Is she your daughter?" he asked, scanning Sofie's passport.

How had I not anticipated this? My daughter looked nothing like me—her brown skin and dark hair contrasted sharply with my fair skin and blonde hair. I could very well look like someone kidnapping a child that wasn't mine.

"Yes, I have the scar to prove it. Do you need to see a birth certificate?" I asked, pale as I reached into my bag for the clear document folder. He glanced at his computer again.

Fuck. Did Amir already find out we were missing and report us to the border patrol? All he had to do was see which flight I had gotten on and call in a kidnapping in progress.

"No need, welcome back to the States," he said, handing back our passports.

I froze.

"That's it?" I asked. *Stupid—why did you ask?*

"Yes, that's it—unless you have anything else you want to tell me?" he asked.

"Oh, no! Happy to be here! Thank you," I said in one breath. His head was already turned to the next victim in line.

I clutched our passports and strolled through the gate, finally exhaling the breath I'd been holding for fourteen hours. My heart pounded in my chest, and my head felt like a balloon as I approached the baggage carousels. I needed to grab our two bags and roll them through customs. Struggling to manage the luggage, diaper bag, and baby stroller, I caught the attention of a man dressed as a janitor. He quickly ran up with an empty baggage cart. I thanked him, tears pooling in my eyes.

"You okay?" he asked.

"Yes, I *am* okay. We're okay. I-I'm so happy to be home," I replied, my voice cracking.

18

ALCHEMY OF PAIN
INTO PURPOSE
(WINTER 2018)

The late November streets of Reno were empty and cold, a striking contrast to the chaos of Cairo. That first-twenty-four-hours-in-a-foreign-country feeling hit me again—order and stillness felt strange, almost surreal. No one walked the sidewalks, there were no mopeds buzzing around, and traffic lights hung above road crossings. Four years and five months had passed since I'd last seen Reno, and in that moment, everything about the city felt gloomy. Yet, I knew the initial shock of my rough landing back on US soil would soon wear off. All my five senses were in overload, as we drove to Becca's home in silence.

When we arrived at Becca's one-bedroom apartment in Midtown, Reno, it was 8:42 a.m. on Friday, Cairo time—twenty-five hours after we had left. By now, the Sabry family would be preparing to reach out to arrange our usual Friday visit. Leaving on a Thursday had given me a one-day window before they would notice I wasn't answering. Even so, as we hauled my luggage up the concrete stairs, I stayed mostly quiet, gripped by the fear of someone chasing us.

"I can see you're in shock right now. Maybe you should eat something. I have some leftovers in the fridge," Becca mothered me, her voice sounding like it was coming from a distant dream.

I sat on her couch, curled up with Sofie in my arms, a petrified look on my face. "I can't believe I'm here," I said, surprised by how small and fragile my voice sounded.

"You did it, Katya. You got away," Becca said gently from the dining table. The silence that followed, free of the usual small talk, felt just right. Becca sat cross-legged on a chair, her long brown curls framing her face, her gymnast's posture perfect, as she let the weight of my actions settle around us.

As I nursed the fussy Sofie, I understood how much baggage I had just brought to Becca's table. I silently admired her bravery for taking us in without question. A bit of sadness crept in as I thought about how I'd brought my mess into her life, but I reminded myself; I knew how to be a good roommate. Determined not to take her hospitality for granted, I would be on my best behavior.

I watched Becca move about her apartment and felt completely disconnected from my friend. Part of me felt Egyptian—quiet, poised, and kept in my bubble—yet in another sense, I felt like a criminal, holding the Sabrys' only grandchild. I was caught between two worlds—one where I was free in the USA and another where I had just kidnapped my own child—and I belonged to neither. Like a baby bird fallen from an abandoned nest, I was unaware of my ability to fly, still in shock from the initial fall.

"You're okay. Sofie is okay. You both just need some rest," Becca reassured me, walking us to our room. My expression and silence must have revealed the turmoil in my head.

Becca gave up her bedroom for me; she'd cleared space in her closet and placed a wooden crib beside it for Sofie. I stared at the space in disbelief, overwhelmed by gratitude for her generosity.

"Thank you so much, Becca! Thank you..." My voice broke as I sobbed. After holding back my emotions for twenty-five hours, I finally let them spill out. I fell into her arms, and she held me tightly on the edge of the bed.

"Oh my God, Katya, you must be like eighty pounds. We will get you better," she said softly, pulling me close. I felt small and fragile in her arms, noticing my protruding hip bones and the way my tan suede pants sagged, barely hanging onto my hips. Someone had noticed me—truly noticed me—and that made the tears fall even harder.

My tears eventually exhausted me into sleep. Before closing my eyes, I turned off my phone and didn't turn it back on for the next twenty-four hours. When I finally did, over one hundred missed calls from Amir lit up the screen. I wasn't ready to talk to him yet, so I turned the phone off again. Maybe he was already taking legal action, but I couldn't let myself process that yet. I had to focus on the basics for Sofie and me: food, sleep, and safety.

On the third day, I sought closure for 2014—for the choice I had made to move to Cairo four years ago, a decision that had brought me full circle. Being back in Reno forced me to confront the life I'd once had and the person I used to be.

I distracted myself from Amir and the kidnapping by watching travel videos I'd made with Lucas and kept on the external hard drive I'd carried around for the last five years. I watched the carefree, smiling girl in the videos and saw the turmoil behind her eyes and the mask of opioids she wore to hide her sadness and desperation. *Why did I put myself through all this hell just for someone to acknowledge my worth? Why did I care what they thought of me? Why didn't I care about myself back then?*

Motherhood is relentless. It doesn't wait for healing or give time for the mother to figure things out. I wanted silence to mourn my life and myself, but Sofie demanded my attention and unconditional love. She distracted me while anchoring me to reality. 'Love me now,' her giggles and stretched-out hands seemed to say, pulling me back to the present when I wanted to sink into the past. Sofie put everything into perspective and saved me. The girl in those videos was not worth saving anymore; she demanded I save the mother in me.

I cannot erase my decisions, but through my daughter, I can be saved from them—we can both be saved from them. I've made my mistakes, and now I cannot afford to make any more for Sofie's sake. Did I want my daughter to pay for my mistakes? No. Her story doesn't have to be like mine.

I stopped the videos and slammed the laptop shut. *I am worthy and proud of how far I've come!* I proclaimed silently, bouncing Sofie in my arms. I had been strong enough to flee Cairo and brave enough to risk my freedom for a better life for my daughter, and I had done it all by myself. Sofie was the only witness to the strongest, most resilient moment of my life—and I didn't need any other witnesses. With that realization, I vowed never to seek validation from others again. I owed my daughter more than our survival—I owed her my growth.

That night, Becca and I made dinner and sipped red wine. We caught up on her life and touched on the elephants in the room regarding mine. The wine left me more exposed, intensifying the vulnerability I already felt about finding money to support Sofie and me. I asked Becca for a week to collect myself even though she wasn't pressuring me—I was pressuring myself to stand on my own two feet. I promised to work on my resume over the weekend and start job hunting. She reassured me that I didn't need to contribute to rent until I had a job and a paycheck. I vowed not to let her down.

Survival is relentless. It forces you to keep putting one foot in front of the other even when you can't see where the next step will lead. With jetlag keeping me awake, I quietly slipped out of my room and passed Becca asleep on the fold-out bed in the living room, seeking a moment of solitude to process my situation. Grabbing my cigarette pack, I sat on the cold concrete stairs outside.

The sky that night was scattered with glittering stars, and the chill in the air felt thick, almost like Jello. *This is what adulting feels like,* I thought—not just figuring out how to survive after kidnapping your daughter from a Muslim country, but sitting outside at 3 a.m., staring at the stars.

"Now what, God?" I said to myself, lighting my fifteenth cigarette of the day. "Please fall. Please fall," I whispered in a smoky breath.

Moments later, a star did fall.

"Okay, God, you are here," I said aloud, deeply moved as I felt the validation of our eternal connection. Even in this darkest hour, God had not abandoned me. He had not forgotten me.

I was back on the steps in Reno, looking up at the stars, just as I had been in May 2014. Something enormous shifted inside me. It was painful and raw. Maybe it was the random breeze that blew by. Maybe it was the shooting star and feeling God's presence. Fearful thoughts entered my mind: *Will Sofie forgive me for taking her away from her father? What can I do so she doesn't feel that pain? What do I do with my pain?*

I started to weep, choking on the cigarette smoke. I let out a silent scream and dropped to the ground.

But did you forgive? a voice spoke inside me.

I'd heard this confident, peaceful, motherly voice before. Long ago. That voice was Kateryna.

But did you forgive? Kateryna asked again. *Your mother? Amir? Yourself?*

I sat up again, paying close attention to my inner thoughts. My tears stopped abruptly, as though a faucet had been tightened.

"But you never loved me," I said out loud to the thick air, wiping tears from my face.

We did the best we could, Kateryna replied.

"So, what do you want me to do?" I sobbed.

Forgive, she said again. *Break the cycle. You have always been enough.*

I finally understood my mission—to live for myself and for Sofie. It took twenty-nine years and nine months to reach that realization. Sofie was my clean slate, my second chance. She would grow up knowing what it meant to be loved without conditions. Lies, border crossings, self-harm, painkillers, and so much self-destruction had brought me to this moment: carrying the torch for the next generation. Standing on those steps, caught between my past and present, I realized I had carried responsibilities that were never mine to bear, yet I'd taken them on anyway.

For so long, I thought my struggles made me weak. But that night, under the Reno stars, I saw the truth—I was never the problem. I was strong, standing beside people who needed healing, taking on their pain while ignoring my own right to peace and unconditional love. I lost myself in the chaos, bleeding myself dry to prove my worth to those who never saw it. But my struggles and pain weren't signs of failure; they were what shaped my resilience and revealed my true strength: the power to overcome.

I didn't choose resilience willingly—I paid for it with scars on my soul. I didn't ask for my childhood or my addiction to unfold the way they had, but it was still my responsibility to turn things around, just as it was my responsibility to shape my future.

Forgive yourself, Kateryna. Forgiveness meant seeing that holding onto anger, pain, and resentment only continued to harm me and everyone connected to me. Even though others had wronged me, forgiving myself for how I internalized that hurt, allowed it to shape my identity, or let it influence my decisions became an act of reclaiming peace. Forgiving myself wasn't about excusing mistakes —mine or others'—but about recognizing them as part of my journey, not the end. They were lessons, not life sentences. And the greatest battle of all was learning to forgive myself for the times I fell short, for the times I let others dictate my worth, and for the times I abandoned my own needs in the name of love.

My crazy mother was right; I couldn't run away from myself. It took me so long to understand that I was meant to break the cycle of generational trauma, to stop seeking validation for the pain life could cause. For years, her words had felt like a curse, a reminder that no matter where I went, the pain, mistakes, and burdens would always follow. But now I saw they weren't curses—they were sources of strength. My problems were weapons in disguise.

I am enough. For the first time, I felt it in the core of my soul. The self I couldn't escape wasn't my pain or my failures—it was my resilience, my strength, my ability to endure and grow. That self was my greatest ally all along.

"I forgive you," I said aloud with full confidence.

Become the mother you never had, Kateryna said.

"I will."

I woke up the next day with a new light inside me. It was as though I'd been under anesthesia for years and had finally woken up. The wave of self-love and respect I felt came from within. This journey had taken me deep into my soul, to the virus corrupting my life: pain. I'd found it, studied it, accepted it, cried about it, and then hit delete. It hadn't been my responsibility to raise myself as a child, but it was my responsibility to forgive the parent who couldn't do it. And it was my responsibility to ensure Sofie didn't suffer because of my pain or the pain her father chose for us.

"Are you sure you want to see it now?" Becca asked, concerned.

"Yeah, I need to see it." I smiled.

Holding ten-month-old Sofie as she slept in my arms—unhappy with her car seat—I sat in the back of Becca's Scion, giving her directions. Moments later, we rounded the bend, and there it was: the roll-out fence gate, the Joshua tree peeking from behind it, the same perennials I had planted on the street corner, and the red door we had painted. They all stood as evidence of the stability I had once craved. This was the place I'd longed to return to whenever life had spiraled out of control. But it wasn't mine anymore.

"Stop here," I said. We parked across the street, and I stared out, capturing a photo for my memory.

It was a nostalgic moment. I needed to see this place I once called home and finally put that chapter to rest. That story, that home, was never meant for me. I needed to say goodbye—to the hope I'd once held on to, to the dream of building a family there with a partner I'd thought would see me through it, and to the younger version of myself who'd never appreciated her own worth. I had left Egypt and closed that chapter; now, I had to close this portal of my spontaneous Cairo move.

We're meant for more than this home could ever offer, I thought. *I'm a blank canvas now.*

I remembered what the house looked like inside those stucco walls: the art, the granite bathroom countertop where I'd once snorted opioids, the Chinese character for 'soul' on the wall, the paintings I had created and hung myself.

"Nothing has changed," I told Becca. *But I have.*

The woman I had woken up to that morning was the pinnacle of strength and self-worth. For the first time in my life, I loved myself—my courage, my persistence, my ability to forgive, and my resolve to start a life away from everyone who had weighed me down. Seeing that home confirmed it: I no longer recognized the woman I once was.

I fulfilled my mission of experiencing life on my own. My character grew stronger, and my soul broke and healed again. I lived fully in another culture, gained everything, lost it all, and still found the determination to keep going. I faced my drug addiction, endured being beaten, raped, and abandoned, and survived being trapped in a country with tight reins.

I've become something far greater than the woman the men in my life expected me to be—I've become a mother. A mother no one can destroy or exploit, but one who gives her best to my little Sofie. She gets the version of me that only we deserve.

"Goodbye," I waved to the friendly ghosts at the stained-glass red front door.

"You okay?" Becca asked.

"Yeah, I'm more than okay," I said. "Let's go. Sofie should nap in her crib," Kateryna added.

We were home—a home I had the courage to find within myself. It is free from the chains of generational trauma, in a country that values women and their right to choose. It is the supportive, loving home Sofie feels when she falls asleep in my arms.

———

EPILOGUE

God—the universe, destiny, whatever you call it—puts His best warriors on the front lines. The ones who bear the heaviest burdens are the ones chosen to carry the weight of humanity's curses. Pain, like a viral disease without a cure, spreads from generation to generation. No one is immune. My mother passed on her pain, but I vowed to break the cycle. Enough was enough. I was ready to fight for my daughter's future with every broken part of me, determined to create something whole.

About a year into writing this memoir, I began therapy. I learned that acceptance was the only way forward—I had to accept my addiction, my childhood, my lack of self-worth, my first husband's betrayal, the abuse I endured, and all the bad decisions along the way.

And there were many. But before you judge me, pause: what would you have done in my place? How would you carry the pain? When survival is on the line, choices are never simple. They are messy, desperate, human.

At the end of this journey of hard truths, I realized I was privileged—not because life was easy, but because I had the courage to stand in the face of suffering. After all, a warrior is only forged in battle.

And today, life still has its challenges, but they are ours—and I'm proud to say I've been sober for ten years. Since 2018, I've rebuilt one day at a time, believing that rock bottom can be the foundation to build upon. Out of those broken parts, I've created a safe, thriving, and loving home for Sofie. My path is steady now: writing these words, studying medicine, and choosing peace over chaos.

I am not defined by the story I came from but by my power to rewrite it. You are not defined by your past, either. Trust your inner strength. Let go of toxic influences, and reimagine a life on your own terms. That's your mission. Trust me—otherwise, life would be too simple.

I've walked through fire, and I kept the match. So can you.

Katya Dunko

ABOUT THE AUTHOR

Katya Dunko was born in Kyiv, Ukraine, and has lived in Egypt, Portugal, and the United States, while traveling to more than thirty countries. For her, travel has always been a form of growth and therapy, revealing the common thread that connects all cultures—the grounding ties of shared humanity. She often reflects on her time in Egypt, India, Myanmar, and Indonesia as transformative in shaping how she views struggle and what truly matters in life.

Her writing blends psychology with raw honesty and an unflinching eye for self-reflection, even in moments of failure. *I Drank From the Nile* is both a reclamation of her story and a light for those who feel lost, showing that pain is part of life but never its end. She hopes her work encourages others to face their inner world with honesty and courage, and to claim their healing for themselves.

Now based in Nevada, she is raising her daughter, working part-time in real estate, and pursuing her long-held dream of becoming a nurse. She is also in the early stages of a tragic romance novel set in Southeast Asia, weaving together cultural knowledge, experiences of heartbreak, and her belief that every struggle carries the chance to create a future worth living.

Connect with her online at www.katyadunko.com

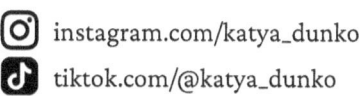
instagram.com/katya_dunko
tiktok.com/@katya_dunko

www.ingramcontent.com/pod-product-compliance
Lightning Source LLC
Chambersburg PA
CBHW021609120626
46545CB00001B/145